Creme de la Femme

Creme de la Femme

A collection of the best contemporary women writers, lyricists, playwrights and cartoonists.

Concept Developed by Anne Safran Dalin
Edited by Nancy Davis

RANDOM HOUSE
New York

This 1997 edition is published by Reference & Information Publishing, a division of Random House, Inc.

Random House, Inc.
New York ◆ Toronto ◆ London ◆ Sydney ◆ Auckland
http://www.randomhouse.com/

Typeset and Printed in the United States of America

Cataloging-in-Publication

Creme de la femme : a collection of the best contemporary women writers, lyricists, playwrights and cartoonists / concept developed by Anne Safran Dalin : edited by Nancy Davis.

p. cm.

Includes index.

ISBN 0-375-70056-0

1. American wit and humor—Women authors. 2. Women—humor. I. Dalin, Anne Safran. II. Davis, Nancy, 1947- .

PN6162.C74 1997

817'.540809287--cd21 97-25306

CIP

BOOK DESIGN BY NINA OVRYN

COVER DESIGN BY ROBERT ANTLER

ISBN 0-375-70056-0

9 8 7 6 5 4 3 2

To the talented and generous women whose work filled this volume with humor and my heart with joy, my unending gratitude.

A. S. Dalin

Authors' Acknowledgments

Michele Brourman & Robin Brourman Munson: We are especially grateful for the opportunity to support the Susan G. Komen Breast Cancer Foundation. Our mother, Liz Brourman, has fought successfully against breast cancer for these past twenty years. We're so proud of her spirit and courage, and wish to dedicate this contribution to her.

Sally Fingerett: To all our friends who've gone on...use your purse, use your bookbag, use your wings...just save me a seat!

Luisa Leschin: Thank you to David Smoot, Louise Leschin, and Lisa Loomer.

Jane Read Martin: Neil Leifer, Caroline Aaron, Susan Greenhill, and Anne Dalin.

Heather McAdams: Chris Ligon - loving husband. John Mullen - Secret Agent. *The Chicago Reader* - 1st Break.

Amanda McBroom: Jerry Sternbach, whose music made the words sing. George Ball, my husband and constant inspiration, and the women of Texas, who taught me how to *really* laugh.

Diane Rodriguez: Heather, Bev, Robin, Chloe, and Mr. L.A.

Kate Shein: Much thanks to Richard LaGravenese who brought me to Joan Micklin Silver. Thanks to Joan Micklin Silver and Julianne Boyd who brought me to *A....My Name Is Still Alice* and Lisa Loomer. Thanks to Lisa Loomer for giving my phone number to Anne Dalin at Random House.

Debi Smith: The other three of "The Four Bitchin' Babes" (Christine Lavin, Sally Fingerett, and Megon McDonough), through whom my contribution to this book was made possible.

The editor would like to thank Estelle Parsons and Joan Micklin Silver for supporting this project from its very beginnings. Thanks also to Bonnie Brook Associates and Kathryn Soman for their extraordinary help in putting together this anthology.

Credits

Sybil Adelman's "Nanny Tyrannica" first appeared in *Child* magazine.

Linda Barry's "Oh Darling!" was originally published in *Mother Jones* magazine.

The cartoons from *Adult Children of Normal Parents* are reprinted by permission of Pocket Books, a division of Simon & Schuster. Copyright © 1994 by Jennifer Berman.

"Psychic Economics" by Mary Kay Blakely © 1981 by Mary Kay Blakely. Originally appeared in *The New York Times* and was included in Nancy Newhouse's *Hers: Through Women's Eyes*, Villard Books/Random House, 1985.

Excerpt from *A Marriage Made in Heaven* by Erma Bombeck, © 1993, reprinted with the permission of the Aaron Priest Literary Agency.

Ellen Byron's "Just Say Purl" was originally printed in *Playgirl* magazine, June 1989. Reprinted by permission.

Roz Chast's cartoon "Natural Phenomena of 15E" first appeared in *The New Yorker*. Drawing by R. Chast; © 1989 The New Yorker Magazine, Inc.

Cindy Chupack's "The End" originally appeared in *Glamour*.

The excerpt from *When My Parents Were My Age They Were Old* is reprinted with the permission of Simon & Schuster. Copyright © by Cathy Crimmins.

"Typical Japanese Woman" and "Typical Japanese Women," excerpts from *36 Views of Mount Fuji: On Finding Myself in Japan*, by Cathy N. Davidson. © 1993 by Cathy N. Davidson. Used by permission of Dutton Signet, a division of Penguin Books USA Inc.

Leslie Dormen's "85 Things Every Young Woman Should Know" originally appeared in *Glamour.*

"I Am the Green Lollipop" and "How to Talk to Your Stepmother," excerpts from *Funny Sauce*, by Delia Ephron, © 1983, 1986, by Delia Ephron. Used by permission of Viking Penguin, a division of Penguin Books USA, Inc.

"TV Talk Show" © 1995 Sally Fingerett.

"Ida Mae Cole Takes a Stance" originally appeard in *A. ...My Name Is Still Alice*, conceived by Joan Micklin Silver and Julianne Boyd.

"It Ain't Over" originally appeared in *A. ...My Name Is Still Alice*, conceived by Joan Micklin Silver and Julianne Boyd. Music and Lyrics by Carol Hall © 1992 Daniel Music, Ltd.

"My Sort Of Ex-Boyfriend" music and lyrics by Carol Hall © 1986 Daniel Music Ltd. & Otay Music Corp.

CREDITS

The excerpt from *Breaking the Silence* by Mariette Hartley is reprinted by permission of the Putnam Publishing Group. Copyright © by Mariette Hartley.

"Good Morning Fort Worth" from *Nothin' But Good Times Ahead* by Molly Ivins. Copyright © 1993 by Molly Ivins. Reprinted by permission of Random House, Inc.

FOR BETTER OR FOR WORSE © 1993 Lynn Johnston Prod. Inc. Reprinted with permission of Universal Press Syndicate.

"Welcome to Kindergarten Mrs. Johnson" originally appeared in *A. . . . My Name Is Alice*, conceived by Joan Micklin Silver and Julianne Boyd.

"It's in the Male" and "The Silent Partner" from *1-800-Am I Nuts?* by Margo Kaufman. Copyright © 1993 Margo Kaufman. Reprinted by permission of Random House, Inc., and the author.

"Accelerando" by Lisa Loomer was first produced by the Odyssey Theater in Los Angeles.

"Juanita Craiga" originally appeared in *A. . . . My Name Is Still Alice*, conceived by Joan Micklin Silver and Julianne Boyd.

"Rural Delivery" from *History on a Personal Note* by Binnie Kirshenbaum, copyright © 1995 by Binnie Kirshenbaum. Reprinted by permission of Fromm International Publishing Corporation.

"Some Thoughts on Being Pregnant" from *Operating Instructions* by Anne Lamott. Copyright © 1993 by Anne Lamott. Reprinted by permission of Pantheon Books, a division of Random House, Inc., and the author.

"What Was I Thinking?" Words and music by Christine Lavin © 1993 CL^2 (ASCAP).

Nancy Lemann's "Excuse Me For Inviting You to the Plantation" originally appeared in *The New York Observer*.

Gail Machlis cartoon © Chronicle Features Syndicate.

"Let's Party" and "Life 102," excerpts from *How to Be Hap-Hap-Happy Like Me*, by Merrill Markoe, © 1994 by Merrill Markoe. Used by permission of Viking Penguin, a division of Penguin Books USA Inc.

Patty Marx's "Why I Hate Spring and Everything Else" and "Over My Dead Wet Body" originally appeared in *The New York Observer*.

"Three Dreams: South Bronx" © Susan Montez was published in *Hanging Loose 63*, Hanging Loose Press, New York, New York, 1993.

The excerpt from *Just in Time* is reprinted with the permission of Simon & Schuster. Copyright © by Phyllis Newman.

"The Days of Gilded Rigatoni," "Babes in Toyland," and "Bears with Furniture" by Anna Quindlen copyright © 1990/91 by the New York Times Co. Reprinted by permission.

CREDITS

"The Story of Z" by Elizabeth Rapoport copyright © 1995 by the New York Times Co. Reprinted by permission.

"Non-Bridaled Passion" originally appeared in *A. . . . My Name Is Still Alice*, conceived by Joan Micklin Silver and Julianne Boyd.

"Spiro Agnew and I" by Cathleen Schine Copyright © 1995 by the New York Times Co. Reprinted by permission.

"10 Things in Little Rock" and "Will I Ever See a Picasso Again?" from *New Times in the Old South* by Maryln Schwartz. Copyright © 1993 by Maryln Schwartz. Reprinted by permission of Harmony Books, a division of Crown Publishers, Inc., and the author.

"Henry" by June Siegel is from *Metamorphoses*, originally published in *Facing Forward*, ed. Leah D. Frank (Broadway Play Publishing, Inc.)

"Caroline's Cremation" by June Siegel was published in *The Dramatists Guild Quarterly*, Winter 1996, ed. Ben Pesner.

"Letter to the Editor" by June Siegel was performed by Judith Hiller in the revue *Things My Mother Never Told Me*, dir. Shari Upbin, Theatre East, N.Y., 1993.

Catherine Siracusa's cartoon appeared in *Movies, Movies, Movies*, ed. S. Gross, HarperCollins 1989.

"Who's Calling" and "Sleep" (© Debi Smith) Degan Music, ASCAP. "Talking Want Ad" by Debi Smith can be heared as performed by the composer on the album *Virgo Rising* (Thunderbird Records, out of print) and on *Penelope Isn't Waiting Anymore* on Rounder Records, performed by Peggy Seeger.

Carrie St. Michel's "Ode to a Love as Strong as an Emery Board" and "A Perfect Model Keeps Her Full Mouth Shut" originally appeared in *The Los Angeles Times*.

Judith Stone's "The Coast Is Not Clear" originally appeared in *Self* magazine.

"Can We Tock" from *Light Elements* by Judith Stone copyright © 1991 by Judith Stone. Reprinted by permission of Ballantine Books, a division of Random House, Inc., and the author.

"You Say Dumbo, And I Say Rambo" by Judith Stone copyright © 1995 by the New York Times Co. Reprinted by permission.

"Exit Laughing" by Patricia Volk copyright © 1995 by the New York Times Co. Reprinted by permission.

"Trudy the Bag Lady" and "Agnus Angst," from *The Search for Signs of Intelligent Life in the Universe*, by Jane Wagner. Copyright © 1986 by Jane Wagner. Reprinted by permission from HarperCollins Publishers and the author.

"They Just Don't Get It," "Mood Swings" and "Dear Edith" from *My Life, So Far: Edith Ann*, written and illustrated by Jane Wagner. Copyright © 1994 Jane Wagner. Reprinted with permission by Hyperion.

CREDITS

Wendy Wasserstein's cartoons were drawn by Blair Drawson.

Contents in Brief

Contents

Chapter 1

It's All in the Attitude 1

CONTENTS

Chapter 7

Are You Having an Interesting Life? 283

CONTENTS

Creme de la Femme

CHAPTER 1

It's All in the Attitude

You

(Woman on telephone)

But Fred, I can't get home for dinner. The meeting of Women in Advertising is tonight and . . . They are not all ball-busters . . . well, so Mary is but . . . No, Liz is not pushy—aggressive, maybe, but not pushy . . . It's not the same thing . . . You're aggressive, Fred . . . No I am not comparing you to Liz I only mean . . . Oh, Fred . . . I'm sorry . . . Fred?

Please do not think I am strident
Humorless, whiny, or shrill
It's true that I voted for E.R.A.
But *you* give me a thrill
I admit that I joined a committee
It was something my mom made me do
I signed a petition for equal pay
But I love *you*

Fred, you remember

I went to that beauty pageant
But you know I didn't protest
Some of the girls say those things are unfair
But I said that *you* know best
Now and then I may go to a luncheon
Where women can speak entre nous
But I swear I would never burn underwear
And I love *you*

We are post-all-that-nonsense people
Designing our life style neatly
Sharing the bed and the chores
And the rent
(You spend half your salary
I spend every cent)
The equality of our commitment
Fulfills me completely

You've got to look at history, Fred

Gramps dominated my grandma
He made her stay home with a child
Alimony still keeps my mother in chains
But *you* let me run wild
Free to be a new-century woman
Who can paddle her own canoe
I am grateful for all my political gains
I recently heard we can fly combat planes
Where are you now, Nancy Drew?

Oh Fred, I insist
I'm femin*ine* not femin*ist*

I perfume, I powder, I shave, and I tweeze
I hated "Thelma and Louise"

Fred . . . I'll be home for dinner

And Fred
I *LOVE YOU*

~ *Georgia Bogardus Holof*

CHAPTER 1

I Think, Therefore I Am

~Anne Gibbons

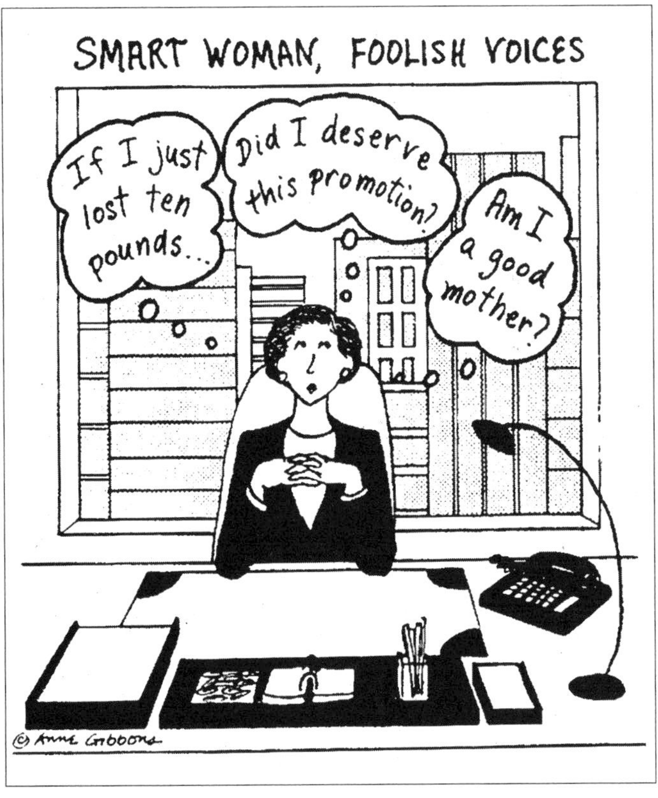

Welcome To Kindergarten, Mrs. Johnson

Lights up on simple schoolroom set. MS. THOMAS is at her desk, stage L. She is wearing a bright smock. As MRS. JOHNSON enters, MS. THOMAS crosses to her.

MS. THOMAS: Welcome to kindergarten, Mrs. Johnson.

MRS. JOHNSON: How do you do? It's a pleasure meeting you. Janie has told me so much about you.

MS. THOMAS: It's a shame you couldn't make it last week with the other mothers.

MRS. JOHNSON: I'm sorry. I was speaking at a conference in Zurich.

MS. THOMAS: Well, come along. *(crosses back to her desk)* I've been observing Janie very closely. Have a seat. *(MRS. JOHNSON starts to sit in a miniature kiddy chair and nearly falls off onto the floor. MS. THOMAS, oblivious to her difficulty.)* Sit straight. *(She sings.)*

She's a very bright girl, Mrs. Johnson.
She works beyond potential-
A model for her peers,
Exploring at a level
That's way beyond her years.
And I'm sorry
But it's getting on my nerves.

MRS. JOHNSON: *(speaking)* I'm sorry . . .

MS. THOMAS *(speaking)* Don't fidget, Mrs. Johnson.

(crosses to MRs. Johnson, singing)

She's a difficult girl, Mrs. Johnson.
She helps the other children—Lord knows where it will lead,
And I've learned that when my back is turned
She's teaching them to read.
I'm to say the least dismayed—
What does she think this is, third grade?
She's independent.
She's assertive.
She's always self-assured.
Now I don't know where she's getting that,
But it's not to be ignored—
And it generally starts at the home.

(MS. THOMAS sits back at her desk. Speaking—) Did you know that Janie's the only child in class with an even reasonable self-image? Now who's responsible for *that*?

MRS. JOHNSON: *(a bit thrown)* I am.

MS. THOMAS: I'm sorry?

MRS. JOHNSON: *(louder)* I am.

MS. THOMAS: I am *what*?

MRS. JOHNSON: I am, Ms. Thomas.

MS. THOMAS: Good. Well, how do you expect her to be intimidated by simple authority?

MRS. JOHNSON: Well, I . . . *(starts to sit on her hands)*

MS. THOMAS: Keep your hands where I can see them.
(MRS. JOHNSON jerks her hands up. MS. THOMAS sings.)

Now, I'm not saying you're a bad mother,
Even though you missed our pageant
And the Halloween parade.
No, No one's saying you're a *(produces Bad Mother flash card)*
Bad mother,
But your cookies at the bake sale,
Well, they clearly weren't homemade

MRS. JOHNSON *(abashed; speaking):* They were Pepperidge Farm Mint Milanos.

MS. THOMAS: The other mothers baked.

MRS. JOHNSON: I know, but . . . but I hate baking.

MS. THOMAS: Janie was humiliated!

MRS. JOHNSON: She never said a thing to me!

MS. THOMAS: Well . . *(singing)*
You're a busy little bee, Mrs. Johnson,
Zipping off to Zurich.
I hear next week it's Rome.
Is there really any wonder
Things are suffering at home?

(MRS. JOHNSON starts to protest.)

Oh, there's no need to object.
It's all here in Janie's artwork—
You can see that I'm correct.

(She produces a large pig made out of a Clorox bottle and decorated with hearts. She shows it to MRS. JOHNSON.)

MRS. JOHNSON *(speaking):* It's a pig! Made out of a Clorox bottle!

MS. THOMAS: Oh, come on, Mrs. Johnson. There are domestic problems written all over this pig. I know what I'm talking about. I've taken psychology courses.

MRS. JOHNSON: *(starting to stand)* But . . .

MS. THOMAS:*(raising pig over Mrs. Johnson's head)* If you have something to say you raise your hand! *(MRS. JOHNSON sits abruptly, MS. THOMAS sings:)* Now, no one wants to be a—
(MS. THOMAS flashes card at MRS. JOHNSON.)

MRS. JOHNSON: BAD MOTHER.

MS. THOMAS: And I think we can do better
If we just make up our minds,
'cause we all know what happens to a—
(She flashes card again at MRS. JOHNSON.)

MRS. JOHNSON: BAD MOTHER!

MS: THOMAS: And there's every indication
That this suits your situation.
Here is my evaluation—
Take it home and have it signed!
(She picks up an evaluation with "Bad Mother" marked on it and pins it on MRS. JOHNSON, who is crushed.)
Now, wasn't it nice meeting and getting a chance to chat like this?

MRS. JOHNSON *(fighting back tears):* Uh-huh.

MS. THOMAS: Did you know we have these parent-teacher conferences every Monday at four o'clock?

MRS. JOHNSON *(shaking head):* Uh-uh.

MS. THOMAS: Well, I hope I'll be seeing you again very soon. *(She replaces the pig.)*

MRS. JOHNSON Ye-yes, Ms. Thomas.

MS. THOMAS: That'll be all. *(MRS. JOHNSON tears out of the classroom.)* No running in the halls. *(She sees the next mother waiting.)* Welcome to kindergarten, Mrs. Feldman. Have a seat.

(BLACKOUT)

~Marta Kauffman

Somewhere a Time For Us

~Roz Chast

CHAPTER 1

Here a Streep. There a Streep. Everywhere a Streep, Streep.

It all started January 7th, 1980, at 11:23 P.M., but who's counting? Patrick and I had gone on a second honeymoon, had just arrived in Palm Springs, and were racing through the aisles of the local 7-Eleven, getting our various eggs and milk, hoping we could hole up the entire lascivious weekend and never come out, when my grocery cart screeched to a halt and I nearly fell into it.

There, on the covers of—not *Star,* not *Us,* not *Family Circle*—on the covers of *Time, Newsweek,* and *Life* magazines, was Meryl Streep, and underneath her picture it said, "Actress of the '80s." *Time, Newsweek,* and *Life* magazines: "Actress of the '80s." And I said to myself, "Well. There go the eighties."

It was not a good weekend. I was depressed; I was forlorn; the Jacuzzi felt cold. We didn't ... I didn't ... smile much. And I felt so petty that I couldn't talk to anyone. So who do you talk to when you can't talk to anybody? You talk to God, right? I talked to God a lot.

I'd say . . . "God. Okay, even if she is the actress of the '80s, I bet she never gets married. She's obviously a compulsive worker, and somebody that compulsive doesn't have time to develop a relationship. I, on the other hand, who have not been compulsively working much at all, have a wonderful relationship." By Sunday, God was answering back:

"*Mariette. Meryl Streep just married a successful sculptor and is blissfully happy.*"

That's everybody's dream, right?—To marry someone who's not only creative, but making a small fortune at it. Anyway, there she was on the cover of *Time, Newsweek,* and *Life* magazines, Actress of the '80s, married to a successful sculptor; but I got past it, I was really okay, then....Wanna hear the review? *Los Angeles Times* on *Sophie's Choice*:

> Nothing you know about acting quite prepares you for the amazing Meryl Streep as this sensual, feverish, kittenish, beautiful, tragic woman. Even though he thought it was a risk, Alan Pakula gave Streep the part. She was given a Polish coach, studied an accent for two months, and reported, 'Mr. Pakula? I'm beginning to feel the character.'...The only regret about Streep's matchless work is that *it ends*.

Well, I figured, even if she does get an Academy Award, I'll bet she never has kids. Her husband's obviously very creative, but what? He sculpts all day. She's constantly on location, constantly shooting movies at the end of some sea-sprayed jetty. How can they ever have kids? I, on the other hand, who have not been working at the end of any jetty at all, have two wonderful kids. I was actually feeling sorry for her. But God kept talking back, a voice that boomed from the heavens, sounding a little like Stan Freberg.

"Mariette."

"Yes?"

"Mariette, Meryl Streep and her husband, a successful sculptor, have begotten two gorgeous children. A boy and a girl."

"When!"

"On hiatus."

Well, I thought at least I've nursed my kids. I didn't want to sound judgmental, but how could Meryl Streep find time to nurse her children? I'll bet they're career orphans, latchkey...

"Mariette."

"Hm?"

"Meryl Streep is a terrific mother. Her children get equal love and attention; never eat with their mouths open; and will never blame their mother in analysis, twenty years down the road."

"Never blame their mother!"

"There's more."

"Gosh."

"Meryl Streep's son will graduate from Yale with honors and be weaned the following week. Meryl Streep's daughter will marry Prince Harry and bequeath her two royal grandchildren. A boy and a girl. Want to see the wedding photos?"

"Not particularly."

Okay, so I was thrown. But I finally got past it; I was really all right. Then I noticed they were doing a remake of *Gone With the Wind.* I ran to the phone to call my agent, practicing all the way. "Oh, Fiddle-dee-dee, Melanie, aren't things bad enough without you talking about dyin'?"

"Mariette!"

"Yes?"

"Sit down, Mariette."

"Scarlett O'Hara! Meryl Streep will play Scarlett O'Hara?"

"Better than Viv."

"Swell. It says here Paramount's shooting the life of Sonja Henie. She can't be playing Sonja Henie."

"Not only that, but she does her own skating."

"What about Esther Williams?"

"Does her own swimming."

"Maureen O'Sullivan?"

"Does her own vines."

"What about Joan of Arc? Does her own burning? Hell, what's left? Wouldn't surprise me if she did '*The Story of Barbie and Ken.*'" God was silent.

"Who plays Ken?"

"Robert Redford."

"Tell you what. Just stop me if she's not going to play these parts, okay? Okay?"

"Roll 'em."

"Alida Valli, Dame May Whitty, Minnie Pearl? You can jump in anytime. Gisele MacKenzie, Lena Horne? LENA HORNE! She couldn't. She can't. It's against Screen Actors Guild. Actors can't play blackface anymore."

"Doesn't have to. She'll just study her color for two months. Want the rest of it?"

"Sure, why not?"

"Sandra Dee, Lu Ann Sims, all the presidents' wives, Audrey Hepburn, Kate Hepburn, Ruth Hepburn . . ."

"Ruth Hepburn?"

"Isn't famous yet."

"What about Larry, Mo, and Curly?"

"Does her own hitting. Zasu Pitts, Fay Emerson, Mariette Hartley, Zizi Jeanmaire . . ."

"Hey!"

"Hm?"

"Would you back up a little, third from the left there? Mariette Hartley?"

"Right."

"The life story of Mariette Hartley?"

"Right."

"Mmm . . . mmm . . . mm Meryl Streep will play my life?"

"That's right."

"But she can't do my life! That's not fair! That's my part!"

"Can't be helped."

"Why?"

"You're too tall."

"Anything else you want to tell me?"

"Can you take it?"

"Sure. Roll 'em."

"Meryl Streep will take over the Today Show; *chair a round table on advanced metaphysics; be the first American awarded the OBE; and on July 22, 1998, Dame Meryl, and her successful sculptor husband, will go on "Tattletales" and win for the banana section."*

"Boy, I mean, I gotta tell ya. Sometimes I think (I mean, I have a terrific career, I know that) but sometimes I think, well . . ."

"You know, Mariette. When someone's in the position that I am—with so many children . . ."

"Oh, I know that . . ."

"So many animals . . ."

"I respect that."

"So many mountains, so many rivers . . ."

"I know all that, but . . . well . . . Do you like her better?"

"Yes, Mariette. I've always liked her better."

"Is that why she gets to stay up later?"

So here it is. The story of my life. Soon to be a major motion picture starring Meryl Streep.

No holds barred.

~*Mariette Hartley*

Hostess with the Mostess

SHE WAS AMAZING
SHE WAS THE HOSTESS AND YET SHE HAD MANAGED TO HAVE A DEEP, MEANINGFUL CHAT WITH EVERY SINGLE PERSON AT HER PARTY.

~*Mary Lawton*

Let's Party

About once a year it occurs to me that I owe a lot of people a social debt and really ought to have some kind of party to try and pay them back. I'm not saying I *act* on this impulse. I'm just saying it occurs to me.

And when it does, it is followed immediately by a sense of panic that makes me feel like one of the members of that Chilean soccer team that survived an air crash and had to contemplate eating a former teammate. In other words, I freak. The next thing I do is begin paging compulsively through books on the subject of "entertaining at home."

Of all the volumes in print on this topic, none fill me to overflowing with as much simultaneous loathing and secret envy as the combined oeuvre of Martha Stewart. Each one of these intimidating tomes is expensively bound and bursting with many, many beautiful color photographs featuring captions such as "a dramatic croquembouche surrounded by fresh flowers makes a spectacular centerpiece on the table in the library" or "Hepplewhite chairs, grandmother's plates, old silver, and long-stemmed Italian poppies grace the dining table set on our porch."

The author is a pretty blond woman with good bone structure and an uncanny ability to make whoever is her closest competitor for the title of Little Miss Perfect appear to have a learning disability. Her chapters have titles such as "Cocktails for 50—a festive occasion!" or "Summer Omelette Brunch Outdoors for 60!" I didn't even scan that one, since it is nearly impossible for me to get even one omelette out of a pan not looking like something I found at the bottom of my purse. But these are not the kinds of problems that plague Martha Stewart. "I always have baskets everywhere filled with fresh eggs," she tells us, perhaps while relaxing on the veranda of one of her summer homes in the mountain region of Neptune where I believe she spends a good deal of her time. Why? Because she simply gathers "eggs of all shapes, sizes, and hues from our Turkey Hill hens." She *has* her own hens. She has her own bees. She probably has a trout stream and a cranberry bog. She's always somewhere picturesque ladling something steaming into something gleaming.

The most pernicious thing about her is the way she makes the thing she recommends appear somehow vaguely doable. "To entertain at home is both a relief and a rediscovery," she says offhandedly, perhaps while seated pertly in the spacious living room of her weekend place on one of the moons of Jupiter. "It provides a good excuse to put things in order. Polish your silver. Wash forgotten dishes. Wax floors. Paint a flaking window sill." Of course it does. Especially during those long Jupiterian winters that I understand can go on for decades. *Nothing* puts *me* less in the mood for thankless chores than the swelling sense of panic that comes from planning a party.

So here at last is advice for people such as myself, busy, frazzled, with no innate hosting abilities or graces.

Merrill Markoe's Home Entertaining Guide for the Panicky Social Debtor

Chapter One: Planning the Event

The Guest List. Martha Stewart says, "When you meet someone interesting at a party it is a natural reaction to think of all the other people who would like to meet him too. Sometimes I do this years in advance—putting people together in my mind." And I say to her, "Have a licensed professional sit you down and tell you all about lithium." *I* begin by inviting only those people I am so sure like me that virtually nothing I could say or do would sway their opinion. If this total does not get you beyond the fingers of one hand, add a select number of others who you know suffer from weight problems and/or eating disorders. These are people for whom heavy calorie consumption is always a problem so if you screw up the food it won't matter. If it does happen, your guests will be secretly relieved.

2. The Menu Checking back in with Martha Stewart we learn that "a dramatic spicy taste is an inappropriate way to begin dinner." Therefore, it only makes good sense to begin by offering each and every arriving guest an enormous peppery bean burrito. "Cocktails that last much longer than an hour jeopardize the shape and momentum of the evening," Martha

cautions. Since these are the very things that are most terrifying, figure on a two-hour cocktail period minimum. Now you've got everyone right where you want them: feeling fat and sleepy with a limited desire or ability to eat anything.

3. The Theme Martha Stewart says, "Your own dishes, possessions, and personality will determine the style and tone of the occasion." That is why I like to use as my theme "the breakup of the Soviet Union," my table settings and decorations reflecting with amazing accuracy the chaos, poverty, and desperation of a culture in the throes of disintegration.

Chapter Two: Day of the Party Preparations

1. As soon as you awake, begin your futile attempt to remove the vast quantities of pet hair that have settled over everything in your house like a gentle dusting of snow on a wintry morning. Pick up as many of the saliva-coated pet toys as you can find and hide them somewhere. Anywhere. Especially the squeaking vinyl turkey leg with a face.

2. Martha Stewart thoughtfully reminds us to "Remember to empty a coat closet" to accommodate the outerwear of your guests. So, take all the stuff you have in there and move it to the . . . no, the garage is full. So is the bedroom closet. And the hall closet. Which is why I recommend that you just put everything *back* into the coat closet and lower the heat in the house so that your guests will not be inclined to take off their coats or sweaters.

3. Begin to anesthetize yourself. It may be politically incorrect in this day and age, but as much as you might like to, you *aren't* going to be driving anywhere. So isn't it worth it just this once to provide yourself with an impenetrable smokescreen between your problems and anxieties and your own ability to perceive them?

4. Don't forget that "music can establish and sustain an easy mood." I prefer a simple loop tape of AC/DC singing "Highway to Hell." But select your own favorites, depending on your theme.

5. Clean the pet hair off everything *again*, making sure to notice that there is just as much this time as there was before you spent all those previous hours removing it. But this time, if you are sufficiently sedated, you may enjoy taking all the saliva-coated pet toys and assembling them into a colorful centerpiece surrounded by fresh flowers and grandmother's old silver. Place the squeaking vinyl turkey leg with a face proudly in the front. Or go directly to

Plan B

Turn out all the lights in your house and greet arriving guests in your bathrobe and pajamas. Wearing an expression of sympathetic, quizzical bemusement, say to them, "Geez—this is kind of embarrassing. The party was *last* night. But hey—come one in. Can I get you a cup of tea?" They will probably stay only a few minutes—just long enough to get angry about already getting pet hair all over some cherished item of clothing. But because the error will seem to be *theirs*, your social obligations will be paid in full!!

~ Merrill Markoe

Living Legends

IT WAS NEVER EASY BEING A HOUSEWIFE, BUT AT LEAST WE DIDN'T HAVE MARTHA STEWART.

~ *Yvette Jean Silver*

Let Me Call You Sweetheart

What can I do for you, sweetheart?" He is talking about cheese, sort of. But the other implication is there. He knows it and I know it, and so does the other customer, a man. He is my cheese man, or was, until this moment. Believe me, I have my regrets. He had great pâtés, too, and baguettes. Also, three kinds of tortellini. And we had been so close.

"I'm not sweetheart!" I say, turn on my heel and walk away from the hunk of feta I need for tonight's Greek salad. I don't look back, but my peripheral vision catches him slackjawed, above a round of morbier. Of course he's surprised. I've let him call me sweetheart before. Also baby, doll, and hon. Always before I'd been runny, semi-soft, but today the anger of years suddenly permits me this reckless, existential act, gives me the courage to stand firm and tell this cheesy man to mind his curds and whey. "*I'm not sweetheart!*" That's what I said! You got the wrong gal, hon! It ain't me, babe.

I imagine him and his customer shaking their heads and laughing softly into their chins, bewildered at women. One of them probably said it: "Women!" I'm sure my ex-cheese man thinks its very amusing that I, a woman in my forties, would ever think he really meant anything sexual by it. He seems to be in his forties as well. (I date him in part by his atavistic, anachronistic d.a. cut.) He didn't, probably. Or he'd never admit it. Heck, I'm way too old for him.

What he wants is power over me. When he calls me hon, he's really saying, "I could have you if I wanted, hon." And I am supposed to be submissive before this expression of power. Indeed, I am supposed to be complimented by it. Especially now that construction workers and truck drivers have fallen silent as I pass. Maybe this cheese man wants me! Maybe he thinks I'm cute. And, if it's a man much younger calling me babe, I should *really* be flattered, and never think how condescending he's being.

It's happened that, during these, my forties, I've been carded by young men in liquor stores. In my twenties and early thirties, that bit of chivalry used to confuse me. Were they kidding? Did they really think I was under age? Now I just raise my right eyebrow and grab my booze.

It's raining outside the cheese store. I don't have an umbrella, and I must go two blocks out of my way to the next cheese store, my new cheese store. I see wearily down all the long years ahead when I will have to trudge these two blocks extra for cheese. The price I must pay for the courage of my convictions, I tell myself. But my righteousness lifts before the first block. What good did it do? Probably just made him angrier at women. And unless I picket the store with a sign "He Calls Women Sweetheart!" my boy-womancott is not going to hurt his business. Actually the attention would probably sell a lot of Emmentaler. Biting off my nose to spite my face. My mother always said I did it and I shouldn't do it, and here I am doing it again.

I should have been calmer, talked to him. "Sir, women don't like strange men using diminutive terms of endearment. They find it demeaning . . . Sir." I know a woman who did exactly that: a chef who took the young man who delivers soft drinks aside. She said he was mortified and never did it again. In that case, of course, she had the power. He was the one who needed the cheese, so to speak.

Am I responsible for the cheese man's education? His father should have taught him manners. His father probably did. How successful would a black man be explaining to an offender why he didn't want to be called boy? But, really, is there anyone left, even the most benighted bigot, stupid enough to call a black man boy these days? To his face, I mean.

Maybe if I just marched back there and explained that I had a master's degree?

My husband tries to conceal his annoyance. He liked the foie gras, and the prices were good. Now he'll have to shop there himself, and he doesn't know from cheese. He doesn't like the owner much either.

"But I couldn't tolerate it anymore!"

"C'mon, women call me 'honey' all the time . . . every day when I get my bagel."

"They do?" Maybe honey has become an honorific for the nineties and I'm too strident to realize it. "They do? Wait . . . the women who call you honey . . . are they older than you or younger?"

"Older."

"Always older, right?"

"Yes, OK?"

"That's different. It's a waitress thing. They're being motherly."

"Yeah, you wish."

"Young women would never dare. You can't do that until you're sixty at least. Men would find it upsetting otherwise. I would never dare! I couldn't even call the cheese man sweetheart back." It had occurred to me. But really, I was frightened. "Does anyone call you hon or dear at work?" I ask him.

"No. Absolutely not. Never at work. You?"

"Of course. At every job I've ever had, there've been men who have. A boss, the janitor, the elevator operator . . ."

"So? Sexual harassment! Tell them off like you did the cheese man."

"Yeh! You think I'd mess with someone who's fixing my fluorescent light?" That's the thing. One has to be selectively righteous. For instance, in the summer I stay in a small town with only one cheese store, where the bread is advertised as "Imported from Arthur Avenue in The Bronx!" The proprietor always calls me darling. His brother Gus calls me luv. The pathetic truth is, I'd probably let them call me anything. I need the bread.

My friend says that's nothing. She kissed a merchant in Greece so he would take $50 off a ring she wanted.

"On the lips?" I ask.

"On the lips. He didn't speak English, just made these little smacking sounds to show what he wanted. He was ancient. He smelled. He had no teeth and a tracheotomy."

"Oh. That's got to be worse than letting them call you sweetheart for bread."

"Yeah, well . . . you didn't see the ring."

Who am I to judge? On one of my jobs the boss, at the end of another stressed-out, alcoholic day, came up to me, held out his arms, sighed and said, "Give me a little sugar, Kathy." And I did! Hugged him and kissed him in front of his secretary. Probably on the mouth . . . who remembers? I was a lot younger then.

C H A P T E R 1

The day after The Feta Incident I get into a cab. "Where ya goin', sweetie?" The meter's down, the door is closed, we're moving fast. I'm his hostage. So I tell him Grand Central without picking a fight. But I have a plan and I am determined. My hands are clammy holding the fare. When we arrive, I say, "Thanks, sweetie!" and jump out, fast. Of course, not before leaving the tip.

~*Kathleen Rockwell Lawrence*

Battle Lines

ALL FEMINISM TRANSLATES INTO — "MEN ARE JERKS... MEN ARE JERKS... MEN ARE JERKS!"
HEY!

"PRO-FEMALE" DOES NOT TRANSLATE INTO "ANTI-MALE"! FEMINISM PROMOTES THE STRENGTHENING OF THE STATUS OF WOMEN— NOT THE DEMISE OF MEN.

OH RIGHT— THAT'S WHAT YOU SAY! BUT FROM WHERE I SIT, ITS AN ATTEMPT TO IMMASCULATE MEN, AND THREATEN THE VERY FABRIC OF SOCIETY!

MEN ARE SUCH JERKS...

~*Jan Eliot*

On Censorship

The American Senator from North Carolina, Senator Jesse Helms, became totally obsessed with the photographs of naked men by Robert Mapplethorpe. Can you imagine this? An Artist? Making pictures of Naked Men? I thought, "Wow, it's a good thing that Jesse Helms has never been to Italy. "There are pictures of naked men EVERYWHERE there. . . naked men on the walls, naked men on the floors, naked men on the ceiling, they even have little tables with statues of naked men, so that you can be innocently walking down the street and then suddenly you turn and WHAM, you've got a big Schwanz right in your face. Jesse Helms would die there! (Hey, good idea! Send Jesse to Italy!)

Anyway, Helms became so obsessed that he got his own book of the photographs of naked men by Mapplethorpe and kept them in a drawer in his desk in his office in Washington, DC, so that every time someone came into his office he would say "Do you want to see something REALLY DISGUSTING? Look at this!. . . And this!. . . Oh! Oh! Oh!. . . I HATE THIS ONE THE MOST! OH!. . . Oh!. . . aaahhhhhhhhhh!"

In fact, in the end, Jesse Helms showed these photographs to more people than Robert Mapplethorpe ever did.

~*Janice Perry*

Blank Canvas

Bülbül © 95 MAR 7
... AND HERE IS AN EXAMPLE OF CULTURAL LIFE AFTER FUNDING CUTS TO THE ARTS !

~ *Bulbul*

Typical Japanese Women

As soon as I arrive in Shirahama with the members of the Japanese Women's Studies Society, I realize that this is not going to be a typical three-day vacation by the sea. Instead of being shown to my room, I'm shown to *our* room, a gigantic tatami room. Except when we're at the beach, I'm told, this is where we will be meeting during the day and

sleeping at night, all fifteen of us. Now we need to hurry to take our bath together because our dinner will be served in this room in an hour and a half.

"You've had a Japanese-style bath before, haven't you?" Kazue-san asks a little nervously as we head down the hall to the women's bath.

"Oh, of course," I shrug off her comment.

Of course I haven't, but I'm not about to give that away. I know the basics from the guidebooks: wash thoroughly before you get into the bath; make sure never to do anything to spoil the communal, clean bath water. I figure I can wing it on the details.

We undress in a small anteroom and fold our clothes neatly into baskets on the shelves. We walk into the bath with our tiny white terry washcloths. Along one wall is a row of faucets for washing, with drains in the sloping tiled floors. On the other side is the mosaic-tiled bath, as blue as the sea, beneath a cascade of tropical plants.

I've seen naked women before in showers in various gyms in America, but the mood in this Japanese bath is entirely different. I've never seen people more comfortable with their bodies. There are twenty-five or thirty women in the room, our group plus a group of obasan (grandmothers) here on vacation from the countryside and some members of an Osaka teachers' association having an annual meeting. The oldest woman is probably close to ninety; the youngest is three. The mood is quietly happy, utterly relaxed.

We sit naked on low wooden stools, soaping ourselves with the terry washcloths, rinsing with red buckets filled from the taps and poured over the body. The conversation is lulled, languid, like the water, like the steamy air.

I finish washing my entire body and notice that most of the women from my group are still soaping a first arm. I slow down, going back again over my entire body, washing and washing, the soapy cloth, the warm water, the joking talking laughing atmosphere, the bodies. The women in my group are now washing a second arm. I slow down again, deciding I will try to do it right this time, Japanese-style, concentrating on a leg. I baby each toe, each toenail, each fold of flesh, noticing for the first time in years the small scar on the inside of my ankle, a muffler burn from a motorcycle when I was a teenager. I'm fascinated by this ritual attention to the body, so different from the brisk Western morning wake-up shower. When I finish (again) and go to shampoo my hair, I see that most of the women in my group are still scrubbing. I give up. It must take practice. I have never seen such luxuriant pampering of bodies.

The bath is a revelation for another reason. I read once that a one-hour bath has the same physiological effect as four hours of sleep. Maybe this is how the Japanese do it, I think, a ritual stop in the otherwise frenetic day.

As I watch these women soaping their bodies with such slow concentration, it is almost impossible for me to remember what they are like most of the time, raising families, working full-time, responsible for all of the household chores and the household finances, as busy as any American women I've ever met.

I tell this to my friend, Kazue-san.

"It's hard to be busy when you're naked," she says smiling. "It looks too silly!"

I find myself laughing. Everywhere around me are the bodies of typical Japanese women, every one different, every one alike.

"May I help you wash your hair?" Kazue-san asks, as I struggle to pour some water over my hair from the little red plastic bucket.

"Please let me!" interjects one of the obasan who has been watching me for several minutes. She is very old, probably in her seventies or even eighties. Standing, her face comes even with mine as I sit on the tiny stool. Her body is bent over, almost parallel to the ground. Kazue-san says she's probably crippled from malnutrition during the War years and the chronic lack of calcium in the traditional Japanese diet as well as from bending to plant and harvest the rice crop every year.

"I bet she still works in the fields," Kazue-san whispers in English,

and I smile back into the old woman's smiling face. Her hair is pure white, her face covered with spidery lines, but her eyes are absolutely clear, sparkling. The old woman introduces herself, bowing even more deeply. Her name is Keiko Doi. I'm too self-conscious to stand up so I introduce myself sheepishly, trying to bow as low and respectfully as I can without getting up from my little stool. The other old ladies in the bath are watching us. They seem abashed by Doi-san's forwardness, but they also look thoroughly delighted. One of the old ladies says you can never tell what Doi-san will do next. She is their ringleader, a real character.

"She has no shame!" one of the grandmothers says half critically, half affectionately of the mischievous Doi-san.

"Too old for shame!" Doi-san retorts, and the other old lady starts laughing so hard I'm afraid she might hurt herself. She pulls up a stool and sits down next to us, watching intently, still unable to stifle her laughter.

Doi-san squeezes shampoo into her hand and then rubs her palms together briskly. She's a pro. She massages the shampoo into my hair, the thick pads of her fingers making circles against my scalp. Then she lays one hand on my head, and starts clapping up and down on it with the other hand, making a sound like castanets as she works her hands over my head. It feels great. After about ten minutes, she chops with the sides of her hands over my head, my neck, and my shoulders, a kind of shiatsu massage.

I think I could die at this moment with no regrets. I feel about four years old and totally at home, this tiny grandmother massaging my back and shoulders, my scalp and forehead. "Do you like this?" she keeps asking. "Is this comfortable?"

Yes, yes.

The other old ladies are cutting up, making jokes, and Doi-san douses one of them with a bucket of water. The woman douses back, and someone else flips at Doi-san with a washcloth. Kazue-san says we've run into a group of eighty-year-old juvenile delinquents. She's never seen anything like this in her life, and she tells Doi-san, jokingly but admiringly, that she's the most outrageous old lady of them all. In English,

I start calling Doi-san the "Leader of the Pack."

"Shuuush!" Doi-san admonishes us to stop talking English to one another. She hands me a cloth to put over my eyes and motions to her friends. Each fills her bucket and comes to stand in a circle around me. They take turns; one pours a full bucket over my head like a waterfall. I take a breath, then the next bucket comes. The water is exactly the right temperature.

When they finish, I just sit there for a while, feeling cleaner than I've every felt in my life.

The old ladies can't stop laughing, and several of them are slapping Doi-san on the back, chiding her for her outrageousness, but also beamingly proud of their brazen friend.

I ask Doi-san if I may wash her hair but she refuses. Now, she commands, I must soak in the bath. It's time for me to relax.

I say that I can't take water as hot as most Japanese, and one of the strangers already in the bath motions me to a place beside her where the water, she says, is coolest. I lower myself slowly, allowing my body to adjust to the heat.

When I look around, Doi-san has disappeared. The rogue and her octogenarian gang from the countryside have all departed. A new group of bathers is coming in. They look startled at first to see me, a *gaijin*, but then go about their business. They are probably high school or junior high school girls, many of them still at the last stages of chubby adolescence, utterly unself-conscious about their nakedness.

"That was her," Kazue-san whispers, absolutely deadpan, as she slips into the water beside me.

"Who? What do you mean?" I ask, puzzled at first, then skeptical as Kazue-san smiles impishly.

"Why, the typical Japanese woman," she teases. "Doi-san. I think you finally found her."

~ *Cathy N. Davidson*

CHAPTER 1

I Can See Clearly Now

~*Martha Gradisher*

Typical Japanese Woman

I am the typical Japanese woman," my neighbor, Mrs. Okano, insists a few mornings after the newspaper interview comes out. It's been at least two or three weeks since we've seen each other. I'm coming back from shopping and she's at the foot of the apartment stairway waiting, she tells me, for the mail carrier.

"I'm serious," my neighbor says, "if you want to know anything about typical Japanese women, you can ask me."

Ted calls Mrs. Okano "the mayor" of Maison Shōwa, our apartment complex. She's there at the mailboxes at eleven o'clock most mornings, exchanging gossip, news, and information with the other women in fifties-style housedresses and slip-on plastic street sandals. I am the outsider in this group, the only foreign woman in Maison Shōwa, but she makes a point of including me in their conversations. She tells me when a neighbor has twins, an event for Maison Shōwa, and is delighted when I respond that I have stepsisters who are twins. She says she will make sure to tell the neighbor and perhaps we can talk together sometime about twins, in America and in Japan. ("Do you know," she asks me, "that twins are twice as common in America? Some scientists think it is because of our diet. Maybe too much soy sauce," she jokes.) Often, Mrs. Okano passes along more mundane information: she warns me of an upcoming earthquake drill one day and another time, tells me that a woman from NHK (the national public television station) will be by to collect a "voluntary but required" user fee.

Twice she's invited me into her apartment for afternoon tea. It's 2DK just like ours but seems smaller. It is crammed with furniture, including several large, freestanding wardrobes that hold clothes for herself and her husband, their two children, and Mr. Okano's mother, who has just moved in with them. Their housing situation is not atypical, even for this affluent suburb. I have gathered that Mr. Okano is an executive at a major corporation; they drive an Audi and own state-of-the-art electronic equipment. But housing costs are astronomical here. A new apartment in the Kansai area can be hard to find and often requires exorbitant "key money," sometimes up to a year's rent paid in cash in advance. Mrs. Okano occasionally hints that they will be moving soon but always abruptly

switches to some more immediate topic, so we never discuss the new home.

I've never seen her husband or children. From our conversations, I've learned that her son is in junior high and her daughter in high school. Both are enrolled in *juku* five nights a week.

"It's necessary" is all she says, putting an end to any further questions I might have about her children spending so much time in school, studying so hard. "Besides," she laughs self-consciously, gesturing around the crowded living room, "at *juku* they can stretch their legs."

Over tea, she tells me I am the first *gaijin* she's ever had in her apartment. She taught high school English briefly before she got married but this is the first chance she's had to practice her English in years. She is one of the few Japanese in our apartment complex to put out a Japanese flag on national holidays, so I assume her politics must be fairly conservative, but it's not a subject we discuss. We talk about our town, Japan, children, America, and anything else that happens to come up. Since neither of us is fluent in the other's language, we spend a lot of time riffling through dictionaries, gesturing, pointing. We speak a strange language, somewhere between English and Japanese, and sometimes find ourselves frustrated that we each know exactly the same words in each other's language.

"Interesting," she'll say.

"*Omoshiroii*," I respond.

"*Muzukashii*," I'll say.

"That's difficult, complicated," she'll translate.

She's been to tea in my apartment too, and has told all of the neighbors how I hang old kimonos on my walls like art and use *soba* to make spaghetti. We have learned from one another, enjoyed each other's company.

"Why do you consider yourself 'typical'?" I ask her.

"Because I am," she laughs. "There's nothing unusual about me at all!"

"I think it's unusual," I say admiringly, "for someone to admit she is typical. Most people think they are pretty special."

"Oh, maybe in America," she laughs. "But in Japan, every woman thinks that she is typical."

As we are laughing, the mailwoman zooms up on her red motorbike. Mrs. Okano excuses herself and goes out to meet her.

She reminds the mailwoman that she will be moving today and that from now on her mail should be delivered to her new address.

"You're moving *today*?" I ask, surprised at how disappointed I feel.

"*Gomen nasai, gomen nasai*," she apologizes, realizing that I'm outside the information loop. Probably everyone else at Maison Shōwa has known for weeks.

I tell her I'm sorry to hear that she is moving, but that I hope she will enjoy her new apartment.

"It's a *house*," she says, unable to conceal her pride.

She is expecting the movers this afternoon but insists on inviting me in so she can give me a copy of a map she has neatly drawn, marking the way to her new house.

"Now you can come visit me," she beams, handing it to me. "I gave my husband a map this morning so he can find his way to our new house tonight after work." She says this casually, as we start to make our formal goodbye bows.

"I don't understand. you mean, he doesn't remember the way?"

"He's never been there."

"I don't understand," I repeat, this time in Japanese. "He's never been there?"

Now she's confused by my confusion, and repeats again, in her best English, that she's drawn him a map because he's never been to the house itself.

"Excuse me, please," I say, upping the politeness level of my Japanese. "I do not understand how he could have bought a house without seeing it?"

"He didn't buy the house, *I* did."

"And he never saw it before you bought it?"

"Of course not. That's woman's work. I told you I'm a typical Japanese woman. Isn't this how women do it in America?"

Mrs. Okano is shocked when I tell her that few American married women make major financial decisions without consulting their husbands and that I don't know any married woman who would go out and buy a house on her own. There might be some, but I don't know any.

"Really?" She's as incredulous as I am.

"Never."

"What about a car?" she asks me.

I shake my head no.

"Appliances—refrigerator, television?"

"Not usually."

"Furniture?"

"Probably not. Most American husbands would be mad, I think, to come home and discover their wife had just bought a new couch or dining room set without consulting them."

"I thought all American women work, earn their own money?" She knows me well enough to know I wouldn't lie about this but she's finding the whole conversation bizarre.

"It's true many American women work outside the home," I begin again, slowly. "But even the ones who earn their own money often consult their husbands about big purchases."

"This is what Americans call 'women's lib'?" Mrs. Okano laughs out loud, then covers her mouth with her hand. She apologizes for her rudeness, but cannot stop laughing.

By noon, everyone in our apartment complex will have heard about how the poor *gaijin* woman works full-time as a college teacher, but wouldn't even buy a measly sofa without first asking her husband's permission.

"*Kawaisō*!" she says finally, exchanging her laughter for the ritual expression of sympathy (How pathetic, how pitiful!). Mrs. Okano reaches out and pats my arm encouragingly, as if I'm a small child badly in need of comforting.

"No wonder you like Japan so much!" she says.

~ *Cathy N. Davidson*

Don't I Know You?

It will be cold at work, the air conditioner perpetually conditioning. My work. Where I work. My twenty-second job in half as many years. Eeny meeny miney moe catch a job by the toe . . .

I drive down Hollywood Boulevard past tourists in Disneyland sweatshirts taking videos of each other in front of RIPLEY'S BELIEVE IT OR NOT. Sometimes I honk and wave and they turn their cameras on me in my twelve-year-old Honda. The sweet scent of jasmine stains the air this time of year, overpowering all other olfactory sensations. If you suck in air through your nose too hard or too fast at any given moment or place in Los Angeles you could almost fall in love. Smells like paradise feels like Times Square. Left on La Brea, right on Sunset Boulevard. I arrive. Sunset Plaza. One city block of pricey boutiques and crowded outdoor cafés visited at lunch by living dolls with large collagen lips, the eminently sun-glassed, tourists in Toon Town T-shirts, old lady Divas faces sewn into place, young men in Sundance caps and HAIR. Hair gone from home to car to destination. Strands lying obediently next to each other, coaxed, willed into place. I watch everyone eat lunch from the doorway of where I work.

I work at Boutique Morgana on the Plaza. Emily, the manager, is an acquaintance of mine. We met in yoga class where I was trying to rid myself of the angst I'd experienced in my last job . . . my twenty-first. I needed a new job. She had just fired a salesgirl for screaming in the dressing room at a naked customer. That's how it happens.

CHAPTER 1

"Clients, not Customers." Emily reminds me.

I never actually touch any money. No dirty green bills. Just plastic. And no dollar signs next to the three and four figures on each price tag. And that is *not* a short wool jacket, that's the DALAI. All the clothes have names. Longer wool jacket—LAMA, longest—HIMALAYA. Long jersey tee—AIR, short sleeved—VALERIAN. There's APOLLO and ATHENA, MERLIN and GAIA. And ATLANTIS and SUN and MOON and VENUS and the History of the World in silk chiffon. The FRIDA KAHLOs—diaphanous medieval velvet gowns—slip off their hangers (trying to run away?). I feel a special bond with them.

Ten-oh-two. My days begins.

SHE enters. She with well trained hair of gold streaks perfectly haphazardly spaced, aubergine wool pant suit, matching pumps. Emily nudges me, "Sarah Lynn Gold, very good client."

I squint as I walk towards Ms. Gold. "Hello, let me know if I can be of help today." Haven't dropped the squint, now I am staring at her. In my head I add twenty pounds, color the hair mousy brown and frizzy, tie-dyed shirt, hooded zipper sweatshirt, earth shoes.

Emily whispers into the back of my head. "You heard of her? She's a big producer."

I drop my squint and watch she-with-aubergine-armor in profile. I casually circle her. She smiles. I smile back. The Doctor Diamond nose. I recognize it. Doctor Diamond, nose doctor plastic surgeon to entire neighborhoods of a certain well-to-do New York suburb. Girls, my friends, a cousin, all owing their eighteenth birthday present to Doctor Diamond. Dr. D., known for a signature diamond tipped nose. A generation of girls with the same secret cousin nose. Girls with names like Sharon Berg and Missy Feinstein and Janet Levy.

Sarah Lynn Gold is stuck in her smile. I'm stuck in my squint. She says, "Gee you look familiar."

Sarah Lynn Gold. Drop the Sarah, bump the nose. Twenty years and no longer tying lengths of incorrigible hair around empty orange juice cans. No longer a baby fat princess proudly revealing a sixteenth calico patch on threadbare bellbottoms. Lynn Gold. Sat next to me. We shared a lab table in Al the Frogman Fishbine's sixth-period eighth-grade Biology class. Al the Frogman specialized in magic tricks with vital pig organs and Borsht Belt stand-up while he showed the class how to pin a lizard to a cork board. Al the Frogman . . . smelled of Wrigley's spearmint and Southern Comfort. Killed the lizards with his breath. Hit poor Amy Funicello over the head with a goat bladder when she couldn't commit the table of elements to memory. No one came near Amy for months after that. Word spreads quickly in eighth grade as do cooties. Lynn and I started a petition to get Al Fishbine's tenure revoked. We whispered together. Got nearly the whole eighth-grade class to sign . . . and some ninth graders. Lynn was well connected even back then. She knew ninth and tenth graders.

Ms. Sarah Lynn Gold holds a GUINEVERE to her chin. "I LOVE this. This is a great dress."

I nod. Never saw her or spoke to Lynn after eighth grade. I moved. She made new friends . . . eleventh graders, TV producers, movie directors.

She hangs up the GUINEVERE. "I know you. Didn't you work at Luma Café?"

"No."

"The one in New York?"

"Sorry."

"The Brooks project. The one that got canceled? You cut your hair."

"No, I don't think so. I'm . . . uh, a biologist. Normally, I am."

Emily stands nearby making the hangers equidistant on the silk rack. She coughs. Sarah Lynn and I watch Emily cough. Emily could be coughing up lightbulbs considering how intently we stare at her.

"I could have sworn . . ." Sarah continues. "I'm very good with faces."

Inside I'm shouting. Remember how we organized the class? I was smart. Made you laugh. Introduced you to Bette Midler and Three Dog Night. Aloud, "Oh well." I begin to make the hangers equidistant on the tropical wool rack.

Sarah Lynn Gold leaves the store and crashes into Blythe Danner. They hug noisily.

Al the Frogman still has tenure although I heard he died a few years back.

~*Karen Rizzo*

Water

A Monologue

[Darkness. A cacophony of Republican voices. An exhausted, dazed, and thirsty woman enters the stage and stands in the middle of a tub of water. She is fully dressed and dripping wet. Lights up. Sound out.]

November 8, 1994.

The Republican tide hit me hard.

I miscalculated.

Quite frankly, I didn't expect the tide to get so high.

It was a wall of water that came towards me. The wave knocked me off my feet. Kept turning me over and over. This huge wall. This huge tide coming straight towards me. I was drowning, gagging on names like Rush Limbaugh, Newt Gingrich, Pete Wilson. Thank God, his doctor shut him up. Oh God! Why am I so thirsty. *(Pulls out a bottle of water from tub. Guzzles some of the water in the bottle.)* The salt water, I guess.

Every time I think I'm drying off, I get hit by another wave. Pete Wilson fundraising for his presidential campaign . . . Slash Affirmative Action . . . California voting for 187 . . . Sylvester Stallone making another movie. Nooo!

I'm not giving up. I am no victim. I'm going to beat them at their own game. Water! *(As she guzzles you can see her body relaxing)*

(She sits at the edge of the tub) I'm a big fan of Crystal Geyser's. I carry a bottle of Crystal Geyser wherever I go. I know, they *say*, we can drink the L.A. water. But don't you trust *them*. *This* is pure and clean. It's ideal. A couple of weeks before the November election, I noticed that Crystal Geyser had developed this new twist-off bottle cap. I hated it. I'd try to open the damn thing and my hands would turn . . . Red. Sweaty. Sore. So, in a fit of frustration, I wrote them a letter. *(Pulls soggy letter out of tub. Reads letter as if doing a Shakespearean monologue.)*

To Whom It May Concern: I buy the Crystal Geyser, 1.5 liter bottle, by the case, on a weekly basis. So, in some ways, I feel this is *my* product, just as much, as it is *yours*. I feel it is my *duty* to tell you this twist-off bottle cap, *(beat)* is just not working. It's as though, when I try to open it, I have *no* strength. And *that* doesn't make me feel good. Much to my humiliation, I have to give it to my husband, the man of the house, and he opens it for me. Sometimes, I have to wait for him to get home before I can have another drink of water. That is totally unacceptable. I wait for no one. *What is going on*? Sincerely, D. Rodriguez. *(bows)*

I just folded that little sucker up and sent it off. *(Throws it out into audience.)*

You guys heard that Jerry Rubin died, right? Yippie man from the sixties. He was crossing in the middle of the street and got hit by a car. They didn't bother pressing charges against the driver because Jerry was *jay-walking*. Yeah, right. And JFK wasn't wearing a seatbelt. Now, strange thing is Jerry got hit by this car only *two days* after the so-called *Republican Revolution*. And the car that hit Jerry Rubin was a *German* car.

The question is: was Jerry crossing from the right to the left, or from the left to the right? Do all us counter-culture types have to start using the cross walk? A dark moment indeed.

I am certain there is a conspiracy going on here. Let's look for a grassy knoll! And while my inkwell is still full, I'm writing a letter to Angela up in Santa Cruz, and Dolores at the UFW to tell them to: Cross at the light! Look both ways. Hire yourself a political crossing guard. *(singing like Dylan) Cuz the times, they are a changing*. Oh, yes, they are. The times they are a changin'. *(sings)* Signs, signs, everywhere the signs. You've seen that sign, right? You know the one? By the border . . . in Oceanside. I don't have to do it for you, do I? *(reluctantly imitates a man running across the freeway)* People, there is obviously a foot traffic problem in that area, right? You'd think they'd build an overpass or a light. But, no there's just a sign warning us: Don't hit the Mexicans! Could it be there is a plot to get rid of us all? *(shakes her head)* I'm not going there.

I pick up the mail on December fifth, *(pulls out a soaking envelope from the tub)* and there is a little five-by-seven manila envelope, from Crystal Geyser spring water. I tear it open.

Dear Ms. Rodriguez: We are always trying to improve our product and we appreciate your input and concern. Our new twist-off cap is more tamper-proof for your safety, though we are still in the process of making improvements. Please accept our Crystal Geyser coasters *(pulls out coasters from envelope)* and an invitation, whenever you're in town, to take a tour of our plant, here in Calistoga, California.

I can't believe it! They wrote me back. They actually listened to me and sent coasters. This is so deep. But don't you see? There still may be hope to make change. Oh ye of little faith. Because, I've been meaning to tell you, when I take my bottled-at-the-source Crystal Geyser natural Alpine spring water, and open it, I feel the difference. Yes, I do!

I open it, with just the *tiniest* of pressure. It's so easy. *I* made a difference. *Me. My* letter made a significant change. Therefore, I am significant. *(She finishes the rest of her water and tosses the bottle offstage. She reaches down into the tub and grabs a new bottle.)* Don't you see. This letter from Crystal Geyser proves it! There's still hope. I'm not going to go down drowning. This is my life jacket! I'm saved. *(Victoriously, she tries to open bottle of water, but cannot. She looks up in utter shock.)* They lied.

~ *Diane Rodriguez*

Polite-itis

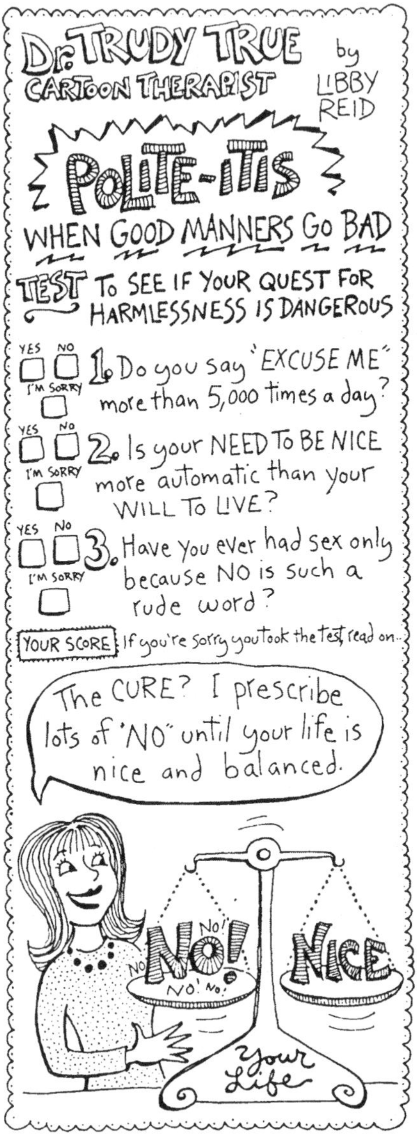

Dr. TRUDY TRUE CARTOON THERAPIST by LIBBY REID

POLITE-ITIS

WHEN GOOD MANNERS GO BAD

TEST TO SEE IF YOUR QUEST FOR HARMLESSNESS IS DANGEROUS

YES NO I'M SORRY 1. Do you say "EXCUSE ME" more than 5,000 times a day?

YES NO I'M SORRY 2. Is your NEED TO BE NICE more automatic than your WILL TO LIVE?

YES NO I'M SORRY 3. Have you ever had sex only because NO is such a rude word?

YOUR SCORE If you're sorry you took the test, read on...

The CURE? I prescribe lots of "NO" until your life is nice and balanced.

No! NO! NO NO! No!

NICE

Your Life

~Libby Reid

Psychic Economics

I used to be an unbeliever. I questioned the integrity of an economic system that valued women's work only half as much as men's. I was—and this seems almost preposterous to admit now—dissatisfied with the lot of women.

Before I reached enlightenment, I suffered from a common form of math anxiety caused by statistics from the Department of Labor. I was easily susceptible to depression whenever the words "supply and demand" came up in conversation. I kept getting lost in the void of the earnings gap. Years of investigation about women revealed many things to me, but didn't make sense of those numbers: Women earn 59 percent of what men earn. Until last week, I was like a haunted woman—devils of injustice chasing me, demons of inequity plaguing me.

My conversion happened unexpectedly, during a business meeting with a highly placed administrator. I had noticed—because skeptics habitually pay attention to damning facts—that the women employed by his prestigious institution were being paid much less money than the men. Like most unbelievers I was there to complain about the inequity. That's the major problem with those who don't have the gift of faith in our economic system. They have their visions trained on the temporal facts of their lives.

The discussion began predictably enough. With benign paternal tolerance, he reviewed the intricate principles of economics, the baffling nuances of budgets, the confounding factors behind the salary schedules. With the monosyllabic vocabulary educators use to address slow learners, he explained the familiar platitudes.

He invoked the dogma of salary surveys—the objective instruments used to determine what "the market will bear." They prove, beyond a shadow of doubt, that women workers are "a dime a dozen." That's reality, he reported almost regretfully; that's how life is outside of Eden. Practitioners of sound business—the members of the faith, so to speak—can in good conscience pay them no more. If he didn't adhere to the precepts of salary surveys, it would cause economic chaos. Other women, in other institutions, would begin to think they were worth more, too. The brethren in other administrations would expel him from the faith.

"You have to think about what the job is worth, not the person in it," he cautioned me. It always gets you into trouble, thinking about what a person is worth. He warned me against engaging in the fallacy of "comparing apples and oranges," a comparison odious to the members of the faith. It is only the unbelievers, the kumquats, who try to argue for the fruits of their labors. Mixing the categories would produce uncontrollable hybrids on the salary scale. Men are men and women are women and their paychecks are just further evidence of their vast biological differences, the powerful influence of the X and Y chromosomes.

I confess, I had heard these tenets of the faith many times before. It was the kind of conversation that might inspire the vision of a lawsuit. So it wasn't with an open heart that I asked the question one more time. How could he accept women's invaluable contributions to the success of his institution, witness their obvious dedication, and withhold their just rewards?

He paused, regarding me carefully, deliberating, apparently, on whether I was prepared to hear the truth, to embrace the amazing mystery of women's wages. Then slowly, respectfully, he revealed the fantastic reason.

Women came seeking positions with an intense longing for work, but with a paucity of credentials and experience. They were filled with gratitude when they were offered a job. They worked in a pleasant environment, doing meaningful work, and had the privilege of writing the name of the prestigious institution on their résumés. They received such an extraordinary sense of well-being, it would be almost a violation of female sensibilities to compensate them with cold, hard cash, Instead, they received something much more valuable; they earned a "psychic income."

I heard my voice becoming hysterical. Hysteria is not at all uncommon during conversations. I was loud—perhaps I was even shouting--when I asked him how much of his income was "psychic." Like many doubters, I didn't immediately see the light. I thought one of us was mad.

~

But not an hour later, enlightenment came. I was in a car dealership, chatting with the amiable mechanic who had repaired my transmission. He seemed to enjoy his job, especially when he handed me the bill. I gasped, knowing that the balance in my checkbook wouldn't cover the charge. Then I remembered my "psychic income" and that people who love their work, who are dedicated to it, are better paid with congratulations and a pat on the back. I told him what a wonderful job he did, how much I appreciated it. And then I wrote a "psychic check."

Suddenly, I was filled with the spirit. A happiness, a release flooded over me. I realized that every act of spending my "psychic income" was an act of faith. I had so much catching up to do I worked steadily to increase my state of grace. Immediately, I applied for a loan at the employee credit union at the prestigious institution, authorizing payments through "psychic payroll deductions." I used my "psychic credit cards" to charge two pairs of spiritual Adidas for my kids, whose real toes were poking through their real tennis shoes.

I was filled with a fervor to spread the Word. At a rally of working women, I brought them the message of "psychic incomes," and many converts came into the fold.

Nurses, who had an extraordinary love for their work, felt "psychic bonuses" coming to them. Their sense of self-esteem expanded miraculously, and they no longer bowed down to the false gods in the hospitals.

Clerical workers grasped the theory of "psychic work for psychic pay" and began typing only intangible letters, filing transcendental folders, and making celestial phone calls.

Prior to their conversions, working mothers thought they had to do all the housework, because their earnings were only half of their husbands' salaries. But when they learned how to bank on their "psychic incomes," they never cooked dinner again. They served their families supernatural pot roasts.

Of course, everyone will not accept the gift of the Word. There are those who will try to persecute us for practicing our faith. We must learn to smile serenely at the unfortunate creditors who lack the vision. We must have a charitable attitude toward the bill collectors whose interests are rooted in temporal assets. Beware of the Pharisees who pay spiritual salaries but still demand physical work.

And judge not the angry women who file the interminable lawsuits, who still rail against the status quo. Their daily struggle to exist prevents them from accepting the good news. Remember that there, but for the gift of "psychic economics," go we.

~ Mary Kay Blakely

Fly Me

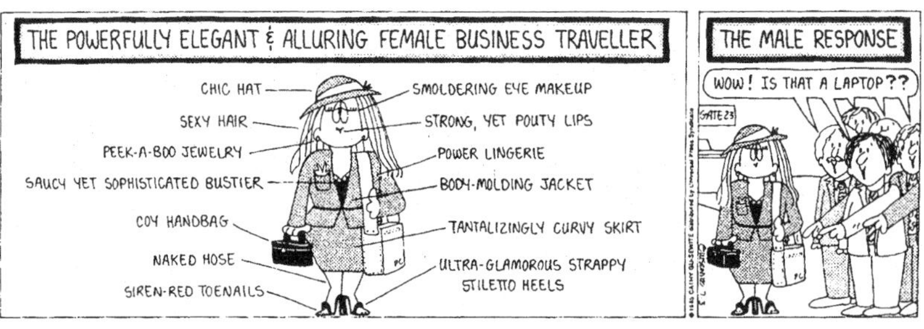

~ Cathy Guisewite

Striking Out in the British Empire

Heidi's first stop was England. After an hour of going through customs, the officials unanimously thanked her for coming across. She told them not to mention it, and slipped them another half an hour to insure it.

After that she set out for London, where she suffered one of the major disappointments of her life: she learned that Big Ben was a clock.

Trooper tart that she was, she took this in her stride, along with several bobbies, two palace guards, and a cross dresser who called himself Boy/Girl George.

It didn't take long for Heidi to find out that the British had a lot more to offer than stiff upper lips. Unfortunately, she made this discovery with a lamppost in a London fog and was hauled into the Old Bailey for soliciting a public utility. As she told me later, "I could have beat the rap if I hadn't made advances to the judge. Who knew it was a woman under that wig?"

Before she left the country, she managed to give a command performance at the House of Lords and a whole new meaning to the term "bed and breakfast."

~*Joan Rivers*

"Any woman who fakes orgasms too often winds up not knowing whether she's coming or going."
~*Heidi Abromowitz*

Broad Comedy

Somewhere out there in the universe is a very funny woman named Kerry O'Brien. Actually, I'm assuming she's still funny. The last time I saw her we were three and best friends at All Souls nursery school. My report cards attest to our joint comedy prowess: we appear to have spent most of our time rolling around on the floor cracking each other up. Or putting on "movie shows" where we would make the rest of the class sit quietly in neat rows and watch as we performed our shtick in the block corner (trying out the show in the sticks, as it were).

At four we split up the act and I went solo to an all-girls school. There, with a drama department devoid of boys, I was able to sink my teeth into the choicest comedy roles, and on a real stage no less. My gravedigger in *Hamlet* was rivaled only by my bad drunk in a bad fedora in *Ten Little Indians*. We were such smart girls. But we were so naive: no one ever bothered to tell us women weren't meant to be funny.

Not surprisingly, ten years later I found myself on a shrink's couch uttering these fateful words: "If I could just be a comedy writer I'd be so happy." I am now a Hollywood sitcom writer. Studios, on an alarmingly regular basis, pay me to be funny. I'm pretty sure they know I'm a woman. And I wouldn't necessarily say I'm happy. Call me bemused.

My first hint that I wasn't in comedy Kansas anymore came when my agent phoned me to tell me about my first break. "Mango Man," (all sitcom titles have been changed to protect the innocent and the guilty) she said, "is very interested in you. You're the best woman they've read." "The best woman?" I asked. "Sure," she said, exasperated. "They had to hire a woman. You're the best. (Pause) What. You're not happy." "No," I explain in my best girls'-school logic. "I'm not a funny woman. I'm just funny. Period." "Welcome to Hollywood," said my agent. "Go to the gym. We'll do lunch tomorrow and talk."

What I learned that day has stuck with me. The female writer quota, like male waxing, is a lot more prevalent in Hollywood than you'd care to know. What's fascinating is that while sitcoms will fight over a handful of women writers, once hired they rarely know what to do with us. We're like that goldfish you diligently tossed rings to win at the school fair: once you got it home you realized you have nothing to put it in and you have no idea what it eats.

There is an unwritten understanding in sitcoms. Women are very good at coming up with stories and writing "treacle scenes" (that ubiquitous part of any bad sitcom, usually act 2, scene 3, when someone says "I think we need to talk.") They are also good to have around to answer general questions about the female anatomy and to field fashion questions. ("No, Amanda can't wear linen in that dinner scene. It's December.") What women, in general, are not hired for is the real stuff of comedy: jokes.

For the most part, writer's rooms are still the denizens of young male writers practicing what I call the Stooges Principle: if you like the Three Stooges, you're funny and can bring in your toys and play. If you don't, you're probably a girl and have cooties. Since appreciation of the Three Stooges does, I'm scared to admit, alarmingly often divide down gender lines, this rule has been quite effective at keeping most women at the comedy water cooler. (By the way: note how many times a Three Stooges joke makes it into your favorite sitcom. They're stealthy.)

Recently I had a (male) boss tell me, point blank, that women aren't funny. When I pointed out to him that he hired me to be funny and, last time I checked, I was a woman, he thought for a moment and then answered with boss-like aplomb: "Yeah, but you're not a woman." With that he turned on his heels and exited, off to make his next executive decision. On more than one occasion I have had the following "compliment" from a fellow male writer: "You're good. You write like a guy." What they mean is: I'm confused. You're actually funny and you have breasts.

Male writers apparently aren't the only ones I'm confusing. While comedy has done wonders for my check book, it has been hell on my dance card. As my friend Karen likes to point out, being a woman in this business is like playing the children's game "Careers." You get sixty points and you get to decide between a family and career. Unfortunately, the guys still get both.

I have a friend here in L.A. He is neurotic. He is losing his hair. He wears bad clothes. He is a classic nebbish. He is also a TV Producer. And women flock to him like swallows to Capistrano. On any given day he is entertaining another would-be model, or struggling actress. His position and paycheck shriek "big break" to this girls. In Hollywood, a guy's producing credit on *Seinfeld* is better than any Spanish Fly.

Now when you're a female comedy writer, it doesn't exactly work the same way. Here's the scenario. You enter a bar. You think you look pretty good. A man with a goatee approaches you. (In Hollywood, a goatee is a necessity. Like milk or toilet paper.) You trade meaningful glances. He approaches. You flirt madly. He asks what you do. Women writers have learned to answer this question as if discussing the very ill: "I write (hushed whisper) comedy."

There is a long pause. During this pause he is thinking the following: "She's probably gay. She's too smart. She won't laugh at my jokes. Oh God, she probably makes more money than me. Hey, maybe she has another gay friend and the three of us could . . . Whoa, is that Michelle Pfeiffer?" He exits quickly to the opposite end of the bar. Really. This happens.

Don't get me wrong, I don't just blame the men of Tinseltown. There are plenty of women happy to uphold the stereotype. Why, right now, there are two very successful comediennes with hit shows who are very vocal about not wanting women writers on their staffs. Both have been victims of bad men throughout their lives. One speaks out against domestic violence. Ironically, while society has come to uncomfortable terms with the image of women being punched, women doing the punch lines still scare them.

Conversely, not all men are scared of funny women. God bless them. In fact, my first benefactor was a man of some stature. It was Robert Lowell, the famous poet. I was five. He was judging a smart writing contest I entered with a touching poem in verse about a crab with a weight problem. He found my piece joyous and effervescent and funny. And better than the boys'. I won. But then again, he was clinically crazy at the time and I had a pageboy haircut so it probably doesn't count.

I have a recurring dream. Kerry O'Brien and I are running a show. I enter the writer's room and it is full of bright, funny women. (Okay, and some enlightened men.) We don't spend hours writing jokes about PMS. We don't talk endlessly about our sexual conquests. We write brilliant, witty repartee for a brilliant, witty sitcom that wins many brilliant shiny awards. Then we go home to our husbands who have spent all day polishing our Emmys. And we make them laugh till they cry.

~Jenny Bicks

Position Available

~*Linda Eisenberg*

If I Produced The Oscars

I was watching the news the other night, getting more depressed by the minute. Just when I was feeling that the world's problems are beyond my ken, there was an interview on the news with Jeff Margolis about directing the Oscars. He said when he thinks of the Oscars, the word that comes to mind is "family." (Oh yeah, me, too. I was up for Best Sibling once.) Well, that explains a lot. Suddenly the heavy feeling of hopelessness that descends after a few minutes of the news was lifted. "The Oscars," I thought. "*That* I think I could fix."

If I could choose anybody to host the Academy Awards, I'd want Groucho, Chico, Harpo and Margaret Dumont. I mean early Groucho, before *You Bet Your Life* and certainly before he wouldn't eat his peas. He had a particular way of wearing a tux that the Oscars deserve.

I think Billy Crystal is great; he's gone a long way toward making the Oscars less embarrassing to watch, but I'm choosing from dead or alive. Leave me alone, I'm trying to have a fantasy.

One year's theme for the gala was "The Year of the Woman." I might throw up. This was the year women in a film shot people and drove off a cliff. Why was that our year? Maybe we should take turns. Maybe we should go back and forth every day, so that Saturday, January 1, is the day of the woman and Sunday, January 2, is the day of the man and whatever day the Academy Awards falls on that's how we know what the theme is.

The year I produce the Oscars the theme will be "Announcing the Academy's Choices for the Best Work in Film for the Year While Being Entertained by Film Stars We Like to Have Talk to Us Because They Make Us Laugh, They Say Things Like We Wish We Could or We Just Like Looking at Them." That way we could have presenters like Rosalind Russell, Cary Grant, Bette Davis, W.C. Fields, Sidney Poitier, Thelma Ritter and Jack Lemmon.

Academy Awards night is the only night of the year that Hollywood dresses worse than Washington. The men do just fine, but the women are out of control. I'd like to be able to use the honor system and just ask them not to look totally silly, but I know at least one person would come wrapped in designer plastic and ruin it for everyone. The year I produce the Oscars everyone will wear usher uniforms and we'll put the money saved in gowns into low-income housing. If someone had an absolutely fabulous gown in mind, she is welcome to bring a picture and show everyone. I'd like to leave it at that, but this lack of emphasis on attire may cause women to overcompensate with their hairstyles and someone is likely to get hurt.

Therefore, like those signs at carnivals indicating how tall you must be to go on a ride, as the stars arrive to greet their fans and quickly take their seats inside, there will be a silhouette of a head at the door. If their hair is too big they cannot enter. With the energy and money we save on hair mousse, we can go a long way toward relief efforts in Somalia.

The last celebrity butt will have hit its seat, we hope, when the red velvet curtain lifts to cue a chorus of "Hooray for Captain Spaulding" and reveals a set like the one the Marx Brothers entered on in *Animal Crackers*. After our four hosts come to the front of the stage, the curtain is lowered and a podium is wheeled out. That's the big production number—I hope you enjoy it. From then on, people come out the side of the curtain or the center of the curtain, like we did in the school play—no long stairs.

It's important that the presenters not be concerned with negotiating long stairways balancing on high heels or monitoring their straps and cleavage, because there aren't going to be any cue cards or writers. I am going to supply people like Judy Garland, Sammy Davis, Jr. and Ed Wynn to present and some new rules:

Rule 1: The presenters have to memorize the names of the nominees. I love Judy Garland, but if she locks herself in her trailer and says she can't work that way, then she can't do the show this year. These people memorize entire movie roles, but they have to read five names off a prompter?

Rule 2: The presenter runs the clips that identify the nominees' work. When Ed Wynn comes out and says, "The nominees for best sound are . . ." he can pop a tape into a machine or push a button so that the right film clip comes on at the right time; if it doesn't, he doesn't have to just stand behind the podium and look helpless. In this modern world there's gotta be a way to bring that off better than when Mrs. Kastier, my junior high Home Ec teacher showed "The Cranberry: How Does it Get to Your Holiday Table?" with a film-strip projector and a narration record with a bong sound when it was time to turn to another frame.

Rule 3: No dancing. I don't want to seem like the mean dad in *Footloose,* but this dancing thing at the Academy Awards almost always gets us in trouble. The people we are supposedly honoring are threatened with being drummed out of the business if they don't keep their acceptance speeches short, and meanwhile the best costume nominations are displayed in a totally unrelated dance number. Remember the guys in loincloths creeping across the stage in a presentation for *Dances With Wolves?* You know they had families and friends they had to face again.

I will make an exception and have the Nicholas Brothers do a number while Jack Valenti says whatever he insists on saying each year, but that's it.

I've eliminated the show's writers in order to make it a night of fairly sincere tribute. If a guy can't come out and say "It's nice to be here" without squinting at his lines just below the camera lens, then it's probably not nice to be there at all and he should begin with that.

Rule 4: No fake witty banter between the presenters. I'm gonna have Julie Andrews and Dick Van Dyke present the award for best song and if complying with Rule 4 seems difficult for them then perhaps they should avoid seeing one another ahead of time so that a simple "nice to see you" falls naturally and believably off their lips. I believe it's called "method presenting." (All of the nominated songs will be sung by Aretha Franklin, because she will do it beautifully.)

The time we shave off in phoniness we'll spend enjoying a tribute to the Three Stooges as well as clips of the great work of the presenters. Since they will include people like Myrna Loy, William Powell, and Cicely Tyson, I know the evening will be richly entertaining. I don't want to break the spell by leaving the stage, so Cher will do her Equal commercials live.

Another happy effect of losing the show's writers will be that when Maggie Smith and Humphrey Bogart present the best screenplay award, they won't be forced to read the obvious line about how "without the writer there are no words . . ." and "the loneliness of staring at a blank page." Since we all pretty much know what a screenwriter does, we can just move right to the award and then have a real movie usher come onto the stage and explain that plastic drink lids at the movies can be recycled.

Rule 5: No cameras at honorees' bedsides. If we want to recognize publicly someone who has made important contributions to the film industry, but is too sick or weak to appear at the event, we may not have them on camera. We can film a nurse or loved one standing outside their closed door and they can take a message.

The enforcement of Rule 5 will allow us time to have Ella Fitzgerald and Louis Armstrong sing "Summertime" before Louis Armstrong eases forward to the podium and, with that wonderful voice, makes an impassioned plea for the *L.A. Times* to stop running commercials in movie houses.

Hollywood is such a tough audience, I almost feel bad for the stars when I see how nervous they are speaking in front of one another. I would, therefore, forbid the camera operators to cover Jack Nicholson's reactions so frequently. I love Jack Nicholson's work, but the poor guy gets a camera shoved in his face every time we want to know if something is hip. Unless he wants to actually sit on stage and give "The Jack Nicholson Report," I would prefer, if it's OK with her, that the camera turn to a reaction shot of Imogene Coca when we're not sure what to feel. She is grace and charm personified.

After Katharine Hepburn and Alec Guinness bestow the best actor and actress awards, we show a little film. It begins with a clip of:

Tom Hanks scraping the caviar off his tongue in *Big*.
The grown-up Salvatore watching the kissing montage
from *Cinema Paradiso*.
W.C. Fields looking for his gun in *The Man on the Flying Trapeze*.

A whole series of movie shootings.
News footage of the scene of the high school shooting in
Chicago and the new metal detectors.
News footage of the schoolyard in Stockton.
News footage of the Luby's incident in Texas.
The grandfather talking to Lukas Haas about the gun in *Witness.*
And closing with a black screen with the daily gun-related
U.S. death toll in white.

That way, if Charlie Chaplin gives away the Oscar for best picture to *Unforgiven,* someone somewhere might notice that something's not right.

~ *Paula Poundstone*

Two By Two

"YOU MEAN NOAH DISCRIMINATED ON THE BASIS OF MARITAL STATUS?"

~*Martha Campbell*

Ida Mae Cole Takes a Stance

IDA MAE COLE, stands at the bus stop counting the change in her purse. SHE snaps her gum furiously, then sucks her teeth when she realizes that she is twenty-five cents short. Ida stops abruptly to gaze at the passersby, cutting her eyes as SHE meets unwelcome stares. Her clothing is overstated, though clearly color coordinated.

Go on look! Go on! *(Resumes counting her change.)* Does anybody know if this is the bus that go downtown, 'cause if it is I need another quarter. Anybody got an extra quarter? *(Places her hand on her hip and steps forward.)* Well? WELL? CAN'T ANYBODY HEAR ME? *(Freezes in her pose for a few seconds.)* I'm one of those loud-speaking women you walk around and say excuse me to at least three times . . . *(Raises her eyebrows.)* I dare any of you to tell me otherwise . . . Yeah! 'cause you see . . . I'm the loud-speaking woman who pushes her way forward and always grabs the last potato . . . peel it, slice it, and eat it right there so that everybody knows that it's mine . . . Ain't no trace of attitude here, 'cause attitude is passé. What I got is *Posture*! *(Hits a pose.)* Punctuated! *(Rolls her neck.)* PERIOD! There are three postures that I'm known to assume . . . Numero Uno. Head cocked, eyebrows arched, lips pursed, hand on hip, finger pointed and a waving. *(Assumes posture number one. Without taking a pause.)* This is the tell me why I was docked a day's pay for coming in an hour late 'cause my daughter had a fever. This is the get off my stoop and go on home position. This is the try me stance, the tell me stance, the why don't you take your fingers off me muthafucka stance. *(A moment.)* Lawd, I stepped on into this posture just the other day. I'd pulled number twelve down at the health clinic, and then had to wait eight hours for the doctor to tell me he . . . ain't . . . gonna . . . see . . . me . . . Well, I marched on in his office. I stripped down to the paper robe, oh yes, which covered everything but the bootie. MMM! . . . You have to leave, he said, like he'd just been served the last pig's foot in the jar, and you know how that taste after it been sitting in the sun for a few months. *(Moves into position number one.)* Try me! I said . . . And he did, he tried me . . . And you know what happened . . . *(Takes two definitive steps forward.)* I GOT EXAMINED! The first time in four years too, and waited eight hours for the doctor to feel my ti . . . toddlytutus *(Touches her breast.)* and ask me how come I hadn't come in sooner, sooner? sooner! Only day off in the last year and he's going to ask me how come I didn't come in sooner . . . Shoot . . . *(Stares, then releases posture number one, eases into posture number two, a more relaxed position.)* Posture number two. Legs spread, smile taut, head swaying . . . The go 'head ask me girl, I won't tell. The oh really, the oh no, oh but it ain't true that he wears her panties beneath his suit. That's what I told her, least five times that he was no good, 'cause I know his type. He gonna make you clean up then won't show. He gonna make you full up, then won't stay, make you pay out, then won't go. And I know what I'm talking about 'cause if you shift the posture on just one foot it becomes a welcoming posture, a thank you posture, the yes I will marry you, the no, I love only you . . . The where were you, the what do you want looking at me that way? I need you, I'm sorry, I'm here stance . . . The one that receives the drunken blows and the casual insults, that took an extra shift in the factory to pay for his new suede coat from Vim's, that prayed the siren wasn't going to bring me no bad news about my child, that . . . *(Counts her change again.)* Shucks . . . that don't forget, no punctuation needed . . . Not even that time on the bus when . . . when . . . *(Smiles, then laughs.)* I turned my head, and here comes one of them big-thighed women traveling in my direction, and I'm not in the mood to move . . . bump! She slaps one of her thighs up against mine and the vibration sends a tremor on through my body. *(Shakes her body.)* Excuse me! We say in unison. I strike posture number one.*(Assume posture number one.)* She don't move. I don't move. Her finger starts a waving, *(Begins to move her finger to emphasize her words.)* my finger starts a waving. Her head starts a moving, my head starts a moving. You going to let me by? she says, deep like Barry White. No place to go! I say smooth like Anita Baker. I eased on into posture number two to let her know that I'm flexible. Then she had the nerve to pull a posture on me I'd never seen before. So I tried all variations. *(Explores a range of positions.)* And she kept throwing them back at me. *(Gives a long penetrating stare.)* We locked eyes, and I thought oh lawd we're gonna throw down right here on the bus heading out to Kings Highway. Then I saw her eyes the night she'd gotten drunk, the vacationless year, the death of her youngest child, the *(Touches her side.)* the mammogram results she hadn't told anybody about, and the new suede coat she bought at Vim's for her man . . . I turned away quick, damn if we didn't have the same posture, damn if we didn't. *(A moment.)* I took two steps to the side, and said GO ON SISTER! GO ON! And that big-thighed sister shoved on down to the back, until she disappeared behind a bus full of attitude. *(Assumes her final position.)* And it all leads to head tilted, muscles relaxed, arms crossed, and feet firmly planted, this is the just so position. It's the just so position you see on the bus . . .Yes, I'm the loud-speaking woman you avoid on the bus, with the steadfast posture you can't get around. *(Counts her change again.)* Anyone got a quarter? I don't have change . . . *(Assumes posture number one.)* I said does anyone got a quarter?

~ *Lynn Nottage*

Where I'm Coming From

~ *Barbara Brandon*

Pisser

It never changes. Yet still you forget, particularly if you are an infrequent theater-goer, as you finish wolfing down your "pre-theater" meal, throw your money on the table and say, "Oh, I won't take the time to use the restaurant bathroom here, I'll wait till I get to the theater." Then you get to the theater and you realize that the line of tight-lipped women spilling into the lobby isn't for will-call. And you can't believe, as you take your place in line by a continuously used water fountain whose flowing stream relentlessly reminds you of your calling, that you forgot again. That rule, ironically golden, that in any public gathering place, despite their differences in anatomy and under attire, despite the fact that society doesn't treat them equally, there are always an equal amount of bathroom stalls for men and women. You watch men walk past no line, return in twenty seconds, buy a drink, furtively have a smoke, buy some candy, read the whole fucking playbill, and you've moved up three feet. You wonder if maybe (and with increasing fear) the women in front of you have somehow cosmically started their periods the same time as you, something to ponder, and also something that would add at least fifty seconds to each woman's bathroom time (BT). In fact, you start calculating the amount of time it will take each woman ahead of you, given their age, layering of their attire, size of their purse, and connecting children. A kind of BT profile. So a ninety-year-old woman in a jump suit with a poncho treating her six-year-old grandchild in tights and petticoat to an afternoon of culture is off the charts. While waiting for what could only be such a duo (who've tauntingly flushed the toilet about an hour ago, but who still have not emerged from the stall), you silently design the perfect theater, with one stall for the men, just to show 'em, and fifteen hundred stalls for the women—no, no—a catheter with every playbill—no, no—twenty-minute intermissions—no, no—each theater seat is actually a porta-potty. You start wondering if the women in the other three stalls (for a thousand seat house) are all pregnant. You wonder if you're pregnant. You start thinking pregnant women shouldn't be allowed to experience the wonder of theater, they embody wonder. You start thinking, from now on, no fluids for three days prior to show time. And then, suddenly, it's your turn for a stall and you're so overcome with opportunity, you can't go. The house lights start flashing, the bell starts dinging and you go to your seat, dissatisfied with your output, and you spend the whole first act plotting your intermission exit. Sure, I'm three seats away from the aisle, but those three people are, again, old, and even though you remind yourself you'll be old someday and have some empathy for what is in your future (no matter how well you take care of yourself), the seven shopping bags at their feet is not encouraging. You study the playbill every time the lights come up on stage to see, first, if there's going to *be* an intermission, and if it's a musical, if there's a production number big enough to cover your exit before curtain. Of course, if it's a play, and it's *Death of a Salesman*, you're dead. You start

avoiding tragedies altogether, knowing any attempt to leave for the restroom will become part of the show. *Oklahoma* is a very good play for weak bladders.

It's not enough that we don't have equal pay, that we age faster, that we have to go through childbirth, that we're missing the gene for computer literacy, that we're ultimately responsible for birth control, that we can't have it all no matter how many articles tell us we can, these same people who are writing those articles are designing public bathroom facilities. They either have a false sense or absolutely no sense of our needs. They don't realize that women tend to pee in pairs, one going along with the other for company. That they often are busy giving the babysitter last minute instructions, or helping their husband find his keys or doing any one of the myriad things required to just get out of the house, and often their bodily needs are left to the last minute. That they don't know what it is to do only one thing at a time, so it just doesn't seem natural not to make fuller use of an evening of theater. In short, women need more porcelain when they've paid for a ticket. No doubt this tradition got started on the Titanic. It wasn't just lifeboats they ran out of.

~ *Lissa Levin*

City Woman's Home Companion

~ *Libby Reid*

Accelerando

She talks to the audience. A long horizontal calendar is projected on the scrim behind her. Each month lights up as she comes to it. Each is a different color, and filled with drawings and notations. She might be filling in last touches as she speaks.

I've been making this—calendar—on the wall in my apartment, a Human History Calendar, the major events of the world from fifty-three hundred B.C. till now. It runs from January to December, and each month is the equivalent of six hundred years. I'm making it to find out what's important.

(Ravel's Bolero *fades up slow and soft.)*

The only thing in January is a picture of a fairly naked guy with a bow and arrow—that's it, that was the big thing till about forty-seven twenty B.C.—and then February is completely blank. Six hundred years like a weekend with nothing on TV. March brought round mud brick houses in Egypt and domesticated animals . . . And in April, there was the Mayan Calendar and settlements along the Nile! So April picked up, and May was really hopping—Stonehenge, the Pyramids, the Sphinx. And in June—the old testament, and indoor plumbing in the Indus Valley. July saw irrigation in China, Greek gods, the arch—and in August the concept of karma was born and so was Buddha—

(noticing someone in the audience)

a smile from the lady in the third row with the crystal in her purse and we're up to four-sixty B.C. In September there was the Golden Age of Greece, the Coliseum in Rome—Jesus Christ—

(noticing, in the audience)

a gay couple in the back and several born-again Christians just smiled almost simultaneously—and we're into A.D. now, and the year, our Human History, is three quarters over.

*(*Bolero *is building now, and She takes a breath and speeds up too.)*

October: Attila the Hun, the Goths, Visigoths, Vikings and Vandals—Mohammed—the decimal system—*(incredulous)* Two months to go till the present, we've covered five-sixths of time as we know it, and we're just up to the DECIMAL SYSTEM! *(pressing on, faster)* November: The printing press, the windmill, the clock, the plague, firearms, Zen . . . And finally—*(The month of December begins to pulse.)*

December, the last six hundred years *(fast as she can)*: the Renaissance, the Industrial Revolution, the Electronic Age—Shakespeare, Bach, Cortes, Hitler—Michelangelo, Fats Domino—the Taj Mahal—the theme park! Einstein, the radio, and the Bolshevik revolution all on the same Human History Calendar day! The airplane, the steamboat, the television, the Chunky—TWO world wars, Two-faced tape, the Space Age, the New Age, ANOTHER plague, ANOTHER war, and any millisecond now, some dictator who got kicked around in grade school gets —The Bomb.

*(*Bolero *cuts abruptly. She takes a breath, exhausted.)*

Jesus, what a busy month. If this was what your date book looked like this month, you'd take a gun and blow your brains out. And maybe that's how we feel as a civilization. We've been overbooked for about six hundred years, we have a giant collective

migraine, and we're real close to blowing out our brains.
(an afterthought) Forget the planet. The planet is like one big disgusting apartment. Who has time to clean it up?
(pause) And I can't slow this down, any of it. I can't stop the scientists from discovering, or the viruses from spreading, or the computers from computing, or the farmboys from making the chickens grow too fast. I can't even take drugs to keep up or drugs to slow it down like I did yesterday in the eighties, because I'm so much older and wiser now, I know I'd just come down or die, and time would just keep speeding up without me. The only thing that takes any time these days is cancer. And the only thing that counteracts time . . .

(like a kid discovering shells)

is love. Because love is the one thing man can't make a profit on. See, take war. With war you make a fortune. You can get rich as hell on disease, make a bundle on sex—art's a good investment—but nobody makes jack shit on love. Because it's the one thing they can't speed up, beef up, or mass produce!

(to a guy in the audience)

I'm not talking about sex here, I'm talking about love, okay? Since fifty-three hundred B.C. there's been no progress in the area of love at all. There's no more of it, and it's no better, and therefore, it's the one sure way to defy time. Who's going to tell you, "Hey, couldya just hurry up and love me a little faster?"

So, thinking practically for the first time in my life, love is the only practical, reasonable conclusion I can come to. It's the one thing worth spending my time on.

(glances at her calendar)

I figure I've got till sunup . . .

(gathers courage)

And I'm going to a party to find it.

~*Lisa Loomer*

Black + White = Gray

~*Signe Wilkinson*

PTA

~ *Signe Wilkinson*

CHAPTER 2

Kill Me, I'm Yours

Dear Kenny Rogers

"Lady . . . I'm your knight in shining armor, and I love you. You have made me what I am, and I am yours . . ."

Dear Kenny Rogers, or anybody like that: I want to be exactly what you want. And after I am, I want you to promise me, and mean it, that you'll love me forever. I'll be strong . . . in an attractive, weak sort of way . . . and independent, without crossing that line of unappealing, and sweet with genuine niceness to everyone. And you watch me decorate the tree and you notice I look great . . . in a subtle, I have no idea I look great kind of way. And you pick me up and carry me off to the bedroom that I have decorated in classy yet folk artsy colors and calico. And we make passionate love, with me exuding just enough need but being careful to be distant enough for you to wonder about. And you brush the hair from my forehead, and I weep faintly into your chest . . for no other reason, other than how fragile and sincere I am.

I want to be a Mrs. Kenny Rogers kind of woman. You know . . . the kind of lady he sings about: "Oh, Lady, I was just scum in the sewer until you came along and made me a man." With hair that's light, but not really blonde, that would be too cheap. Instead, sort of a wheat-and-sunstreaked affair with not a lot of hairspray. A ninety-five dollar cut that looks like your hair just naturally grows out of your head like that. The kind of woman who always, no matter what, has that I-understand-and-am-knowing-without-being-threatening kind of always smile.

I don't need a lot of makeup or jewelry. I was born with diamond studs permanently pierced in my ears. Fun, yet mature; spiritual, but never kooky or culty; and always understanding, yet firm and moral. I am equally comfortable on Walton's mountain or in a Rolls Royce. My legs are long . . . like the horse I ride every morning. And sometimes . . . sometimes, when I'm reading an old classic that I've had rebound in light leather, I glance over at Kenny and chuckle, 'cause he's still such a little boy. Last night I wept when I heard his grandmother's neighbor's sister died. But quietly, on the bed, until he came in and held me for hours, admiring my natural foal-like beauty.

I never gossip or talk about Kenny to anyone. I just smile knowingly, and hang that handmade ornament on the Christmas tree. While Kenny admires my ass.

~*Kathy Najimy*

Lowest Common Denominator

~*Jennifer Berman*

CHAPTER 2

Ode to a Love As Strong As an Emery Board

I knew we were right for each other the moment we met. And for five years we had a wonderful relationship—talking for hours, laughing, and yes, at times, crying.

Now it's over.

I'm not making excuses, but I was fragile, vulnerable. A once-vibrant woman, I'd grown haggard and hostile, each day a rerun of kids, cooking, and cleaning. I hungered for attention, understanding, and, perhaps, just a hint of excitement.

I had tried talking to my husband. Tearfully I told him: "My life is meaningless."

He picked up his head, having been intently examining the plant growth on the bottom of his tennis shoe, and asked, "What? You're going to enlist?"

"That's right babe," I replied. "I think the military could really use me. I've been practicing with the kids' remote-control helicopter, and I'm sure I could handle one of those Apaches. What do you think?"

"Sure, I'll take a drink," he said.

With that, our conversation ended, and I walked out the door.

It wasn't as if I was looking for someone. It just happened. Actually, a friend had innocently introduced us. But that's all it took. From then on, we had a standing appointment of sorts. We'd see each other every week or two, usually just for a couple of hours unless it was a special occasion. Then we'd take longer.

But that's all in the past.

My manicurist has gone onto a career in banking, and I'm left with a heavy heart, hangnails, and cuticles that are completely out-of-control.

Oh, I know what you're thinking: "Geez, she was just your

manicurist, get over it."

Well, you couldn't be more wrong. No, this was not a simple she-has-a-file-I-have-fingernails relationship. We truly enjoyed each other's company. Granted, she was getting paid, not to mention a big fat tip. Nevertheless, I think we had something special.

Who else would give me their undivided attention for a couple of hours—truly listening, allowing me to share my innermost thoughts, my deepest concerns? More importantly, my manicurist never disagreed with me. She was the first person who recognized what had been obvious to me for years: I'm always right.

She was also insightful. I'm convinced that if you have a good manicurist you'll never need a therapist. And, unlike many of-course-this-is-completely-confidential shrinks, manicurists can actually be trusted.

How often do you hear of a manicurist speed dialing "Hard Copy" the minute her client leaves, or splashing their sordid secrets all over the tabloids? Admittedly, the fact that the details of my life are about as compelling as your average toaster-oven manual probably limited such opportunities.

And did I mention I got to leave the house? For two hours every other week, I entered a world where people addressed me by my first name? This initially took me by surprise, having assumed that immediately after giving birth, the state automatically changed your name to Mom, which is most frequently pronounced *M-high pitched scream-O-even higher pitched scream-M!*

In this dream world, other odd things happened. I was able to sit down. For many consecutive minutes. I almost fell off my chair the first time I was asked, "Would you like a cup of coffee?"

"You're a saint," I replied, throwing my arms around her, weeping. "I have never experienced such kindness." (In time I learned a simple "thank-you" would suffice.)

And when I left this other world? I felt renewed, invigorated. And, my nails looked darned nice too.

So please, don't even show me an orange stick. The pain is still too fresh. The mere sight of an emery board can send me reeling. And I will never again look at a bottle of Moscow Red the same way.

It was, after all, *our* color.

~ Carrie St. Michel

Talking Want Ad

In a casual, free, off-handed manner of speaking

```
         C                        F
I'm looking for a man to wash my clothes
     G
Iron my shirt and blow my nose,
     C                    F
Sweep the floor and wax the kitchen
          G
While I sit around playing guitar and bitchin'.

          C
          Mud all over my boots,
          F
          Cigar butts on the rug
          G
          Beer cans lined up around the wall
          C
          . . . That kind of thing.
```

I'm looking for a man to cook my meals,
Wash my dishes and take the peels
Off my bananas with a grin,
And ask me how my work day's been;

C
Insufferable
F
As usual;
G
Playing the guitar
C
Is such a struggle.

I'm looking for a man with curly hair,
Great big muscles and a nice derrière;
To get up nights and feed the baby,
And have my coffee when I'm ready;

C
I've got to feel good in the
F
Morning
G
That's when I make my best
C
Music.

So if you feel you'd like to apply,
Just send a photo or drop on by;
And you can shine my shoes today
And if you do that good, I'll let you stay

C
And cook my supper;
F
And after you've finished the dishes,
G
If you're lucky, I might let you listen to me
C
Practice my guitar.

~*Janet Smith*

Cafe Society

~*Jan Eliot*

My Sort Of Ex-Boyfriend

My sort of ex-boyfriend . . .
Who I kind of lived with . . .
Has said that we ought to be
Living more sensibly,
Possibly separate?
(Only a month or two),
Seeing if all of this
Tension and bickering
Ends . . .
He says that's the way we can
Always be sure to stay
Friends.

My almost ex-lover . . .
Who I kind of liked once . . .
Has told me he thinks I have
Lots of potential, and
I should explore it, like
Start my own business, or
Study karate,
Or learn how to put up a shelf . . .
He says that's the way
That a woman survives
By herself.

My nearly ex-roommate . . .
Who I kind of miss now . . .
Was very intelligent,

CHAPTER 2

Full of suggestions, and
Always so rational,
Still as I think now, I'm
Starting to wonder,
Do I blame my heart or my head?

My sort of ex-boyfriend . . .
Who I kind of lived with . . .
And liked once
And miss now . . .
I guess that
I wish he was dead.

~ *Carol Hall*

Happy Hour

Savannah and Robin watched Gloria eat and occasionally looked around the room, waiting for someone to ask them to dance. But no one approached them. Three more songs came and went, and still no one invited them. Savannah was tempted to ask somebody, but she didn't see anybody she wanted to meet, let alone dance with. If the men in here were a representative sample of what was available in Phoenix, she might as well forget about it.

"No," Robin moaned.

"What do you mean, 'No'?" Gloria said.

"I don't even believe this."

"What?" Savannah asked.

Robin dropped her head.

"Which one is it?" Gloria said; she'd been through this before.

"Michael."

"So what's the big deal?" Savannah asked looking toward the entrance. All she saw was a pudgy, light-skinned man with a nice-looking sister by his side. "That's Michael?"

"Yes, and who the hell is that standing next to him is what I wanna know." Robin's face was now pulsating. She couldn't believe this shit. "He's supposed to be so in love with me, and here it hasn't even been a whole week since I fired him and he's already out in public with another woman?"

"Take it easy," Savannah said.

"Don't do anything stupid," Gloria said. "You're the one who gave him the ax, so try to act civilized. Whatever you do, don't embarrass yourself, and especially us."

"I'm not Bernadine, so don't even think it. That little fat fuck."

Michael had to walk by their table in order to get into the room. When he saw Robin, he smiled and said hello. She didn't say anything. He said, "How are you?" to Gloria and Savannah, and kept on walking. Robin looked as if she was ready to detonate when Bernadine flopped down in the chair, sweating and out of breath. "Girl, did you see Michael?" she said.

"What do you think?" Robin said.

"I just asked. You get what you pay for," she said. "I'm having a good time. How about you guys? You haven't danced yet? The music is jumping. You guys should be dancing. Shit."

"We know that," Savannah said. "But we're waiting for somebody to ask us."

"Don't wait for your ship to come in. Swim out to it!"

None of them could believe this was Bernadine. When did she come out of that cocoon she'd been hiding in all these years? Bernadine had never been a real party girl, but she was turning the place out tonight. She sprang back up. "I need to freshen my makeup. I really needed this," she said, as she walked away. "I swear I did."

Robin sat there as if she was in a trance. Finally, somebody asked Savannah to dance. She didn't care what he looked like at this point, and when she got on the dance floor, she still didn't care. Everything about him was average: height, looks, weight. She didn't look at him until he asked her name, and when he asked her what she did for a living, she told him and, out of courtesy, asked him about his work. When he said he was a mortician, Savannah wanted to crack up. She immediately thought she smelled embalming fluid and was glad she didn't have to hold his hands. They danced through Bobby Brown's "Every Little Step," and that's when she saw Robin come out on the floor with a below-average type, and Bernadine was right behind her, holding Herbert's hand. Gloria, who would not walk through that door at all tonight (and really didn't care), was busy thinking about two things: the fact that she was missing Cagney & Lacey for this bullshit and whether or not Tarik would have his behind in the house by nine o'clock.

Michael was on the other side of the room, dancing with his date. Robin almost broke her neck trying to find him in the crowd, but she was unsuccessful. After the song ended, the three women went back to their table and sat down. They ordered another drink and took their time drinking it. Every now and then, Gloria and Savannah watched Robin scoping the full room, looking for signs of Michael, who in fact had sat down at a table in the dance room. Although they were right in the center of things, no one acknowledged them. An occasional man walking by gave them a nod or a half-smile and kept walking. This was not fun.

"How long does this thing last?" Gloria asked.

"Why?" Bernadine asked. "Are you bored already?"

"You know it. And I'm going home."

"Me too," Robin said. "This is dead."

"It's only dead because you haven't met anybody and you got your feelings hurt tonight. Can't you be satisfied having a little fun and let it go at that? For once in your life. You don't always have to meet somebody, Robin."

"Shut up, Bernadine, would you? I've got a ton of paperwork waiting on my desk for me in the morning. I had no intention of staying out late anyway."

"It's not even nine o'clock. What about you, Savannah? Are you ready to leave too?"

"I'm with Robin."

"You guys are nothing but a bunch of deadbeats, I swear. Go on. Go. I'm not ready to leave yet. I came here to relax and have fun, and that's exactly what I'm going to do."

"Then do your thing," Robin said. "You ready, Savannah?"

"I'm ready," she said.

Robin didn't have to ask Gloria. She was already heading toward the door. When the three of them got there, the same man who had greeted them popped out from behind the partition. "Leaving so soon?"

"We have to get up early," Robin said.

"I heard that," he said. "Try to make it back on Friday. It's going to be even better. But we need sisters like you three here to make it that way."

"Yeah, yeah, yeah," Robin mumbled, as they walked out into the graveled parking lot. Gloria said good night, got in her car, and took off, leaving a cloud of dust.

"Is this how folks party here?" Savannah asked Robin when they were seated in the car.

"It could be worse," she said, and turned on the lights

"You're kidding."

"I can't believe Michael, girl. I can't."

"Well, let it go," Savannah said. "Just let it go."

"That's what I thought I was doing, but you want to know what's weird?"

"What?"

"I'm jealous! I can't even believe this shit."

"I can. You always want what you can't have."

"But I had it!"

"You know what I mean."

"Yeah, you never know how good something is until somebody else has it."

"Remember, you're the one who put him on hold, and all men don't have call waiting, honey."

~ *Terry McMillan*

Alex Phones

~ *Cathy Guisewite*

The Race

Tuesday

I had a blind date tonight. He was really nice, but I'm afraid he may be too much of a noodle. I'd mow him down in a minute! His name is Sam.

Friday

Sam called today and left me this message: "Hi, Lily, it's Sam giving you a call. I haven't heard from you since our date on Tuesday and I just want to tell you I had a really great time with you that night and I'd love to see you again. As a matter of fact, I've been thinking of you ever since and I sure would love another look at those beautiful blue eyes. How about breakfast tomorrow? Or Thursday? Or any day over the weekend? Give me a call. I really think we may have something here. I know we just met but I just have a feeling. I look forward to talking to you. Bye."

I am standing over the answering machine with my mouth open down to my toes. "Gag!" is my first thought. "Who do you think you are? You don't even *know* me!" are my second and third thoughts. Then an enormous grin spreads not merely from ear to ear, but around my whole head, engulfing me briefly before the panic sets in.

The guy was showing a little moxie. I like that. That's what I was worried he didn't have any of, right? Why, then, do I feel like I used to feel in the eighth grade when a boy I liked turned out to like me? Ill. So very ill.

I am overcome with feelings of inadequacy. I should be ecstatic but all I want to know is: "What kind of a dope do you think I am, Sam? You think I just fell off the hay truck? I know your type. I've been around the block, buddy. I've already been married and divorced, remember? I'm not that easy. So if this is some kind of a lousy joke, I'm on to you, asshole, and you can find some other bimbo to stroke your ego!"

I guess I want him bad, huh? Does it show?

CHAPTER 2

I've always wondered what it must be like to be pursued. Now that it's happening I feel completely out of control. And the critical voices in my head are euphorically beating my self-esteem to a pulp in ravenous anticipation of my self-loathing devouring the gooey mass that will be all that's left of me in another twenty-two seconds.

"Why on earth do you think he'd go for you?" the voices sneer. "He must be an idiot, not worth his weight in boogers! And you must be exorbitantly desperate to believe a line of gewgaw like: '. . . I sure would like another look at those beautiful blue eyes.' You know, as soon as he really gets to know you and finds out what a false alarm you are, he's going to dump you. (Actually, you won't have to worry about that because the relationship will never get that far.) 'What on earth was I thinking?' he'll wonder to himself by this evening and you'll never hear from him again."

I am now sufficiently tenderized and ready for consumption by that insatiable soul-snatcher known as "Self-loathing." Before she takes me down, however, I get one phone call.

"Hi, it's Lily calling for Sam, please . . . Thank you . . . Hello, Sam? It's Lily. How are you?"

"Fabulous! I'm so glad you called. I was really hoping you'd call."

(Lily: One. Vicious Voices: Zip!)

"Well, I got your message; how could I not?"

"I don't know. I hung up and I thought, 'I hope I didn't scare her by coming on too strong.'"

"I don't scare that easily," I say laughing flirtatiously to cover up my utter terror of having been found out only four seconds into the conversation.

(Maybe I spoke too soon.)

"Great," he says. I can hear the smile in his voice. "When can I see you again?"

"Um . . . well . . ." (The familiar feelings are lining up at the starting gate in rapacious anticipation of the capital race of the week that is about to begin. Terror, I Need An Out, No Self-Esteem, Just Keep Your Distance, I'm Worthless, Big Liar, and, oh yes, that scrawny little stiff, Contrition, are ready to go. A posse of allegorical horses prepared to stop at nothing for that evanescent moment of glory when they *trample me* like a grape; make off with my senses; and declare world domination!)

"... I'm actually very busy this week with rehearsals for this play I'm doing. We're about to start tech week so I'll be at the theater 'till all hours." (And they're off! It's Terror in the lead; followed closely by No Self-Esteem, and Just Keep Your Distance along the rail.)

"You have to eat don't you? Maybe I could meet you down at the theater during your dinner break?"

"Um ..." (Oh my, ladies and gentleman, will you look at that! This is going to be a very exciting race indeed. Coming from behind, gaining from the far outside; she's an early foot from wire to wire ... It's Big Liar!)

" ... We're not organized enough to know when our dinner break will be ..." (Big Liar breezes past the stands; gaining nimbly on No Self-Esteem and Terror ...)

"How about Sunday? I'm having breakfast with my friend Ellen at 10:30, before my rehearsal, (Big Liar leads by a hair ...) but we could go for a walk before that at 9:00 ..."

(Now it's I Need An Out dusting the railbirds and rounding it out along the back stretch. She's pressing the bet on Just Keep Your Distance *and* getting the edge on No Self-Esteem. I'm Worthless tries to give I Need An Out the hat trick, *but the latter pulls ahead*. She's a cyclone. Neck and neck with that speedball Big Liar. . .) "I just have to be on the road by ten so I can make it to Ellen's on time." (... I Need An Out gets the bat. She's puttin' on the ritz—she's nose to nose with Terror but can't quite steal the lead.)

"Sure, that'd be great."

"I'm sorry it's so early. I'll have more time after tech week is over ..." (Holy moly! Coming from behind—as if out of nowhere, ladies and gentlemen—it's Contrition—*that glue pot without a prayer*. What a race this is turning out to be!)

"I'll look forward to seeing you bright and early Sunday morning, then . . ." beams Sam.

(Contrition picks up speed . . .)

". . . Get my day off to a wonderful start. Shall I come pick you up?"

(Terror still leads by a nose with Just Keep Your Distance now sneaking into second . . .) "Oh, no, you don't have to do that . . . (Big Liar is jammed in the middle. She puts the chill on Just Keep Your Distance and muscles her way back to number two . . .) I'll bring my own car; that way I can go straight to breakfast with Ellen."

(I'm Worthless and No Self-Esteem hang on to a tight tie for third, giving Just Keep Your Distance a bad day at the office . . .)

"Okay, I'll see you Sunday . . ."

(. . . And whatd'ya know? As they come thundering down the home stretch, that neverwuz—Contrition—is all but out of the race.)

". . . Have a great two days," offers Sam.

"Thanks. You, too."

"Thanks."

"Bye."

"Bye . . . Thanks for calling back."

"Oh . . . well . . . my pleasure, really."

(It's going to be a close one . . .)

" 'Kay, bye." Sam doesn't want to hang up, either, but I have no choice. My palms are so sweaty I'm in danger of being electrocuted any minute . . .

"Bye."

(And the winner is . . . Terror, by a breath! Big Liar glides into second. Just Keep Your Distance and I'm Worthless tie it up for show and No Self-Esteem and I Need An Out bring up the rear.

What a race, ladies and gentlemen! What a race!

The horses are walking it off now, already looking ahead to their next heat which could come at any moment. Tireless beasts, these ponies live to win—unmitigated cerebral domination or bust.)

Despite the infinite stamina of the "horses" in my head, I hang up the phone still master of one or two of my senses and feeling relatively intact. World domination is not to be theirs just yet. I take a deep breath and notice that even "Self-loathing" has momentarily lost her appetite for my soul.

Boy, this dating thing is exhausting—and I haven't even left the house yet. If Sam and I ever have sex, I'll probably pass out before we've even popped the first button. I need some milk.

~Yeardley Smith

Oops!

Oops!
I fell in love with a married man.
Oh, not your usual married man, but a dutifully, happily
married man . . . with children!

I didn't mean to do it. I'd NEVER do such a thing. Who was I?
It was a terrible idea, that, of course, wasn't an *idea* at all
—just *inevitable*
Actually it was more like an advanced course in
"The Concept Of NEVER":
NEVER touch in public.
NEVER have breakfast together.
NEVER make any plans.
NEVER sleep together.
But of all the NEVERs we studied,
I NEVER imagined he'd NEVER speak to me again.
One day though, he commanded, "Don't call anymore."
Because I loved him I did what he asked.
But then I got too busy to call—which didn't count.
So I called to remind him that I was *not calling*.
But *that* call ruined everything.
And I had to start *not* calling him all over again.

~ *Flash Rosenberg*

Among Other Thoughts On Our Wedding Anniversary

Over the years,
When the sink overflowed
Or the car ran out of gas
Or the lady who comes every Friday to clean didn't come
Or I felt pudgy
Or misunderstood
Or inferior to Marilyn Kaufman who is not only a pediatric
surgeon but also a very fine person as will as beautiful

Or I fell in the creek and got soaked on our first family
camping trip
Or I bruised my entire left side on our first family
camping trip
Or I walked through a patch of what later turned out to be plenty of
poison ivy on what later turned out to be our last family camping
trip.
Or my sweater shrank in the wash
Or I stepped on my glasses
Or the keys that I swear on my children's heads I put on top
of the dresser weren't there
Or I felt depressed
Or unfulfilled
Or inferior to Ellen Jane Garver who not only teaches constitutional law but is also a wit plus sexually insatiable
Or they lost our luggage
Or our reservations
Or two of the engines
Or the rinse that was going to give my hair some subtle copper
highlights turned it purple
Or my mother-in-law got insulted at something I said
Or my stomach got upset at something I ate
Or I backed into a truck that I swear when I looked in my
rearview mirror wasn't parked there
Or I suffered from some other blow of fate.
It's always been so nice to have my husband by my side so I could
Blame him.

~Judith Viorst

On Being Married

LET'S JUST SAY WE COMPROMISE A LOT... WHICH MEANS NEITHER OF US GETS WHAT WE WANT.

~ *Paige Braddock*

Bears with Furniture

Some of the best comedians right now are women, and the best of the women comedians is named Rita Rudner. She does great bits on men, and in one of them she says: "Men don't live well by themselves. They don't even live like people. They live like bears with furniture."

I always wondered about that furniture part.

Since the observations of female comedians, women lawyers, my aunt Gloria, the entire membership of the Hadassah, the League of Women

Voters nationwide, and the woman who lives across the street from me don't count as empirical evidence, researchers at the University of California at San Francisco have done a study that shows that men need to be married or they starve to death. They studied 7,651 American adults to come to this conclusion.

This is why we think scientists are wasting their research money. This study says that men between the ages of forty-five and sixty-five who live alone or with somebody other than a wife are twice as likely to die within ten years as men of the same age who live with their wives. "The critical factor seems to be the spouse," said a professor of epidemiology and biostatistics who, incredibly enough, seems both to be surprised by these findings and to be female. She also noted that researchers were not sure why men without wives are in danger of an earlier death, but that preliminary analysis suggested they ate poorly.

Let me explain how you might do a study like this. Let's say you have a package of Stouffer's macaroni and cheese, a tomato, and a loaf of French bread. Let's say that it is seven o'clock. Pretend you are a researcher for the University of California and observe what the woman between the ages of forty-five and sixty-four will do with these materials:

1) Preheats oven according to package directions. Puts package in oven.

2) Slices tomato and sprinkles with oil, vinegar, and ground pepper.

3) Slices bread and removes butter from refrigerator.

In about an hour the woman will eat.

At the same time researchers can observe a man between the ages of forty-five and sixty-four living alone using the same materials:

1) Reads package, peers at stove, rereads package, reads financial section of paper.

2) Looks at tomato, says aloud, "Where the hell's the knife?"

3) Places tomato on top of frozen package, leaves both on kitchen counter, watches Monday Night Football or a National Geographic

documentary on the great horned owl while eating a loaf of unsliced French bread.

This can be compared and contrasted with the man living with his wife. When the wife goes out, the result is exactly the same as in example 2, except that when the wife returns and says, "Why didn't you eat dinner?" the husband between the ages of forty-five and sixty-four will say "I wasn't hungry," in exactly the same tone of voice he would use if he were to say, "I have bubonic plague." (These results are occasionally skewed by observed occasions on which wife returns home and finds house full of smoke. Such incidents are particularly reliable indicators of longer life for men between the ages of forty-five and sixty-four, since they enhance the well-documented "I told you not to go out and leave me alone" effect, which promotes a generalized feeling of well-being and smugness.)

Every woman I know finds the California study notable only because the results seem so obvious. But I find it helpful to have anecdotal observations confirmed by scientific analysis, and besides, it gets me off the hook. I am frequently accused of feminist bias for suggesting that the ability to do a simple household task without talking about it for weeks is gender-based. If I were to suggest that a man without a wife is a man overwhelmed by dust balls, pizza cartons, and mortality, I would get an earful from the New Age men. The New Age men appear in many stories about life-style matters; there are five of them, and they are the guys who actually took those paternity leaves you've been hearing so much about. One of them makes a mean veal piccata, which is habitually featured in stories about men who cook.

If they're unhappy with this conclusion, they've got science to arm-wrestle with. E = MC2, some guy once said, perhaps while eating a loaf of French bread and wondering why his wife had to visit her sister. And 1 man minus 1 wife = bad news, according to researchers at the University of California at San Francisco. Bears with furniture. Rita and I have biostatistics on our side.

~*Anna Quindlen*

It Ain't Over

I'm standin' at the supermarket
Next to the cheese...
Noticin' a man in the quick frozen peas...
He seems very physically fit, in his jeans...
I'm full of admiration, I'm snappin' my beans...
Then he turns...
Our eyes lock...
And our grocery carts they knock...
And he asks me, can I tell if his melons are ripe?
He's my type!

I'm in love again!
Yes, really...
I'm in love again!
Sincerely...
I'm in love again!
For the forty-third time today...

It seems that
It ain't over till it's over!...
And you don't see me
pushin' up a clover...

It ain't over till it's over...
There's words that ain't been said yet...
Joy that ain't been spread yet...
Appetites not fed yet
And I ain't dead yet!

I'm waitin' at the service station
Down by the bank...
Lookin' at the fella
Who's fillin' my tank...
I'm thinkin' his body's as tight as a wire...
Maybe I should ask for more air in my tire?
He looks up...
From the pump...
And my heart, it gives a thump...
And he asks me, just how long since my oil has been checked?
And I'm wrecked!

I'm in love again!
Yes, really...
I'm in love again!
Sincerely...
I'm in love again!
For the sixty-eighth time today...

It seems that
It ain't over till it's over!...
And you don't see me
Pushin' up a clover... and
It ain't over till it's over!...
There's words that ain't been said yet...
Joy that ain't been spread yet...
Appetites not fed yet...

And I ain't dead yet!

Someday I will live to be one hundred and four...
Sittin' in a wheelchair, can't dance anymore...
My teeth in a glass and my feet wrapped in socks...
I'll find me an old man who sits there and rocks.
"Sonny boy"...
I will say...
'Gather rosebuds while ye may!'...
That's a poem...
And there's poetry deep in my soul...
So...you rock...
And I'll roll!"...

It ain't over till it's over...
And you don't see me
Pushin' up a clover...and
It ain't over till it's over!!...
I have not expired yet...
I ain't even tired yet...
And I ain't dead yet.

~ *Carol Hall*

Playing by the Numbers

HONESTLY, RICHARD, SOMETIMES I THINK OUR RELATIONSHIP IS NOTHING MORE THAN A GAME TO YOU!
LIEBE

~*Liebe Lamstein*

Letter To The Editor

Editor
Orgy Magazine
Salt Lake City, Utah

Dear Sir or Madam:

As a long-time reader of my husband Howard's copies of your magazine, which he keeps in his old karate uniform at the bottom of his closet under the bar bells which are too heavy for me to lift, I appreciate your sharing with the reading public some of the sincere experiences and relationships that furry creatures can offer to human beings. Yes, indeed, the interesting letters from your readers show us that our little four-footed companions, large and small, can be our very best friends. So, I thought, maybe, I should share one of my recent experiences with you. A few weeks ago, my husband, who has frequent contacts with Arab potentates and others, and is therefore often away on long trips among the trackless dunes of Saudi Arabia, and deserts like that—well, to make a long story short, a few weeks ago he sent me a camel. A bactrian which has two humps because, as he wrote in the letter which accompanied his gift, two humps are better than one, which is a dromedary, but they're both known as the ship of the desert. It was a terrific gift, as I wrote him immediately in a grateful thank-you note, but it's hard to know where to put a camel when you live in a small three-room apartment in Queens with no dining alcove. Well to make a long story short, I let my new pet spend most of his daytime waking hours in the kitchen and various other places with me while I did my household obligations, but at night he seemed very lonely wandering around the living room and having insomnia, and stuff. So, after thinking the matter over, I gave him a place in my bed, seeing as Howard, which is my husband's name, is away chauffeuring that big muckamuck in the state department.

Well, to make a long story short, propriety and an upright sense of decency prevents me from going into details, but all I can say is that camels are the most inventive pets you'd ever want to meet. Every night has been an extraordinary experience, in a wonderful kind of inexpressible way, which my mother always said nice girls don't talk about.

So, anyway, Lynda and I have been spending these very agreeable nights together—oh, I forgot to tell you, I took a look the other day, where my mother always said it's not at all polite to

stare—and lo and behold, I discovered he's not even a boy camel, he's a girl, which makes the whole experience even more extraordinary. But now I'm really upset, because our relationship has progressed to the point where we spend not only a lot of night time together in bed, but also a good part of the day, which is okay because my household obligations are not extensive. The children are in school all day—they have this great lunch program, so I don't even have to make sandwiches, all I do is give them each 85 cents, which comes to only $2.25 per diem, as we have three children, Howard and I, but two of them are twins—so the house doesn't get too messy, and Lynda is quite fastidious, knock on wood, and has adapted very well to American cuisine, though we sometimes send out for falafel.

But, the reason I am upset, is that in the middle of enjoying, and even expanding this newfound relationship, I have received a letter from Howard telling me that he is definitely coming home on Friday—today is Monday—and that means that he is definitely going to want his side of the bed back. But, worse still, he says that the camel was actually just a loan, even though it certainly was meant as a pleasant surprise. But it seems that his boss—the aforementioned gentlemen from the state department, of whom Howard is the chauffeur—plans to surprise his own wife on his homecoming, by riding Lynda into the entrance hall of their large Jeffersonian-style townhouse, in Washington, D.C., when he comes home.

The worst thing is, I don't know exactly how I'm going to explain it to Lynda, who has, I'm afraid, gotten into some habits most camels probably don't have much opportunity to get into, and she may seem a little unusual. And also, I've heard that when camels get frustrated, they spit. Well, Lynda has never had to spit, not for a moment, in this house, knock on wood. But I hate to think what might happen to the muckamuck's wife if she isn't as considerate as I am of her newfound pet.

Lynda, at this very moment, is reclining, comfortably on Howard's Barca-lounger, which is made of real naugahyde, happily unaware of our impending separation. I don't know how to handle this new turn of events, but of course, I want to do what's best for Lynda and I—and Howard, too. I was thinking of writing Ann Landers, whose advice I read daily, every morning, but I think maybe she's better for in-law problems. I am enclosing a photograph of Lynda, me, and the children, which I took with the self-timer button on the Kodak Howard bought last Xmas. Camels are wonderful with children. Unlike Howard. Oh, Lynda, we're going to miss you so very much...

Very truly yours,
Mrs. H.C.

~ *June Siegel*

Healthy Appetites

~ *Anne Gibbons*

"Kill Me, I'm Yours"

Ext. 59th Street Bridge—Night

A black, filthy New York City night. The old bridge moans as cars stream across in both directions. No one notices a YOUNG WOMAN *pull herself up onto the guardrail by a steel cable. She stares out over the river, her face devoid of expression. A few beats and she looks over her shoulder. Sees something across the way.*

YOUNG WOMAN *(shouts):* Excuse me!

POV on a *YOUNG MAN on the other side of the bridge, also standing on the rail, about to jump. The man looks over his shoulder at the YOUNG WOMAN who, one hand cupped to her mouth, holds on to the cable with the other, swaying.*

YOUNG WOMAN: I'm sorry to bother you, but are you about to ... *She gestures "jump in."*

YOUNG MAN: As a matter of fact, I am!

YOUNG WOMAN: Do you think you could help me with something before you go? I mean, do you have a minute?

The YOUNG MAN hesitates, then climbs down. He darts through the traffic and goes up to the YOUNG WOMAN, who looks down at him from her perch on the rail.

YOUNG WOMAN: I'm having a little trouble actually, you know ... Could you just give me a little push.

YOUNG MAN: But that would be murder.

YOUNG WOMAN: Well ... *(thinks)* You could just stroll by and bump into me. Then it'd be an accident.

YOUNG MAN: I don't know. I could go to jail.

YOUNG WOMAN: You'll be *dead. (losing patience)* Look. Just push me. Then jump in. Do you have rocks in your pockets?

He pulls a stone from his jacket. She nods. Good.

YOUNG WOMAN: Okay. So, here we go. *She turns again and faces the river. Closes her eyes.*

YOUNG WOMAN: Okay. . . Now!

YOUNG MAN: I can't.

The young woman groans, looks down at him with disgust.

YOUNG WOMAN: Oh, to hell with it. *And she jumps, but the YOUNG MAN grabs hold of her ankle and she hinges forward, smashing against the rail. She shrieks. Now he's got her by both ankles as she kicks to free herself. He struggles to hang on.*

YOUNG MAN: I'm sorry!

YOUNG WOMAN: Let go!

YOUNG MAN: I can't.

YOUNG WOMAN: LET GO!

He awkwardly hauls her back onto the narrow sidewalk. Her face is cut. He flinches when he sees blood on her forehead.

YOUNG MAN: Oh, God. Look at you.

He takes out a handkerchief to dab the blood when she feels her face, pulls her hand away, dazed.

YOUNG WOMAN: Oh, God... *(looks at him)* I'm still *here.*

She flops back against the rail in despair.

YOUNG WOMAN: I've left suicide notes all over town.

YOUNG MAN: I *am* sorry. I just couldn't let you ... *(fuddled)* Listen, if it's any use, you can come to my place. Get cleaned up.

YOUNG WOMAN: But don't you want to kill yourself?

YOUNG MAN: Well, yes. That's the plan. But I've mucked up your ... thing, so at least let me give you a cup of coffee and ... a Band-Aid.

YOUNG WOMAN: Where do you live?

YOUNG MAN: Not far.

He offers his arm. She manages a faint smile, loops her arm through his, and they hobble back toward the twinkling lights of the city.

—Perry Howze

CHAPTER 2

For the Woman Who Has Everything

The Building

Words by Wendy Wasserstein Drawn by Blair Drawson

Your fairy godmother's on her way up.

Oh no, not her again.

It's me—Gilda. Your fairy godmother.

I've come to make your life perfect.

I have glass slippers, water-processed decaf, the perfect little black dress.

And you also get four weeks at a health spa, new teeth, new eyes, new cheeks.

A new romance, a best friend, a son who wins the Westinghouse science fair.

Honey, you need company.

But I'm perfectly happy.

Don't talk crazy.

—*Wendy Wasserstein*

TV Talk Show

Introduction to the Crossing of Mediums Using Television as Inspiration for Composing

In 1994, I caught one of those colds, so virulent and vicious, all I was capable of doing was lying on the couch, excused from all life and responsibility, finally understanding the joy and power of "manhandling" the television's remote control. I became a flipper, a surfer, a competitor in the world of "power channel changing." I was fearless. I could watch one show, and during the commercials, flip and scan, returning to my original station, without having to miss one word of dialogue, and yet not having to wait while "a word from our sponsor" finished its series of 12 spots. What a talent, what a gift. I see now why men struggle so. I think we can file this special gift and talent under the heading of spatial relation." It's not at all unlike our ability to completely load and stack the dishwasher without wasting one slot. It's a skill that may or may not be genetic. . . I don't care . . . all I know is . . . I surf better, faster, smoother, and more completely than my husband. 'Nuff said.

One small note: I'm addicted to the *TV Guide.* I love the Horoscopes, as well as the small eight to ten word descriptions they give the programs. These small, incomplete sentences are used to hook us into watching. Bait us with such unusual paraphrasing that we can't miss it. No matter what.

This song was written after my daily perusal of one such daytime listing.

9:00 A.M. OPRAH Women with multiple personalities

10:00 A.M. DONAHUE Women who stalk

11:00 A.M. JENNY JONES Women with multiple personalities who stalk themselves.

How could I resist?

CHAPTER 2

TV TALK SHOW

I heard about this man wanted a wife and some children
The problem with this man is he used to be a woman
Now he wants a family, someone to understand
There she is sitting with him, wants a husband and some children
The situation here is she's not a real woman
There they are together the man who was a woman
The woman who was a man:
    How do I know? I seen it on the . . .
    TALK, TALK, TV TALK
    TALK SHOW

Then there was this woman who had a quirky daughter
Forty times a day the kid sticks her hands in water
Doctors say the young girl is trying just to cleanse her soul
She's a prisoner in the bathroom, she's stuck inside the bathroom
She's compulsive in the bathroom, they film her from the bathroom
Mom would like to use the bathroom now and then you know.
    Where does she go? She goes on the . . .
    TALK, TALK, TV TALK
    TALK SHOW
One day Oprah's heavy, next day Oprah's skinny
Next day Oprah's heavy, next day Oprah's skinny
Jenny Jones had big boobs, now Jenny's big boobs are gone
. . . where'd they go?. . . I don't know!
One day Oprah's heavy, next day Oprah's skinny
Next day Oprah's heavy, next day Oprah's skinny
I'm checking in with Donahue, he's got a red dress on
What's going on. . . on the. . .

TALK, TALK, TV TALK
TALK SHOW

They got mothers who are dating their daughters' boyfriends,
Mothers who are dating their daughters' girlfriends
Mothers who are dating guys who like to dress like priests.
They've got ninety-year-old bikers, with rings in their noses
Then there's the bulemic, who ate up all the roses
The anorexic brought along her feeding hoses
Oh, the things they show . . . Do we need to know?
All that they give us on the . . .
TALK, TALK, TV TALK
TALK SHOW

I'm just a simple woman with simple complications
I can be lazy, lacking motivation,
Today I am a voyeur, I cannot let go.
I view the TV for holistic meditation,
Compared to some, my life it is perfection
Does anybody understand our attraction
To people who suffer so, hope I never know
. . . or you'll find me on the TALK, TALK, TV TALK,
TALK SHOW

~ *Sally Fingerett*

Rosebud

ROSEBUD was originally written as a short film with subtitles—but please don't let that discourage you. First of all, only the first couple of pages are hard. And

second of all, if you're old enough to see a movie with subtitles, you're old enough to read one. It was produced and directed by Neil Leifer, starred Caroline Aaron as Carol and Susan Greenhill as Jane, and was selected for the 1992 Edinburgh Film Festival.

The Place: One of New York's many nail salons.
The Time: The 1990s
The Characters (in order of appearance)

PEDICURIST TINA—*A Korean pedicurist in her early twenties*
MANICURIST CHRIS—*A Korean manicurist in her early twenties*
JANE—*A regular salon customer in her late thirties. Married.*
CAROL—*Jane's friend. Also a regular salon customer in her late thirties. Has never been married.*
PEDICURIST PATTY—*A Korean pedicurist in her early twenties.*
NOSEY OLD WOMAN—*A regular customer who passes her time in the salon eavesdropping.*
SONNY—*A regular customer who could easily be confused for John Gotti. Dapper. Italian.*
VARIOUS EXTRA CUSTOMERS AND SALON WORKERS

We open in a New York City nail salon. There is a row of small tables with relaxed customers on one side and stone-faced name-tag-bearing Korean manicurists working diligently on the other. At the pedicure thrones—two chairs, each sitting above a small sink—we meet Tina and Patty, pedicurists who sit hunched on impossibly small and very uncomfortable-looking stools. They are waiting to perform their magic on yet another pair of tired, calloused feet. Manicurist Chris has carved out a little niche for herself near the thrones. As they wait for their regulars, Jane and Carol, to come in for their weekly appointments, they pass the time chatting in their native Korean tongue.

PEDICURIST TINA: *(in her native Korean . . . so this part is subtitled)*
He even has a special little nickname for me when we're in

bed . . . *(then in English . . . and in a gravelly whisper á la Citizen Kane)* Rosebud.

MANICURIST CHRIS: *(in Korean and Subtitled)* He calls you . . . *(in English and incredulous)*. . . Rosebud?

PEDICURIST TINA *(Reaffirming in the same whisper):* ROSEBUD!!! *(and the three giggle uncontrollably for a moment)*

(JANE, who is just getting settled in her chair, has been listening but doesn't understand anything, obviously, except for the word "Rosebud."

CAROL bursts into the salon and up onto the throne next to JANE. They exchange ad-libbed greetings with one another as well as with CHRIS, TINA, and PATTY. Then the manicurists and pedicurists get to work.)

CAROL: Jesus, Mary, and Joseph!

JANE: What?

CAROL: God!

JANE: What?

CAROL *(Rubbing her thighs and indicating something "over there" with her head)* I should have taken a Valium. Followed with a Prozac chaser.

JANE: *What?* Tell me.

CAROL: *(indicates "over there" with her head again)* I'm not kidding! Do they serve alcohol here? I need one of those new martinis I'm always reading about.

JANE: *What happened?*

CAROL: I just had a . . . you know . . . *(Still being secretive)* "Bik Wak."

JANE: Huh?

CAROL *(More deliberate):* A "BIK. WAK."

JANE: What the hell is a "Bik. Wak" *(Then . . .)* Oh . . . a BIKINI WAX!?

CAROL: Oh, thank you! Now the whole city knows. Did you make sure my cousins in Brooklyn heard you?

JANE: Did it hurt?

CAROL: *(Still whispering)* Are you nuts? It's like sex with a sand-blaster.

JANE: Why are you whispering? *(Gesturing towards the manicurists and pedicurists)* They can't understand you. They only speak four words of English; "What color?" and "Cut cuticles?"

PEDICURIST TINA *(in Korean and Subtitled):* Four? Try four thousand. And what are the other customers? Deaf? Pass me the pumice. *(Patty passes the pumice without ever looking up)*

JANE: Anyway, where were you last week? I missed you.

CAROL: Oh, I threw my back out so I went to a healer.

JANE: A healer?

CAROL: This very spiritualistic woman who cures physical, mental, emotional, and attitudinal illnesses with common household rice. It costs a fortune, but it's worth every penny.

PEDICURIST PATTY *(in Korean and Subtitled):* Someone's making money off of rice? Why didn't I think of that?

JANE: Rice? Like in the kind you throw at a wedding?

CAROL: Exactly. Except she's a vegetarian so this is brown rice.

PEDICURIST PATTY *(in Korean and Subtitled):* Oh. Brown rice? Forget it.

JANE: What does she do? Put you on a rice diet?

CAROL: No. No. No. It's not like that at all. First you explain your problem to her—mine happens to be a bad back from sleeping funny. Then, she pokes and prods you a bit, bounces a quarter off your stomach, makes you repeat an ancient holistic chant, and massages lavender oil into your ears.

JANE: You're kidding.

CAROL: I've never been more serious.

JANE: So where does the rice come in?

CAROL: When she's finished, she tapes nine pieces of rice in an upside down "Y" on your diaphragm.

PEDICURIST TINA *(Horrified. In Korean and subtitled):* And she thinks a bikini wax hurts?

JANE *(In disbelief):* Your *diaphragm?!*

CAROL: Not *that* diaphragm. Here. *(Indicating her chest)*

JANE: What the hell does that do?

CAROL: It relaxes your skeletal muscles, enabling your red blood cells to flow more evenly, with a greater awareness of their space. This then allows your white blood cells to prioritize themselves thus discarding any "bad seed" cells. And finally, it reoxygenates your lungs while filtering out the evils of city living. I'm surprised you haven't heard about it. Everybody's doing it.

JANE *(In disbelief):* Not this everybody. *(Pause)* Back problem, huh?

CAROL: Uh-huh.

JANE: Sleeping funny?

CAROL: Yeah.

JANE: Gimme a break, Carol. I wasn't born yesterday. Who is he?

CAROL: Well . . .

JANE: I knew it! Why didn't you tell me?

CAROL: Because every time I start to say I have a new boyfriend, we break up before the words are even out of my mouth. It's my own customized jinx.

JANE: Details. I want details.

NOSEY OLD WOMAN *(Drying her nails in front of a fan and eavesdropping on everybody):* Excuse me. But aren't you a little old to be dating?

CAROL *(Stunned by the woman's rudeness):* If I'm old enough to periodically stop having sex, I'm old enough to date.

(Clearly neither CAROL nor JANE want this woman to enter into their conversation. They do not encourage her.)

NOSEY OLD WOMAN: You were never married?

CAROL: No. *(Then specifically to JANE—because she is still appalled that the woman is trying to join in)*And could she possibly say that a little louder? I'm not sure they heard it in the skin peeling room. The one in Beverly Hills.

JANE: Where'd you meet him?

CAROL: In my aerobics class. He's very fit.

JANE: Go on.

CAROL: Romantic.

JANE: Nice.

CAROL: I-talian.

JANE: Weo!

CAROL: Rich.

JANE: Okay.

CAROL: Oh, and thoughtful!

JANE : Sure sounds like "Mr. Right!" What's his name?

CAROL: Tony. And if he's not "Mr. Right" he's at least "Mr. Right Enough For Now Even Though, Lord Knows I'm Not Making Any Predictions Because I've Done That Before And Look Where It Got Me."

(Tina shoots a glance at Carol for one split second, then quickly resumes working)

PEDICURIST TINA *(in Korean and Subtitled):* Are all Italian men named Tony?

PEDICURIST PATTY *(in Korean and Subtitled, gesturing toward the very dapper Sonny, who is having a manicure):* Not Sonny.

(Sonny smugly smokes his cigar, blowing the smoke in the direction of the Nosey Old Lady)

PEDICURIST TINA *(in Korean and Subtitled):* Sonny doesn't count. He's a thug. All regular Italians are named Tony, and all thug Italians are named Sonny. Didn't you see *The Godfather*?

JANE: So . . . how long have you been seeing this Mystery Man?

CAROL: Two months today. And he sends me flowers at least once a week. You know how I have this thing about fidelity? Well, this guy is f-a-i-t-h-f-u-l.

PEDICURIST TINA *(in Korean and Subtitled):* Ten bucks says he's married.

JANE: You said that about Max . . .

CAROL: Max was a psychotic, insincere cradle robber. This guy's forty-one and his head is screwed on straight. He wants to have a baby, not date one.

JANE: So . . .

CAROL: Who knows. My track record is pretty . . .

JANE: Lousy?

CAROL: Jane! What are you? My friend or my mother? I'm telling you—this guy's different. He surprised me after work last night and took me dancing.

PEDICURIST PATTY: *(in Korean and Subtitled):* Where does your boyfriend take you?

PEDICURIST TINA: *(in Korean and Subtitled):* The park, the movies, Japanese restaurants.

(SONNY gets up to leave. He gallantly tips every manicurist in the salon. In unison, they all bid him goodbye)

JANE: How many nights a week do you see him?

CAROL: Three. Sometimes four. He never cancels unless it's a work thing. Although he did last Saturday.

PEDICURIST TINA *(in Korean and Subtitled):* Haven't we heard this before? She'll find out he's cheating in a month. My guy never cancels.

JANE: Well, then maybe this is it. I know when I met Ed, I had completely given up on men. I was thirty-four and getting wedding invitations from kids I used to baby-sit.

CAROL: Tell me about it. I'm still getting shoved out onto the dance floor to catch the bouquet.

JANE: But this sounds serious.

CAROL: It is. Otherwise, I wouldn't subject my thighs to such torture.

JANE: Remember—the way to a man's heart, even in the 90's—is still through his stomach . . .

PEDICURIST TINA *(simultaneously in Korean. Subtitled)*. . . Through the bedroom door.

JANE *(con't):* Fill him up so much he can't move . . . and then jump on him. *(Pause)* What's his favorite restaurant?

CAROL: Come to think of it, I don't know. We never eat out.

JANE: What is he? A cheapskate?

CAROL: Worse. A health nut. He cooks for me at his place.

JANE: That's an impressive switch. A man saying the way to a woman's heart is through her stomach. A green-light to eat!

CAROL: It's not as great as you think.

JANE: What do you mean?

CAROL: Well, he cooks, but it's not exactly human food . . .

JANE: What is it?

CAROL *(Pausing, as if really trying to figure out what it is):* Hay, maybe? Straw? *(Then . . .)* It's all this weird-ass, macrobiotic, low-fat, high fiber, vegetarian . . . cruciferous . . . Alpha Beta . . . High Octane . . . Retin-A'd . . . trigylceride . . . shit.

JANE: So then look at it this way. You have a boyfriend *and* a personal trainer all rolled into one.

CAROL: I guess. But frankly, I'd kill for a huge plate of linguine with clam sauce, an eggplant parmigiana hero with extra cheese, and a dozen bottles of cheap Chianti.

JANE: Oh, no. He doesn't drink, either?

CAROL: Oh, he drinks. His bar features several beautiful decanters of . . . Perrier, Evian, Seltzer, and Pellegrino.

(A woman gets up to leave the salon. Her freshly painted toenails have cotton wedged between them and Saran Wrap covering them. Her fingernails are still wet, too, so she holds her hands in the air as if someone has just yelled, "Stick 'em

up!" One of the other manicurists piles her coat, purse, and a shopping bag over one shoulder.)

CAROL *(Looking at the woman—who is truly a sight to behold):* Will you look at what we women go through just to try and look like Murphy Brown?

JANE: Hell, I do this for Ed, not me. He has a foot fetish—thus my weekly pedicures. And because of this . . . fetish . . . he likes to, you know hmmmm, hmmmm, hmmmm my toes.

CAROL: What?

JANE: You know . . . da-da-da . . . my toes.

CAROL: *(Loudly and in disbelief):* SUCK YOUR TOES? Edward J. Regent likes to *suck your toes*? I couldn't be more stunned if you said Prince Philip.

JANE: SSSHH!!!

CAROL: Well, my, my, my. I have a whole new respect for Ed.

JANE: What finally hooked him was, I dipped my toes in different flavored liqueurs every night. Champagne one night, peach Schnapps the next—I even mixed up a little pail of Old Fashioneds one night which I kept right next to the bed. Dip. Dip. Kiss. Dip. Dip. Kiss. The next thing you know he's on bended knee proposing.

CAROL: Wow! Really?

JANE: Dating is like fishing. It's all in the bait.

CAROL: I don't know. You think if I dipped my toes in sparkling water Tony would automatically propose?

PEDICURIST TINA *(in Korean and Subtitled):* Are you catching any of this?

MANICURIST PATTY *(in Korean and Subtitled):* Unbelievable.

PEDICURIST PATTY *(in Korean and Subtitled*): I wouldn't suck these toes if my life depended on it. And I'm their grounds-keeper.

MANICURIST CHRIS *(in Korean and Subtitled):* Maybe I should try it on my husband. A nice, subtle Arsenic.

PEDICURIST PATTY *(in Korean and Subtitled):* Forget that! Let's market it! Liqueur flavored nail polish. We'll make a fortune. *(In English)* Rinse please, Carol.

JANE: The trick is to pamper him. All men really want is a mother.

PEDICURIST TINA *(in Korean and Subtitled):* Mother by day. Hooker by night.

CAROL: I *do* pamper him. I gave him a back rub the other night . . .

JANE: Good.

CAROL: It was great if I do say so myself. The rub that broke the bachelor's back.

JANE: What's your hurry? It's only been two months.

CAROL: Two months may be nothing to an old married broad like yourself. But once a woman hits thirty and she's still single, her body and her ovaries start to age the way a cats do. You know, where one human year really equals seven ovary years?

(CAROL pauses to calculate—for the first time—just how old her ovaries would be according to the equation. She is clearly horrified at the result)

CAROL *(con't)*: Oh my God, Jane! My ovaries are almost three hundred years old! I'll give birth to my own great-great-great grandchildren!

JANE: That's nothing. I had one kid and my ovaries went on Social Security.

PEDICURIST TINA *(in Korean and Subtitled)*: Sounds like she's starting to panic. Me, too.

PEDICURIST PATTY *(in Korean and Subtitled)*: You? You're only twenty. She's got fifteen years on you. Pass me the lotion.

PEDICURIST TINA *(in Korean and Subtitled)*: But I'm not married.

MANICURIST CHRIS (in Korean and Subtitled): You're dating someone—that's a start.

PEDICURIST TINA *(in Korean and Subtitled)*: No one I could bring home. He's not Korean. He's not even Asian. Can I have the cuticle cream?

JANE: So, are you doing something special for your two-month anniversary?

CAROL: He wanted to go for a 10-mile run. I wanted champagne and caviar in bed. So we compromised man-style . . . we're going to a Knicks game.

JANE: Remember your six-month anniversary with Gerry? You and I spent it at my house eating frozen pizza and watching *Love Story* while Gerry and his buddies kept company with Boom Boom La Fleur.

CAROL: Men. You can't live with 'em . . .

JANE AND CAROL *(Simultaneously and to each other):*. . . And you can't kill 'em.

JANE So . . . is your *(Mouths the word, "sex"):* life good?

CAROL: JANE!

JANE: Come on! Good as Ed is, after six years of marriage, I'd like to know if there's anything new out there I need to know about.

CAROL: Well, yes, your honor, it's great.

PEDICURIST PATTY *(in Korean and Subtitled):* Of course. It's only been two months. *(Then, in English . . .)* What color?

JANE: Hot Tomato, please, Patty. *(And then . . .)* How great?

CAROL: He takes top honors. Considering all my other relationships have been like Tours of Duty.

JANE: A true Italian Stallion?

CAROL: A true Italian Stallion.

(Chris, Tina, and Patty's interest has been piqued.)

JANE: Really? No weird quirks?

CAROL: No. No weird quirks. Well, he does do one rather strange thing.

JANE: Yes . . .

CAROL: But it's not life threatening.

JANE: Yes . . .

CAROL: Or even relationship threatening.

JANE: Go on.

CAROL: It really isn't that big a deal.

JANE: Tell me.

CAROL: I feel funny saying it.

JANE: Carol! Tell me!

CAROL: But since you asked . . .

JANE: TELL ME!

PEDICURIST TINA *(in Korean and Subtitled):* SAY IT ALREADY!

CAROL: During . . . you know . . . sex . . . he has this little nickname for me.

(At this point, EVERYBODY in the salon is riveted)

JANE: Yeah?

CAROL: He calls me . . . *(in a gravelly whisper)*. . . "Rosebud."

PEDICURIST TINA *(Incredulously):* ROSEBUD?!

(Pop cut to stunned faces and fade out)

THE END

~*Jane Read Martin*

Sixteen Pictures of My Father

1. A small, square black-and-white photograph with a scalloped white edge on which the date May 1959 is printed in small type. I am the curly-headed baby in a white party dress sitting up on Daddy's shoulder eating a strawberry. Boyishly handsome in his crew-neck sweater and grown-out GI haircut, he smiles up at me, squinting into the sun. He is thirty, I am one, we are in love.

2. Twenty-five years later. My father and I at my sister's wedding, a beautiful summer day at the golf club. We are facing each other in profile, mouths wide open, very excited, talking at once. We are running the show. My father looks like Lee Iacocca with his white hair and his wire-rimmed glasses. The day he started wearing those glasses was the day he was no longer young. If you look at this photograph long enough, my father disappears. I am alone in my fuchsia party dress, in profile, mouth wide open.

3. Nights when our parents are out, Nancy and I make Jiffy-Pop and show sixteen-millimeter home movies on the wall of the den. Our favorite is Mommy and Daddy on their honeymoon. They wear matching tennis sweaters and pretend to paddle around the empty swimming pool at Grossinger's. Young and happy, they hardly ever get on each other's nerves.

4. My father in flowered velvet bell-bottoms and a denim safari jacket, his wild gray hair sticking out all over the place. It is very late at night and he is at his discotheque, the Pandemonium, where Brother Duck is playing and everyone is drinking Harvey Wallbangers and smoking pot. The Pandemonium is losing money like crazy. My mother is home, loading the dishwasher and crying, mostly because he looks so ridiculous and he won't cut his hair. I hear her the next morning on the phone: He is a forty-three-year-old man, for Christ's sake.

5. In this picture, my father is writing a check. This check will feed me and clothe me and send me to college, will pay for my eyeglasses, my summer camp, my abortion, my psychiatrist, and my phone bill, will insure my car and fix my nose and take me out to dinner on my birthday. Stereos, TV sets, diet pills, guitar lessons, collect calls from Europe, all covered. This is a very important check, but my father scribbles it out quickly, and hands it to me without looking up. Here you go, sport, he says.

6. This is a twenty-mile-long traffic jam created by New Jersey commuters trying to get into Manhattan. All eight zillion of them have to squeeze in by nine a.m. through two underwater tunnels or over a bridge.

My father is not in this traffic jam—are you kidding! He gets off the turnpike, goes through the underpass, down the frontage road, over a bridge, zigzags through parking lots and shopping centers and the sleeping downtown streets of Union and Weehawken, gets back on the turnpike at a different exit only to cut off again and loop around, winding up ten minutes later at the front of the line. All the while he is listening to Chapter 6 of *War and Remembrance* on his cassette player and figuring out how to do a spreadsheet in Lotus 1-2-3 that will automatically compute the winnings for the Super Bowl pool.

7. My father is in his office at his perennially failing textile firm. He has an unusual group of employees, who have all been there forever and are devoted to him beyond reason. The tiny, ancient bookkeeper; the flamboyant male receptionist; the disheveled, disreputable delivery man; the enormous bald computer operator from Long Island. At his desk, my father yells, Edna! Harold! Junior! Artie! Get in here! And his motley minions assemble to do his bidding.

8. We have the coolest father on the street. He plays war with all the kids on the hill behind the Mahoneys', takes us on Lost Rides in the car, teaches us about schneiders and double schneiders and other secrets of scoring for world-class gin rummy. We have a movie of him jumping rope, totally flat-footed, bringing his knees all the way up to his chin on every jump. He answers the front door in his boxer shorts. When I was very young, I thought he was Fred Flintstone.

9. Fred Flintstone is not amused when I call at two in the morning because the car has broken down on the way home from the rock concert, and six of us are stranded in a police station somewhere near Passaic, a good hour away from home. Morons! he says, stomping into the police station in his pajamas. Get in the goddamn car!

10. My father is having a heart attack in his Cadillac El Dorado during morning rush hour in the middle of the Lincoln Tunnel. He grimaces but continues driving into the city, where he parks his car in his customary spot on the roof of the Port Authority Bus Terminal and proceeds to his dentist appointment. You look like hell, Hyman, says the dentist. My father can barely reply. The dentist calls an ambulance. My father's hospitalization coincides with the publication of *Iacocca*!, the autobiography of his corporate Italian look-alike. He receives about a dozen copies from various well-wishers.

11. Some years later, my father has a coronary bypass operation, after which he will eat nothing but chicken salad. Not just any chicken salad, we soon learn, as the nurses' refrigerator fills up with rejected deli containers. It should have large chunks of white meat! Maybe a little celery! Not this goddamn chicken paste! Soon everyone who visits is bringing chicken salad for his review. Now this is chicken salad, Hy. Try this. We drive in from Jersey with chicken salad made by his mother, the famous Gigi. Although this is certainly the salad against which all others must be measured, even it is not eaten with real gusto. They say my father will recover, as 99 percent of bypass patients do, but they are wrong.

12. I land at Newark Airport upon my return from New Mexico, where I have spent two weeks in the mountains with my guru. I am seventeen years old, barefoot, and wrapped in a Navajo blanket. Where the hell are your shoes, he says. Get in the goddamn car!

13. My father's body is lying in a box at the Bloomfield-Cooper Funeral Home, where my mother, sister, and I go to see it before it is cremated. I have never seen my father dead and I have never seen him wearing a yarmulke either, so this is a double surprise. I fear that this awful picture will stay with me forever and blot out all the other pictures of him in my mind, but later I can remember only that his head seemed too large for his body, the yarmulke, and his closed eyelids.

14. The last time I saw my father alive and well was the ignominious night he bailed us out of jail in New York City. My sister, Nancy, her husband, Steven, my then fiance, Tony, and I (Dey got yuh whole family? a fellow prisoner inquired incredulously) squirmed on the wooden bench, sobered up and scared to death after twenty-four hours in Manhattan's central holding tank. Too impatient to drive back to the apartment after scoring, we'd pulled over on a darkened street with our little packets of powder; the car was surrounded by cops in less than a minute. Out in the courtroom, my father was white with exhaustion and anger. It was after midnight when the judge set our fines and let us go. We were ashamed and miserable, but Daddy took us out to a restaurant, where we ate and drank by candlelight and soon were reminiscing about jail as if it were years instead of hours in the past. At four A.M., he left for home. We watched him drive off through a dense white fog.

15. Before you lose a parent, you think, Oh God, what will I do if one of them dies? Then it happens, and you find out you can't do anything. You just go on. Maybe you can try to become what you miss most. My father is not in this picture, but his shoulders are. I wear the memory of those football-player shoulders like a magic cloak, indispensable for getting through traffic jams.

16. This is the face I remember best. He's in a swimming pool on one of those floating lawn chairs, drinking a Heineken. The two dogs jump in and paddle over to throw themselves into his lap, the gangly Lab pup and the miniature dachsund. The shutter snaps as he begins to topple in, surprised, laughing, holding the beer aloft.

~ Marion Winik

CHAPTER 3

It's in the Male

CHAPTER 3

It's In the Male

Where can I get a male ego? Anyone who believes that men and women have the same mind-set hasn't lived on earth. A man thinks that everything he does is wonderful, that the sun rises and sets around him. But a woman has doubts.

Recently, my husband and I were in an elevator, waiting to ascend from the depths of Parking Level Five to Ground Zero. After a few moments, I had a revelation. "Honey," I said, "we're not moving."

"Sure we are," Duke said with more certainty than I ever feel about anything.

We waited a little longer. The lights on the control panel were dark and there wasn't the slightest sensation of motion. Yet he insisted that everything was under control because, he explained, "I pushed the button."

I hate to argue with a man who has pushed the button (men frequently take it personally when a machine disobeys their commands). But I was getting claustrophobic. So I pushed the button and immediately—noticeably!—the elevator began to rise. Duke was unabashed. "There must be something wrong with that button," he exclaimed.

I don't know one woman (though I'm sure some exist) who would have come to that conclusion. I, for one, would have assumed that I had made a mistake. That's why I want a male ego. Men rarely seem to assume that they've made a mistake.

"You're looking at the basic premise of the male ego," my friend Doug says. "Men are always right." But this implies that when I disagree with one, I am always wrong. "You've got the picture," he replies.

I detest the picture. But "it's the thing that let our ancestors go out and kill woolly mammoths," my friend Rob argues. "If you let any doubt creep in, you're history. You've got to go out like it's the only thing to do and you're just the guy to do it. It's the only way you've ever got a shot."

I don't want a shot. I just want to be treated fairly and paid well. Still, armed with a male ego, I could do battle over almost anything—the placement of my name on a memo, for example, or who gets served coffee first when I'm in a meeting. "Titles are really critical," says my sister, Laurie, who believes that there should be a theme park based on the male ego, only "there's not enough land."

"There's a guy in my office at the exact same level as me," she says. "Yet he fought for six months—screaming!—to be called Senior Media Supervisor instead of Senior Media Executive. Finally, our boss asked if I minded that Harold had this title—did I want it as well? I said, no, the title I wanted was Senior Media Goddess. So he put that on my door. Now Harold is fighting for a bigger office."

My husband isn't surprised. "A man's ego is quite large," Duke says. "But it's very delicate."

He's telling me? In my life experience, the male always seems to be discovering a cure for something, no matter what he's doing. And whatever it is, it's invariably more important than what the female wants to do. I'd be willing to bet that if one day a woman walked barefoot to the moon and back and a man cleaned out his desk, when the two of them sat down to dinner that night, he would groan, "Boy, was that desk a mess."

"It's protective," Rob says. "Would we ever do anything if we couldn't convince ourselves and our loved ones that it was the most critical thing on the planet?"

I don't know. Some guys seem to be without shame. Not too long ago, I was reading the Trump-versus-Trump coverage in the New York *Daily News*. Marla Maples was on the cover wearing something revealing (does she own a regular dress?). The headline read, BEST SEX I EVER HAD. None of my girlfriends (for the record, I don't know Cher, Roseanne, or Madonna) would be flattered to wake up and find that in giant letters on her doorstep. But . . .

"Reading that headline was the best sex Donald Trump ever had," Duke said admiringly. "The male ego can always use an amorous press release." (Actually, any stroke will do.)

I wonder if I could go to Sweden and have ego-change surgery or to Houston and get a male ego transplant. One useful side effect would be that I'd no longer feel the compulsion to straighten up the house. The next time I got lost, instead of asking for directions, I'd drive around in circles, clenching my teeth, trying to read the map while going forty miles an hour. And if I happened to run into an abusive, frothing maniac, I could get into a nose-to-nose shrieking confrontation with him instead of discreetly slipping away.

On second thought, maybe the house isn't big enough for two male egos.

~Margo Kaufman

The Pot Calls the Kettle...

~Sherrie Shepherd

If Men Could Menstruate
A Political Fantasy

A white minority of the world has spent centuries conning us into thinking that a white skin makes people superior—even though the only thing it really does is make them more subject to ultraviolet rays and to wrinkles. Male human beings have built whole cultures around the idea that penis-envy is "natural" to women—though having such an unprotected organ might be said to make men vulnerable, and the power to give birth makes womb-envy at least as logical.

In short, the characteristics of the powerful, whatever they may be, are thought to be better than the characteristics of the powerless—and logic has nothing to do with it.

What would happen, for instance, if suddenly, magically, men could menstruate and women could not?

The answer is clear—menstruation would become an enviable, boast-worthy, masculine event.

Men would brag about how long and how much.

Boys would mark the onset of menses, that longed-for proof of manhood, with religious ritual and stag parties.

Congress would fund a National Institute of Dysmenorrhea to help stamp out monthly discomforts.

Sanitary supplies would be federally funded and free. (Of course, some men would still pay for the prestige of commercial brands such as John Wayne Tampons, Muhammad Ali's Rope-a-dope Pads, Joe Namath Jock Shields—"For Those Light Bachelor Days," and Robert "Baretta" Blake Maxipads.)

Military men, right-wing politicians, and religious fundamentalists would cite menstruation ("*men*-struation") as proof that only men could serve in the Army ("you have to give blood to take blood"), occupy political

office ("can women be aggressive without that steadfast cycle governed by the planet Mars?"), be priests and ministers ("how could a woman give her blood for our sins?"), or rabbis ("without the monthly loss of impurities, women remain unclean").

Male radicals, left-wing politicians, and mystics, however, would insist that women are equal, just different, and that any woman could enter their ranks if only she were willing to self-inflict a major wound every month ("you *must* give blood for the revolution"), recognize the preeminence of menstrual issues, or subordinate her selfness to all men in their Cycle of Enlightenment.

Street guys would brag ("I'm a three-pad man") or answer praise from a buddy ("Man, you lookin' *good*!") by giving fives and saying, "Yeah man, I'm on the rag!"

TV shows would treat the subject at length. (*Happy Days*: Richie and Potsie try to convince Fonzie that he is still "The Fonz," though he has missed two periods in a row.) So would newspapers. (SHARK SCARE THREATENS MENSTRUATING MEN. JUDGE CITES MONTHLY STRESS IN PARDONING RAPIST.) And movies. (Newman and Redford in *Blood Brothers!*)

Men would convince women that intercourse was *more* pleasurable at "that time of the month." Lesbians would be said to fear blood and therefore life itself—though probably only because they needed a good menstruating man.

Of course, male intellectuals would offer the most moral and logical arguments. How could a woman master any discipline that demanded a sense of time, space, mathematics, or measurement, for instance, without that built-in gift for measuring the cycles of the moon and planets—and thus for measuring anything at all? In the rarefied fields of philosophy and religion, could women compensate for missing the rhythm of the universe? Or for their lack of symbolic death-and-resurrection every month?

Liberal males in every field would try to be kind: the fact that "these people" have no gift for measuring life or connecting to the universe, the liberals would explain, should be punishment enough.

And how would women be trained to react? One can imagine traditional women agreeing to all these arguments with a staunch and smiling masochism. ("The ERA would force housewives to wound themselves every month": Phyllis Schlafly. "Your husband's blood is as sacred as that of Jesus—and so sexy, too!": Marabel Morgan.) Reformers and Queen Bees would try to imitate men, and *pretend* to have a monthly cycle. All feminists would explain endlessly that men, too, needed to be liberated from the false idea of Martian aggressiveness, just as women needed to escape the bonds of menses-envy. Radical feminists would add that the oppression of the nonmenstrual was the pattern for all other oppressions. ("Vampires were our first freedom fighters!") Cultural feminists would develop a bloodless imagery in art and literature. Socialist feminists would insist that only under capitalism would men be able to monopolize menstrual blood . . .

In fact, if men could menstruate, the power justification could probably go on forever.

If we let them.

~Gloria Steinem

Wading Waist-High

~Sherrie Shepherd

CHAPTER 3

Why We Can't Stay Married

Many people are making lots of money writing books about why men and women can't stay married. They have titles like: *Men Who Love Women Who Love Too Much, Women Who Love Men Who Can't Find Their G-Spots, Couples Without Time To Love Because She's Always Driving the Car Pool.*

The thing that makes me angry about this is that I'm not one of the writers making money writing these books. And the reason that makes me angry is that I have the answer, which I'm going to give to you right here, for free.

The reason husbands and wives can't stay married is: large appliances.

Large appliances break up far more relationships than do sex, money, household chores, and relatives. My personal historical research proves it. Just watch *Wagon Train* some time (that's how I do most of my personal historical research). Those people had to put up with sex (under a wagon, yet), money, house (or wagon)-hold chores, and relatives. Okay, I'll give you relatives, since most of them were moving away from their in-laws, which saved several marriages right there. But do you see people on *Wagon Train* getting divorced? I think not! And they didn't have large appliances, either. They beat their laundry with rocks in a creek.

If you check statistics you'll find that American marriages started falling apart in the '60s, just a decade after people acquired several types of large appliances.

"Imagine," my friend Lauren said to me, "finding out that there is only *one* correct way to load a dishwasher, and I am married to the *only* man in the world who knows it. And who is more than happy to share the technique with me."

My chin dropped, the way it does when I've found a soulmate (such as someone else whose car clock is an hour off for half the year because they don't know how to change it back from Daylight Savings Time).

"Oh, no!" I gasped. "There is one *other* person who knows the one correct way to load a dishwasher," referring to my own husband of a quarter century. "It must be a secret society."

Lauren and her husband are still married, but then they have a young son to consider.

But I estimate the dishwasher is a minor league marriage-buster compared to that mainstay of American kitchens, the hulking refrigerator.

"Where is the leftover pizza?" calls my husband from the kitchen. I shudder. I know that my answer, "On the right side, second shelf," will only add to his aggravation when he is unable to locate the mozzarella-covered prize. So I join him, feigning puzzlement, in front of the open fridge.

For a while we both stand there in silence, basking in the glow of the light and the chill of the frosty air pumping out at us. Of course, I see the pizza perfectly well because it's sitting right there on a red plate covered with clear plastic wrap; if it were any closer I would be in danger of inhaling the Saran and suffocating to death. But I let a reasonable amount of time pass before I say, "Oh, could that be it?" and my husband, mumbling about how anyone could find anything in "there" retrieves it and I return to the safety of the next room.

Faced with a similar situation, the uninitiated bride too often rolls her eyes, pulls out the pizza, and hands it to her chagrined mate, who attempts to save face by lashing out at her about some unrelated issue, such as the S&L crisis or call-forwarding. She lashes back at him and their marriage becomes another victim of large appliances.

Even if her marriage survives the refrigerator challenge, the "what-were-you-doing-when-you-broke-it?" menace awaits.

"It just started beating itself against the basement wall like it was trying to commit suicide."

"What did you put in the washer?"

("Your underwear and a bag of cement," she mumbles under her breath, gritting her teeth.)

"The laundry," she replies slowly, as if speaking to a small child.

"What were you doing when it started ramming the wall?"

("Plowing into it with the Toyota.")

Did you spot the trend? One spouse, usually the male, forms a series of questions aimed at *finding out whose fault it is.* Large appliances provide the easiest available way for a husband to blame his wife for an expensive inconvenience for which she was in no way responsible. For reasons that no one has been able to discern, this makes him feel better. For reasons that are perfectly obvious, this makes her feel like keeping the washer and trading in the husband.

Large appliance manufacturers do not want you to know any of this, of course, and they will, no doubt, demand that I retract my statements. They'll probably argue that I, a woman who has been married to the same man for twenty-five years, have no right to abuse large appliances, several of which I own and use daily.

However, I stand firmly behind the facts I have presented here and, if you'll excuse me, I have some laundry to catch up on.

May I borrow some rocks?

~*Marcia Steil*

Men Who Like Housework

Catherine deposits five loads of laundry on the bed, erroneously assuming her husband will feel compelled to fold them before going to sleep.
machlis

~*Gail Machlis*

Disneyland

G*LORIA and MARY-MARGARET, two big-haired, fast talking, gum chewing girls from Queens, meet at the bus stop.*

MARY MARGARET: So, you're back. So, where'd ya go?

GLORIA: California. Mr. Man wanted to go to California.

MARY MARGARET: California? Who wants to go there? It's gonna fall off.

GLORIA: That's what I said. I said, what's in California but smog and earthquakes, right? Right. Disneyland, he says. Disneyland's for kids, fer Christ's sake, right? Right. So we go ta Disneyland and it rains for two weeks like we were gonna have ta build an ark or somethin'. Giant soakin' wet mice with three fingers, who needs it, right? So I told him, I said, I told you we shoulda gone to Atlantic City or Vegas or someplace nice like that, I mean, who needs wet people in animal suits and little kids crying all around you, right? I said, if I told you once, I told you a million times this was a dumb idea, but you wouldn't listen. Oh, no. Disneyland, California. We couldn't even go ta the beach, fer Christ's sake. He kept saying, we can still have a good time. Yeah. Right. So then we're comin' back and he got some special plane deal or somethin' and we've got a two-hour layover in Minneapolis, so I go ta the waitin' area, I mean really, what can anybody do in Minneapolis, right? And I go and sit on my suitcase 'cause there aren't any seats, and he says, I gotta go to the head, meaning the john, on account a he thinks he's some kinda sailor or somethin', and then he leaves, right? And two hours go by and he's not back and it's almost time for the plane to leave and he's nowhere. I have him paged, everybody's lookin' for him. I tell you I coulda shit a pickle. So, we couldn't find 'em and I was sitting there with my thumb up my butt on my American Tourister lookin' like some kinda schmuck or somethin' and he doesn't come back and I am stuck in God-for-saken Minneapolis for three days until my Ma wires me some money. When I get home I find out he's gone off to Puerto Rico with this stewardess he bumped into outside the men's room. I felt like some kinda fool let me tell you.

MARY MARGARET: Men. Ya can't leave 'em alone for a minute.

GLORIA: Ain't that the truth.

And the bus comes.

~*Katherine Hewett*

Hare Transplant

ALTHOUGH EARLY TESTS SHOW DR. HOMNIM'S HARE TRANSPLANT HIDES HAIR LOSS AND HAS NO BAD SIDE EFFECTS, ED IS NOT SURE HE LIKES THE RESULT.

~*Theresa McCracken*

The Silent Partner

Can we talk? I'm rarely at a loss for words. As far as I'm concerned, talking is a natural biological function, like breathing—I do it all the time. Yet, my husband can hold his breath for hours, even days at a time.

The silence seems deafening. "Is something bothering you?" I ask, even though I realize that trying to pull words from the mouth of a man in the midst of a mute spell is as pointless as trying to make a telephone call when the line is dead.

Duke shakes his head. "Uh-uh," he mutters.

Unfortunately, talking is like tennis. You need two people to play. "It's a big problem in a lot of marriages," says family therapist Marcia Lasswell, who adds that the quiet one is usually the man.

Why? "Men have an easier time being silent than women," she explains. "Silence is almost a macho characteristic. Clint Eastwood, Gary Cooper—they don't say many words, they're all action. The strong, silent type is a masculine myth. But women get very frustrated."

Yup. My friend Leon was once married to a man of few words. "Not only didn't he speak, but when I did, he said, 'Shh!' " she recalls. "He wouldn't answer things like, 'Let's buy a house' or 'What did you think of that movie?' I tried notes, I tried signal flags; he wouldn't answer. Once, after a prolonged period of his not talking, I went outside the house and rang the bell. He opened the door and asked, 'Where have you been?' "

"At first, I thought all that silence meant that he knew the secret of the universe and that in time he would impart it to me," Leon says. "But when it was not forthcoming, I began to think that if I killed him slowly, at least he'd say something like 'Ouch' or 'Stop it.' "

Nope. Threats won't make him talk. In such extreme cases, "it's like trying to force someone who isn't coordinated physically to dance,"

Lasswell says. "These really silent types are basically shy. Somewhere along the line, they learned that speaking up didn't get them anywhere."

Shutting up doesn't get them anywhere either. "I had a couple where the man was so nonverbal that he really had a terrible time," Lasswell recalls. "His wife yearned to hear the words 'I love you,' and he just couldn't get it out. So, we practiced and practiced. I told her to say it first so that he would feel safe. So she turned to him and said, 'I love you.' And he said, 'Ditto.' "

Recently, starved for conversation, I called my friend Claire. "I'm trapped in the Silent Zone," I said with a sigh.

"He must be angry," Claire concluded. "Fred always clams up when he's absolutely furious. I figure it's just as well, because if he said something, it would be something that I didn't want to hear."

"Duke's not mad," I assured her. (It's easy to tell when a quiet man is mad. He storms into the house, slams the door, and hits the wall, and when you ask what's wrong, he snaps, "Nothing.") "He's just not speaking."

"I'd go insane," Claire said. "I'd send myself into a busy little circle wondering why he isn't talking. Pretty soon, I would start tossing plates around."

We don't have that many dishes. Besides, "you shouldn't take the silence personally," Lasswell insists. "You've got to remember that he didn't just start being silent when he married you."

Don't I know it. After a year of dating, I still didn't know where Duke went to high school. It's not that he conceals anything. He just doesn't go out of his way to reveal it.

Some day, I expect to find a ticket to Stockholm lying on the dresser. "What's this?" I'll ask. After ten minutes of cross-examination, he'll reluctantly inform me that he's won the Nobel Prize.

Now, if I ever won, I'd tell everyone in the city in a matter of seconds. So would my friend Jane, another life of the party, who's been married to a taciturn man for thirty-seven years. She's still trying to adjust. "You can't out-silence them," Jane marvels. "Things come up in this world like 'Hello'

or 'The house is on fire.' You've just got to teach them that it's important to say, 'I'm home' when they walk through the door so you don't have to worry it's a robber."

I suspect that it's easier to teach a dog to "speak." So does Monica. "Jack can go through an entire family outing without saying a thing," she laments. "But it makes me very nervous. So the last time we went to my parents' for dinner, I asked him to please try to act interested. He said, 'I can't. I don't relate.' I said, 'Just try to say something to do with something they're talking about,' and he replied, 'I've got to be me.' Finally, I asked, 'Could you at least lean forward when they're talking?'"

Sometimes I feel guilty for talking more than my mate. But someone has to shoulder the conversational burden. "I suppose the worst thing for a man who doesn't talk would be a woman who doesn't either," Jane says. "He'd go crazy."

Experts agree. "I enjoy someone who's pretty much of a brass band more than someone who's just a flute," declares Glen Esterly, co-author of *The Talk Book: The Intimate Science of Communicating in Close Relationships*. Esterly, a self-described "silent man in a state of flux," admits: "An extrovert takes away the pressure to avoid what's referred to as awkward silence. If I'm going through quiet periods and I'm with a quiet woman, there's a lot of dead air time. I'm not uncomfortable with the silence, but most people are."

Yup. Duke is lying in bed, reading about irregular Spanish verbs. "Soon, he'll be able to be silent as fluently in Spanish as he is in English," I think. "*Buenas noches*," I say, giving him a kiss.

"*Mi charladorita*," Duke says fondly. "My little chatterbox."

~*Margo Kaufman*

Light Reading

"I'VE DATED ELEVEN ENIGMAS—I WANT AN OPEN BOOK."

~*Liza Donnelly*

Berflegump

My lover and I will be out for a ride. He'll be driving and say,
"I'm taking Route 295 to the bridge. What do you think?"
And I say, "Berflegump hipple dip."
He'll say, "I'm hungry. I'm stopping at that diner.
What do you think?"
And I answer, "Quiddy diddle quank blurp."
Why am I speaking gibberish?
Because I understand.
He's one of those new *sensitive* kind of guys,
who knows enough to ask me what I think—
But he hasn't quite evolved to the point
where he *cares* about the answer.

~*Flash Rosenberg*

The End

He would like to close
his eyes and have
you just go away

Men are good at a lot of things. Breaking up is not one of them.

When a woman wants to break up with a man, she invites him over for dinner, cooks his favorite dish, then tells him she's seeing his best friend. It's all very straightforward. But men have this weird aversion to endings. They prefer to take the passive mode, allowing the relationship to end itself. Men can't be bothered with dramatic farewells, the questioning of motives, discussions. They are bored. They want out. Good-bye.

I remember the first time a boy broke up with me. We were in the seventh grade. He invited me over after school, said he just wanted to be friends, then had his mother drive me home. It was all downhill from there. In more recent years, a doorman informed me that my date was not coming down. Ever.

A friend called her boyfriend and found out he had moved to a new city.

A coworker happened upon a personal ad placed by the man she was dating.

Every woman, with the possible exception of supermodel Cindy Crawford, has a story like this. You may have dated the man a few weeks or a few years. You may have shared a cab or an apartment. It doesn't matter. For some reason the man thinks that the decision to break up is none of your business. (Of course, some women do the same thing. But then again, some women mud wrestle.)

Often a woman senses a breakup brewing and tries to get the man to sit down and fess up. No deal. The average male gets this beam-me-up-

Scotty look on his face as soon as you mention the word *discussion.* He treats you as if you were trying to serve a subpoena. Then, when you finally work up the nerve to ask him what the heck is going on, he pretends you're imagining the whole thing. It's all part of the game, and evidently the winner is the one who can quit the game without ever talking about it.

Some men admit they avoid confrontation because they're afraid we'll cry. Of course we'll cry; we cry at Hallmark commercials. What they don't understand is that we're not crying because of them, we're crying because now we have to get naked in front of someone else.

It's a rare and brave man who breaks up in person. Most likely he has sisters and does volunteer work. He'll say things you've heard before: "I'm unable to make a commitment. I don't have time to be the kind of boyfriend you deserve." Then he'll add, "I hope we can eventually be friends. I'd really miss your company." It doesn't matter if he's lying, telling the truth, or quoting something he read in a woman's magazine. At least he's trying.

Most men, however, think that even making a phone call to end a relationship is excessive. "What's the point?" they want to know. The humane thing, they've decided, is not to call, but instead to disappear like the Lone Ranger.

These men believe in "Close your eyes and make it go away." They believe in the Fifth Amendment. They believe in absentee ballots. They may ski black diamonds, walk barefoot on hot asphalt, skydive for fun, but measured on their fear of confrontation, these guys are wimps.

They'll say they're going to the rest room and never return. Then they'll meet friends for drinks and say, "She just doesn't get it" or "What do I have to do, spell it out for her?"

It's not that we don't get it. After about three weeks of shampooing with the water off—*just in case he calls*—we get the picture. But we'd like to feel we're more than just a notch in somebody's bedpost. Stranded without an explanation, we sound like the neighbors of a murderer. "He seemed nice. Kind of kept to himself. This came as a complete surprise."

Underneath, of course, we *know.*

You can spot a woman who knows her relationship is disintegrating, because her answering machine gives hourly updates of her whereabouts. "I'm at work now, but I'll be home by six." "I'm at aerobics." "I'm in the shower." Meanwhile, a man's machine has the same message as always: "I'm not home. Later."

So what happens is this: you refuse to bow out gracefully, and he refuses to confront. His only option is to make you so miserable that you break up with *him.* We're talking emotional terrorism.

During this period he won't laugh at your jokes. He'll ask you out, then act like you're imposing. He'll shred what's left of your confidence by saying, "You're wearing *that*?" or "Didn't you have time to change after work?" He may even tell you he'd like to end the relationship but continue sleeping with you. Then he'll act surprised when you bash in his headlights, stuff his favorite tie down the disposal, and ignite his baseball-card collection.

So what's the right way for a man to break up? I suggest the following steps:

Advice to Men Who Want to Break Up

Step One. Choose a reason. Inevitably your girlfriend will ask why you're leaving, and you should be prepared to explain. If you know that your reason is petty and immature, make up a nicer reason.

Step Two. Select a date that doesn't conflict with birthdays or major holidays. "I didn't plan to break up with her on Valentine's Day," a male friend once explained. "It just happened to coincide."

Step Three. Talk to her. You're both adults. It might go surprisingly smoothly.

Step Four. Hide your baseball cards.

One final note: Since writing this piece I experienced one actual face-to-face, special-trip-to-my-apartment-to-end-it breakup and I am now convinced I may have been too quick to criticize the Lone Ranger method.

~Cindy Chupack

Sister City

~Jan Eliot

Henry

Retirement? No big deal. When the time came, I said goodbye to the bookkeeping field, picked up my pension and went. Pretty soon I was busier than ever. Yoga class, art tours, my great books group, my matinee ladies, and candy-striping at the hospital once a week. But Henry . . . . The firm threw him a big party at Le Bernardin, and the next day he started his life as a vegetable. He was never the great communicator—with his clients, yes, but not with me. I thought maybe being thrown together now, we'd make up for lost time. But instead, he practically stopped verbalizing altogether. Just sat in front of TV, eating carrot sticks and salt-free pretzels, and mourning his lost kingdom. This went on for months. Gradually I began to notice a change in his appearance. Nothing specific. But he seemed softer, rounder, more . . . cushiony. I told him he should get some exercise.

One evening, he emerged from the bathroom with a towel around his middle. It was unmistakable: Henry had breasts! I didn't say anything. Why upset him? But during the next few weeks I observed him closely as, to my—what—horror?. . . astonishment? . . . delight . . . he slowly changed into a . . . woman. And I must tell you, it's made a tremendous difference. Henry is a new person. He's learning macramé, tap dancing, and Mandarin Chinese cooking at the Y; he's taken up the accordion again, which he hadn't touched since high school. And talk! We can't seem to find enough time for everything we have to say to each other. The world has opened up for both of us. I admit I miss the sex a little. But in every other way, Henry and I are much happier.

~June Siegel

Men-o-Pause

I TELL YOU GLORIA, I'M FINDING HIS MALE MENOPAUSE TO BE RATHER EXCITING.

~*Yvette Jean Silver*

You Say Dumbo and I Say Rambo

The ultimate intimacy is an act so fraught and resonant that a couple probably shouldn't do it before they have a candid and detailed discussion, freely revealing personal histories and preferences. They certainly shouldn't do it before the third date. I mean, of course, renting a video together.

Video rental is one of those activities that makes or breaks a relationship, like canoeing. In fact, I (not my real name) have observed a problem on the cusp of becoming a trend and, Oprah willing, a national malaise: Video Incompatibility Syndrome.

When a couple enter a video store, basic issues come into play: Who's going to accommodate? By what route will you reach an accord? Does his fear of leaving Classics for a dip into Cult suggest other timidities? Is it significant that she's happy to rehash her romantic past but reluctant to disclose the fact that she has seen *Jason and the Argonauts* twenty-three times?

Divergent tastes don't always signal disaster; Dumbo and Rambo can find happiness. And yet.

Says my friend K (her real initial, but she's not really my friend): "My ex would only rent pretentious, boring things like *Dersu Uzala,* or *Ursu Derzala,* a Russian film about a Japanese guide or a Japanese film about a Russian guide standing silently in a field of snow for three hours. If I ever see a copy again, I'll crush it slowly."

He automatically vetoed her suggestions, she reports, especially ridiculing her passion for Schwarzenegger classics from his pre-smiling period.

"We took to renting separately," she says, "which I think is a real trouble sign in a marriage." It could also be the sign of a healthy independence. We'll let Oprah decide.

Phil Keller, the manager at Couch Potato Video on East Eighth Street in Manhattan, confirms the spread of Video Incompatibility Syndrome. "*Fried Green Tomatoes* was a big fight-producer," Keller says, "although movie choice generally doesn't fall along sex-stereotyped lines. But it's almost always a guy who gives in." (He has also seen some ugly battles over who's responsible for late fees, and has turned down parents offering cash incentives to say he's out of *Barney* tapes.)

Keller politely declines when sparring couples ask him to referee. "The only intervention I'll make is to say, 'You know, if you rent both of them, you get a third one free.' "

I wouldn't presume to point out a national malaise if I didn't have a suggestion for a solution. I propose that film makers take some responsibility and start splicing up genre-bridging hybrids expressly designed to solve the problems of the renting diad.

Ten Potentially Top-Grossing Films for the Video-Incompatible Couple:

1. "Terminators of Endearment."
2. "My Own Private Benjamin."
3. "Honey, I, Claudius, Blew Up the Kids."
4. "A Few Good Men in Tights."
5. "Henry V, Portrait of a Serial Killer."
6. "Scenes From a Mall and the Night Visitors."
7. "Pretty Woman Under the Influence."
8. "Jennifer 8-1/2."
9. "Shoahboat."
10. "A Guy Named Joe'sliver." (From Reader's Digest Pictures, the only documentary on the list: Spencer Tracy and Sharon Stone get an anatomy lesson they'll never forget.)

These carefully wrought composites will, of course, maintain the artistic integrity of the originals; I'm not advocating an intercut of *Howards End* and *Buns of Steel*, or an all-Smurf version of *The Piano*.

Certainly, the plan is not without risks. Already many a mise-en-scène is marred by prominent product placement; if video blending goes commercial, how long will it be before we're watching "When Amana Loves a Woman" or "The Return of the Monistat 7?" (Actually, I trust the industry to police itself; it's not as if there were three Amy Fisher movies.)

Whether or not Hollywood heeds my cry, full-frontal rental will remain a private matter between (or among; who am I to judge?) consenting adults—and a potential source of friction.

I hear that one Solomonic video incompatibility therapist is using a radical technique: couples who refuse to compromise are forced to choose between *Heaven's Gate* and a head-cleaning tape.

~*Judith Stone*

Sex on the Silver Screen

~*Jan Eliot*

Samuel Espada

There is a long and illustrious tradition of Latino Detectives: Shelock Homeboy, Perry Mexican and Colombian Colombo, but perhaps the finest one of all was . . . Samuel Espada.

(Under the plaintive sounds of a wailing sax, Samuel Espada enters with trenchcoat and fedora, stops under streetlight, reflectively lights a cigarette, as the lights rise.)

ESPADA: It's five A.M. in the A.M. and here I am, walking down these mean streets getting ready to experience another Tequila sunrise. My eyes feel like two prickly cacti. I'd give my left . . . whatever . . . to be home catching some ZZZ's next to my faithful girlfriend, Conchita. But no. I'm on a case. Me, Samuel Espada, P.P.I.—Private Pachuco Investigator—I'm facing one of the toughest cases of my career. I had been hired by the entire Latin female population of this God forsaken Tex-Mex town to find out one thing: why Latin men have this . . . compulsion, this . . . drive . . . this need . . . to date blonde women.

Dames, dames. Damn those dames. Dames are a mystery no one can solve. Except me . . . Samuel Espada, P.P.I.

(A blonde femme fatale slinks across the stage and leans provocatively against a lamppost. As Samuel sees her he lets out a loud Mexican Grito *and slowly circles her.)*

Hello Blondie! I know you. I know your kind. What's your name? Wendy? Debbie? Susie? Buffie? Binky? (He takes her in his arms). The name says it all . . . long gams, blue peepers . . . white girls! What is it about you Aryan cheerleaders that makes us

Latin men feel like piñatas when we date you? What? What? What? *(They begin a seductive Apache dance.)*
First you cling to me like cheap perfume, just because I'm Latino. Yeah. Latino makes me macho. Latino makes me a good lover. Hey, that's no lie. Sure. I'm a good dick *(She reaches for his groin.)* Get your mind out of the gutter! It means detective. I know what the turn-ons are about you ash-blonde babes. You buy all my lines ... not even my good stuff.

(The blonde is wrapped around him, fondling a scar on his cheek.)

What's this? Oh, I got this scar in a bullfight. (Ha!) All I have to do is talk Spanish to her and it's all over. "Wendy, My *amor ... mi corazón*! *Donde está la biblioteca*!" *(She faints into his arms)* This is a definite turn-on!
But the next minute you give me the cold shoulder!

(She kicks him across the stage and pins his hand to the ground with her stiletto heel.)

You give me the deep freeze, the arctic chill. You tell your friends I'm your gardener when you see me at the mall. You make me feel so low I could be sitting on a dime and my feet wouldn't touch the ground. Why am I so drawn to you Blondie? Don't make me bark like a dog! Arf, Arf! I hate that! *(Crawls after her, succumbing.)*

Look at you. Maybe it's because you remind me of wheat fields, of apple pie, of little Kim O'Fleary from my fourth grade class who was so blonde she glowed. You remind me of the American Dream. A dream I am not part of. Ouch ... that cut through me like the bullet I bit in Iwo Jima. *(Disentangling himself and pushing her away)*

Ha! You almost got me, you blonde, black widow spider. But no! I'm going home to wrap myself around Conchita . . . Conchita! She's brown as the holster on my .32 snubnose, eyes so dark you can show a movie in them. When I look into her eyes, I see . . . ME. ME. My family . . . my home . . . My American Dream. *Orale*!

(Lights slowly fade out as ESPADA strikes a pachuco *pose.)*

~Luisa Leschin

Closet Commuter

~Nurit Karlin

CHAPTER 3

Benefit Performance

Eleanor and I had met for a working lunch. I'm a writer. I write lyrics for songs. As I've had two gold albums with Eleanor, she wanted me to help her put together a song for her new album—something inspiring, upbeat, hopeful, and with a disco beat. "A disco spiritual. Hey wow!" I said to myself.

After the waiter had taken our order, I happened to notice a magazine that was on a busboy's cart. On the cover was a picture of a very famous actor—a white actor—and I remarked how much I liked him and how I go to see all his movies.

"Oh yes," Eleanor said, " I did a benefit with him a few months ago."

She asked our waiter if she might look at the magazine. She thumbed though it to the cover story, scanned it quickly, slapped it closed, and suddenly busted out laughing. Now one of the things that can really make me scream is for somebody to laugh out loud like that and not say what about. Just as I was going to ask, "Tell me, what's so funny," she sighed and said almost to herself, "These men, my dear, they mess with you in little ways." Then she followed that deep observation with a definite non-sequitur.

"Too much coffee is no good for the bladder."

Patience sat on curiosity, and I found myself, without breaking out in bumps, waiting for her to continue—to make some necessary connections if conversation was to develop. After a few moments of smiling privately and drawing invisible circles on the tablecloth with a lacquered nail, she told me.

The morning after the big benefit, the stars were assigned limos for a long drive to the airport. Eleanor, lucky thing, was to ride with our very important famous star and another man, evidently his friend. The leaving time was 6:30 A.M. for a two-hour ride to the airport to catch a 9 o'clock plane.

"You know me," Eleanor began, "I'd had my two cups of coffee just to make it out of bed after a long, hard night, what with the benefit running forty-five minutes over and the meeting and greeting after that. We'd been traveling only a little while when I realized I had to go to the bathroom. I crossed by fingers, my legs, said a little prayer, and told the bladder just to 'cool it' 'till we get to the airport.

"It didn't listen, however, and about a half hour into the trip I said, 'Excuse me, gentlemen, but I see we'll be passing a rest area soon and I'd like to stop, please.'

"The silence that had prevailed since we left the hotel deepened. Finally the driver said that we'd stop in about five minutes. Your gorgeous star said to the driver,

'What's our leeway here. No chance I'll miss my plane, is there?'

The driver assured him that he'd allowed an extra half hour, but not to worry because just outside the main terminal was a special flight service where they could hire a private jet—in case.

'Cause man, I got to be in L.A. too-day,' said the star.

"His friend asked me, 'Couldn't you have thought of this before we left, young lady?'"

At the rest stop, I asked, "Don't you all want to come in, grab a bite or something?"

"No, no,' said the star.

" 'You run along,' said the friend.

" 'But make it fast, okay Sweetie?' said the driver.

"I went in and out as fast as I could. I ushered myself back into the limo that started off almost before I'd shut the door. I was embarrassed, but the bladder felt a whole lot better. I settled in the corner, folded my arms and closed my eyes, hoping to sleep. Then it began: two IMPORTANT MEN discussing IMPORTANT affairs—deals, dividends, stock market predictions based on unpublished facts, smart moves, who said what to whom on the tennis court, brilliant financial strategems—"When the head of so-and-so tells me personally that thus and thus . . .' Etc. Etc. Yatata, yatata, yakety-yak. Hea-vy!

I dozed off. When I opened my eyes, there was silence. Then Gorgeous leaned across and whispered something to the friend, and the friend whispered something to the driver. I thought, "They're telling him to slow down. We're going so fast. Oh God, hope we don't all get killed." I could just hear it now—'all on account of the broad; she had to take a leak.' I'd never forgive myself. Shoulda just made a piddle-puddle right on this plush maroon carpet. Maybe they'd have preferred that! If we miss that plane I'll cut my wrists and just bleed all over them. Then they'll see how sorry I am. Maybe I'll just do a super-sister and fly both these dudes to L.A. on my back! Got to get Gorgeous to L.A. too-day! Being gorgeous and famous and all, his time must be worth at least ten thou' a minute.

Suddenly we were screeching to a halt. 'God, where the hell are we,' I thought. The airport couldn't be in these bushes.'

The three guys hurriedly de-limoed. I started to say, "Hey, wait for me!" Quickened perception bit my tongue, however, and I shrank into the seat and closed my eyes tight. But I just couldn't resist a quick peek out the back window where I saw three heads bowed in an attitude that usually accompanies prayer—or pissing in the bushes!

"When we resumed our journey, I found myself telling jokes about my six year old, about my dog—anything. I'm sorry the jokes weren't funny, but I needed an excuse to howl with laughter or bust. I howled, however, all by myself. Gorgeous, sitting now in front with the chauffeur, and his friend seated now beside me, no longer looked or sounded very important. They reminded me of two small boys as they stared straight ahead as if helping the driver keep his eyes on the road. Incidentally, we made the plane with plenty of time to spare."

~Ruby Dee

Road Signs

~Jennifer Berman

Better From Behind

So you're leavin'—forgive my starin'
But, I want to freeze this picture in my mind
Riding out into the sunset
Lookin' for that open sky
Been a fool for your pretty face
and the way your silver buckle shines
But now I know the simple truth, dear:
You always look better from behind.

Yes, you always looked better from behind
It's the view I always knew would linger in my mind
Well, you know I like your Stetson, and the twinkle in your eye
But honey, I can't help it—
You look best from behind.

Better pack for nasty weather
'Cause a cowboy never knows what he might find
Take your lasso and your leather
Take your heart, 'cause you're not takin' mine.
Turn and face me for a minute
So I can see you one more time
Flash that smile with nothin' in it
I confess, you look better from behind.

Yes, you always looked better from behind
It's the view I always knew would dazzle someone blind
Well, you look like you're in movies
And you sing like Patsy Kline

But honey, I can't help it—
You look best from behind.

Git along little dogie, get you gone
But walk a little slower, as you're movin on . . .
And if I see you next December
Waitin' on the check-out line
You'll turn around and I'll remember
How you always looked better from behind

Yes, you always looked better from behind
Pardon me if I must be a little less than kind
You were handsome as the devil, so I took it as a sign
No regrets when you left
Like the sun when it sets
Skip the rest - You look best from behind.

~©1994 Michele Brourman and Robin Brourman Munson

CHAPTER 4

When My Parents Were My Age, They Were Old

They Just Don't Get It—

I wish I had a quarter every time my parents said, "Edith, you are being childish." Excuse me, but shouldn't a kid my age have the right to be childish? It's one of the few perks we have left. Not that I blame them for wanting us kids to act more like grown-ups. I wish my parents would act more like grown-ups, too. But it just does not seem to work. Acting childish seems to come naturally, but acting like an adult, no matter how old we are, just doesn't come easy to us.

~*Jane Wagner*

Agnus Angst from the Pay Phone at IHOP

Hello, Charlotte, listen, it is *vital* I stay
over at your house tonight!
Don't ask me to explain.
You've got to make your mom let me stay over!
Can't you force her to say yes?

Look, my parents think you're a bad influence on *me, too.*

Just for that, you can't run the equipment at my gig tonight.

You are out of my life, Charlotte;

you are *her*story. You are the "crumb de la crumb." Drop off my tapes at the Un-Club, or I'll sue you for all you're worth.
It is vital, Charlotte!

Don't you eyeball me, you *speck!* Can't you see I am USING this PHONE!! And don't you *touch* that cage.
That's my parakeet in there.

Hello?
Look, it's vital I talk to the radio shrink. My name's Agnus.
I'm fifteen. My *parents* locked me out of the house today.
I want to find out if that is *legal.* I'm in the
ladies' room, House of Pancakes. I can't wait long.

Hello? Is this Dr. Kassorla, the psychologist? Look, Doctor,
for years I've been going home after school, nobody
would be there—

I'd take my key
from around my neck and
let myself in.
But today I go home,
I put my key in the door . . .
THEY CHANGED THE LOCKS ON ME!

Yeah, maybe it *was* something I did. I didn't say I was innocent.

Whatever I do is wrong, anyway. Like, last night, my stepmom,
she accuses me of leaving dirty fingerprints on the *cheese.*
Even getting an innocent piece of cheese becomes a criminal act.
But the problem goes deeper: My real mother's not around
much right now. She's in Europe, Germany or someplace,

doing her art thing. She's a performance artist. Like me.
There was this big custody beef, see, 'cause
my real mother's a lesbian. So the *court* gave me to my dad.
He's a gene-splicer, a bio-businessman at this research lab of
*mis*applied science. Where he's working on some new bio-form
he thinks he'll be able to patent.
He doesn't get that *I* am a new bio-form.

I AM USING THIS PHONE!! You IHOP speck!

So today I go by my dad's lab, to get some money for some gear
for my act,
and I see this like glob of bio-plasm
quivering there in this petri dish.
I don't know why I did it.
Maybe it was sibling rivalry.
But I leaned over
and I spit into it.
And of course, my dad had a MAD SCIENTIST ALERT!
He says I've ruined years of research.
The truth is he loves that *bio-form* more than *me.*

Yeah, I thought of calling the hot line for runaways, but I'm
worried maybe they don't take
throwaways like me.
I have other family, my grandparents,
but we have nothing in common, except that we are all
carbon-based life forms.

What?
A commercial?
I can't believe you're brushing me off.

To sell some product
that probably killed some poor *lab rat.*
You've been about as helpful as an acid FLASHBACK!

~*Jane Wagner*

Mothers and Daughters

"IF YOUR OWN HOUSE IS GOING TO LOOK
ANYTHING LIKE THIS ROOM, I'M NEVER COMING OVER!"
Lawton

~*Mary Lawton*

CHAPTER 4

Some Thoughts on Being Pregnant: A Preface of Sorts

I woke up with a start at 4:00 one morning and realized that I was very, very pregnant. Since I had conceived six months earlier, one might have thought that the news would have sunk in before then, and in many ways it had, but it was on that early morning in May that I first realized how severely pregnant I was. What tipped me off was that, lying on my side and needing to turn over, I found myself unable to move. My first thought was that I had had a stroke.

Nowadays I go around being aware that I am pregnant with the same constancy and lack of surprise with which I go around being aware that I have teeth. But a few times a day the information actually causes me to gasp—how on earth did I come to be in this condition? Well, I have a few suspicions. I mean, I am beginning to put two and two together. See, there was this guy. But the guy is no longer around, and my stomach is noticeably bigger every few days.

I could have had an abortion—the pressure to do so was extraordinary—and if need be, I would take to the streets, armed to defend the right of any woman for any reason to terminate a pregnancy, but I was totally unable to do so this time psychologically, psychically, emotionally. Just totally. So I am going to have a baby pretty soon, and this has raised some mind-boggling issues.

For instance, it occurs to me over and over that I am much too self-centered, cynical, eccentric, and edgy to raise a baby, especially alone. (The baby's father was dramatically less excited than I was to find out I was pregnant, so much so that I have not seen or heard from him in months and don't expect to ever again.) At thirty-five years old, I may be too old and too tired to be having my first child. And I really *did* think for several seconds that I might have had a stroke; it is not second nature for me to believe that everything is more or less okay. Clearly, my nerves are shot.

For example, the other day one of the innumerable deer that come down here from the mountain to eat in the garden and drink from the stream remained where it was as I got closer and closer. It was standing between me and my front door. I thought, Boy they're getting brazen, and I walked closer and closer to it, finally to within four or five feet, when suddenly it tensed. My first thought was that it was about to lunge at me, snarling. Of course it turned instead and bolted through the woods, but I was left with the increasingly familiar sense that I am losing my grasp on reality.

One moment I'm walking along the salt marsh listening to sacred choral music on headphones, convinced that the music is being piped in through my ears, into my head, down my throat, and into my torso where the baby will be able to hear it, and the next moment I'm walking along coaching the baby on how best to grow various body parts. What are you, some kind of *nut*? I ask myself, and I know the answer is yes, *some* kind of nut, and maybe one who is not well enough to be a mother. But this is not the worst fear.

Even the three weeks of waiting for the results of the amniocentesis weren't the most fearful part, nor was the amnio itself. It was, in fact, one of the sweetest experiences of my life. My friend Manning drove me into San Francisco and stayed with me through the procedure, and, well, talk about intimate. It made sex look like a game of Twister. I lay there on the little table at the hospital with my stomach sticking out, Manning near my head holding my hands, a nurse by my feet patting me from time to time, one doctor running the ultrasound device around and around the surface of my tummy, the other doctor taking notes until it was his turn with the needles.

The ultrasound doctor was showing me the first pictures of my baby, who was at that point a four-month-old fetus. He was saying, "Ah, there's the head now . . . there's the leg . . . there's its bottom," and I was watching it all on the screen, nodding, even though it was all just underwater photography, all quite ethereal and murky. Manning said it was like watching those first men on the moon. I pretended to be able to distinguish each section of the baby because I didn't want the doctor to think I was a lousy mother who was already judging the kid for not being photogenically distinct enough. He pointed out the vertebrae, a sweet curved strand of pearls, and then the heart, beating as visibly as a pulsar, and that was when I started to cry.

Then the other doctor took one of his needles and put it right through my stomach, near my belly button, in a circle that the ultrasound doctor had described with the end of a straw. I felt a pinch, and then mild cramping, and that was all, as the doctor began to withdraw some amniotic fluid. Now you probably think, like I thought, that this fluid is some vaguely holy saltwater, flown in from the coast for the occasion, but it is mostly baby pee, light green in color. What they do with it then is to send it to the lab, where they culture it, growing enough cells from the tissue the baby has sloughed off into the amniotic fluid to determine if there are chromosomal abnormalities and whether it is a boy or a girl, if you care to know.

During the first week of waiting, you actually believe your baby is okay, because you saw it scoot around during the ultrasound and because most babies are okay. By the middle of the second week, things are getting a bit dicey in your head, but most of the time you still think the baby is okay. But on the cusp of the second and third weeks, you come to know—not to believe but to know—that you are carrying a baby inside you in only the broadest sense of the word *baby*, because what is growing in there has a head the size of a mung bean, with almost no brain at all because all available tissue has gone into the building of a breathtaking collection of arms and knees—maybe not too many arms but knees absolutely *everywhere*.

Finally, though, the nurse who had patted my feet during the amnio called, and the first thing she said was that she had good news, and I thought I might actually throw up from sheer joy. Then she talked about the findings for a while, although I did not hear a word, and then she said, "Do you want to know its sex?" And I said yes I did.

It is a boy. His name is Sam Lamott, Samuel John Stephen Lamott. (My brothers' names are John and Steve.)

A boy. Do you know what that means? Do you know what boys have that girls don't? That's right, there you go. They have penises. And like most of my women friends, I have somewhat mixed feelings about this. Now, I don't know how to put this delicately, but I have never been quite the same since seeing a penis up close while I was on LSD years and years ago. It was an actual penis; I mean, it wasn't like I was staring at my hand for an hour and watched it turn into my grandfather's face and then into a bat and then into a penis. It was the real thing. It was my boyfriend's real thing, and what it looked like was the root of all my insanity, of a lot of my suffering and obsession. It looked like a cross between a snake and a heart.

That is a really intense thing you boys have there, and we internal Americans of the hetero persuasion have really, really conflicted feelings about you external Americans because of the way you wield those things, their power over us, and especially their power over you. I ask you once again to remember the old joke in which the puzzled, defensive man says, "I didn't want to go to Las Vegas," then points to his crotch and says, "He wanted to go to Las Vegas." So it has given me pause to learn that there is a baby boy growing in my belly who apparently has all the right number of hands and feet and arms and legs and knees, a normal-size head, and a penis.

Penises are so—what is the word?—*funky*. They're wonderful, too, and I love them, but over the years such bad things have happened to me because of them. I've gotten pregnant, even when I tried so hard not to, and I've gotten diseases, where you couldn't see any evidence of disease on the man's dick and he claims not to have anything, but you end up having to get treatment and it's totally humiliating and weird, and the man's always mad at you for having caught it, even though you haven't slept with anyone else for months or even years. It is my secret belief that men love their penises so much that when they take them in to show their doctors, after their women claim to have caught a little something, the male doctors get caught up in this penis love, whack the patient (your lover) on the back, and say thunderously, "Now don't be silly, that's a damn fine penis you've got there."

A man told me once that all men like to look at themselves in the mirror when they're hard, and now I keep picturing Sam in twenty years, gazing at his penis in the mirror while feeling psychologically somewhere between Ivan Boesky and Mickey Mantle. I also know he will be someone who will one day pee with pride, because all men do, standing there manfully tearing bits of toilet paper to shreds with their straight and forceful sprays, carrying on as if this were one of history's great naval battles—the Battle of Midway, for instance. So of course I'm a little edgy about the whole thing, about my child having a penis instead of a nice delicate little lamb of a vagina. But even so, this is still not the worst fear.

No, the worst thing, worse even than sitting around crying about that inevitable day when my son will leave for college, worse than thinking about whether or not in the meantime to get him those hideous baby shots he probably should have but that some babies die from, worse than the fears I have when I lie awake at 3:00 in the morning (that I won't be able to make enough money and will have to live in a tenement house where the rats will bite our heads while we sleep, or that I will lose my arms in some tragic accident and will have to go to court and diaper my son using only my mouth and feet and the judge won't think I've done a good enough job and will put Sam in a foster home), worse even than the fear I feel whenever a car full of teenagers drives past my house going 200 miles an hour on our sleepy little street, worse than thinking about my son being run over by one of those drunken teenagers, or of his one day becoming one of those teenagers—worse than just about anything else is the agonizing issue of how on earth anyone can bring a child into this world knowing full well that he or she is eventually going to have to go through the seventh and eighth grades.

~Anne Lamott

The Days Of Gilded Rigatoni

Breakfast will be perfect. I know this from experience. Poached eggs expertly done, the toast in triangles, the juice fresh squeezed. A pot of coffee, a rose in a bud vase. A silver tray. I will eat every bit.

Breakfast will be perfect, except that it will be all wrong. The eggs should be a mess, in some no-man's-land between fried and scrambled, the toast underdone, the orange juice slopped over into the place where the jelly should be, if there were jelly, which there is not. Coffee lukewarm, tray steel-gray and suspiciously like a cookie sheet. I get to eat the yucky parts. I know this from experience.

Today is Mother's Day, and the room-service waiter at the hotel is bringing my breakfast. No handprint in a plaster-of-Paris circle with a ribbon through a hole in the top. Nothing made out of construction paper or macaroni spray-painted gold and glued to cardboard. This is a disaster. Any of the other 364 days of the year would be a wonderful time for a woman with small children to have a morning of peace and quiet. But solitary splendor on this day is like being a book with no reader. It raises that age-old question: If a mother screams in the forest and there are no children to hear it, is there any sound?

It has become commonplace to complain that Mother's Day is a manufactured holiday, cooked up by greeting-card moguls and covens of florists. But these complaints usually come from grown-ups who find themselves on a one-way street, who are stymied each year by the question of what to give a mature woman who says she has everything her heart desires except grandchildren.

It has become commonplace to flog ourselves if we are mothers, with our limitations if we stay home with the kids, with our obligations if we take jobs. It's why sometimes mothers who are not working outside their homes seem to suggest that the kids of those who are, live on Chips Ahoy and walk barefoot through the snow to school. It's why sometimes mothers

with outside jobs feel moved to ask about those other women, allegedly without malice, "What do they do all day?"

And amid that incomplete revolution in the job description, the commercial Mother's Day seems designed to salute a mother who is an endangered species, if not an outright fraud. A mother who is pink instead of fuchsia. A mother who bakes cookies and never cheats with the microwave. A mother who does not swear or scream, who wears an apron and a patient smile.

Not a mother who is away from home on a business trip on Mother's Day. Not a mother who said, "You can fax it to me, honey" when her son said he had written something in school and who is now doomed to remember that sentence the rest of her miserable life.

Not an imperfect mother.

The Mother's Day that means something, the Mother's Day that is not a duty but a real holiday, is about the perfect mother. It is about the mother before she becomes the human being, when she is still the center of our universe, when we are very young.

They are not long, the days of construction paper and gilded rigatoni. That's why we save those things so relentlessly, why the sisterhood of motherhood, those of us who can instantly make friends with a stranger by discussing colic and orthodonture, have as our coat of arms a sheet of small handprints executed in finger paint.

Each day we move a little closer to the sidelines of their lives, which is where we belong, if we do our job right. Until the day comes when they have to find a florist fast at noon because they had totally forgotten it was anything more than the second Sunday in May. Hassle city.

The little ones do not forget. They cut and paste and sweat over palsied capital letters and things built of Popsicle sticks about which you must never say, "What is this?"

Just for a little while, they believe in the perfect mom—that is, you, whoever and wherever you happen to be. "Everything I am," they might say, "I owe to my mother." And they believe they wrote the sentence themselves, even if they have to give you the card a couple of days late. Over the phone you can say, "They don't make breakfast the way you make it." And they will believe it. And it will be true.

~Anna Quindlen

Pre-School Yuppies

The Building

Words by Wendy Wasserstein *Drawn by Blair Drawson*

We're applying to Park Avenue Christian, The Dalton Lower School, & Miss Hewitt's Classes (safety).

We're applying to Little Red Schoolhouse, Hunter College Elementary, & Montessori.

WHAM

Then I'm applying to Harvard, Princeton, Yale, and Smith (safety). And I'm getting a J.D. & an M.B.A. from Harvard or Columbia (safety).

I'm applying to Bennington, Sarah Lawrence & the Rhode Island School of Design, & then I'm dropping out in my sophomore year to become a graffiti artist.

WHAM

Well, obviously then I'll be a lawyer at Sullivan & Cromwell, then an arbitrator at Goldman Sachs, and then I'll marry David Kissinger.

Well, obviously then I'll be going to the Palladium and Area and clubs every night for 2 yrs. before I sell my first painting to Mary Boone for $200,000.

By this point I'm Chairperson at Chrysler, then Secretary of the Treasury before I retire to Seal Harbor, Maine.

By this point I'm starring in a Susan Seidelman movie, & expatriate to Paris where I have children with Max Spielberg, and a retrospective at The Beaubourg.

WHAM

Pamela!

Samantha!

And when I'm 60 I'll come back to the U.S.A. & for my golden yrs. I want to be doorman of this building & tell great stories about my life—just like Mike!.

~ *Wendy Wasserstein*

Nanny Tyrannica

"I used to worry about losing my husband to another woman," the twins' mother confessed at my son's toddler program while stashing two color-coded pacifiers into a diaper bag. "Now," she sighed wearily, taking out two color-coded bottles of apple juice, "I'm more afraid of losing my *nanny* to another woman. She's terrific with Matthew and Molly. Because of her, they sing all of Gilbert and Sullivan's *Pirates of Penzance.* She's taught them Chinese stretching exercises. Anyone seeing her in the park would want to snatch her right up. They don't know she's a health-food fanatic. I can't bring a potato that wasn't organically grown into the house. She forbids us to eat chocolate. Did you ever binge on *carob?"*

The kids moved from story time to singing time. My son launched into monotonous rounds of "Row, Row, Row Your Boat." Without missing a syllable the twins, not yet two, piped, "When constabulary duties kill enjoyment, kill enjoyment . . . a policeman's lot is not a happy one."

Their mother looked at me and shrugged. "So tonight we're having free-range chicken and hydroponic yams."

Nobody can ever realistically anticipate the changes brought about by a new baby. Double those when the baby is followed by the arrival of a nanny. It's not easy having a stranger come into your house. Gone is the freedom to raid the refrigerator naked; you have to put on a trench coat just to get juice. Sex, of course, is now restricted to the bedroom.

And along with your privacy, you relinquish control of your baby. Each time you go into the nursery for a little kiss and nuzzle, you find yourself asking permission of the nanny.

At baby gyms, swim schools, and Suzuki lessons, mothers complain about their help, all of whom are in varying degrees intrusive. Even if they initially appear eager to please, soon they evolve into tyrants and bullies.

Whether she's a British-trained nanny, a French *au pair,* or a Salvadoran housekeeper, she's the one who sets policy, determining her hours and responsibilities, dictating how your child will be fed and disciplined.

In the canyons of Wall Street, a junior partner this assertive would certainly be dismissed; but in tiny-tyke America, a nanny quickly gets tenure. Once she's established a warm relationship with her charge, the nanny has nothing to fear. The love of the child is her job security. She can beg, borrow, and belittle without risk of reprisals. Rather than change nannies and perhaps upset the child, parents will tolerate affront after abuse.

"I don't know what to do!" a mother at the ice-skating rink wailed. "After eighteen months, Jessica is very attached to our live-in. We were okay with her too until she got a boyfriend. Our arrangement was she could leave for her day off once Jessie was asleep. Last week her boyfriend showed up early and started honking. She tried to put Jessica to bed at five o'clock!" She shook her head, baffled. "Her last employer said she was a gem."

Former employers have been known to lie—maybe they want to dump this "gem" before any more sterling vanishes—and besides, each household has its own quirks. You can interview like Mike Wallace and study her chest X-rays to make sure she's not a smoker, but it's still impossible to predict how she'll fit in. Landing the right nanny is all luck, which is why some parents are brave enough to import from abroad someone they've never met.

Hiring a nanny sight unseen is an act of faith, today's version of an arranged marriage. How do you know you won't wind up with a subversive? A Madonna clone? A slob?

A mother at the park who'd flown over a French *au pair* smiled impishly when I asked if she'd been concerned about surprises. "I wanted a wallflower," she admitted. "That's why I had the girls send pictures. The last thing I needed was someone like Catherine Deneuve moving in when I didn't have my waist back yet. The homelier, the better! I wanted the *kids* to fall in love with her, not my *husband!*"

The mother at the next swing laughed. "We brought a young nanny over from England," she reported. "One morning, maybe eight months after she'd started with us, she looked up from feeding the baby and said, 'I'm quite fond of life here in America.' I didn't know what she was driving at. 'I think I'd like to become a permanent resident,' she continued. 'But there's a bit of a problem with my papers.'

"She was great with Alexandra," the woman went on. "Certainly we wanted her to stay. I offered to find a good immigration attorney for her. 'Oh, I've spoken to a solicitor,' she said. 'It would make things much simpler if I were married to a citizen.' I figured she was telling me she'd need a morning off to do this," the mother laughed. "Wrong! She then said, 'I thought maybe your brother would marry me. We wouldn't have to *consummate* the marriage . . .' "

She laughed again, an edge of hysteria creeping into her voice. "My brother won't even let me fix him up on a blind date! I should tell him to marry our nanny?"

Listening to mothers, one suspects there's a course in *chutzpah* at nanny school. A nanny, particularly a British-trained one, assumes the status of Chairman of the Board. If she's willing to do laundry at all, *she'll* pick the wash cycle. As far as child-care is concerned, she looks upon parents, pediatrician, and relatives as obstacles to the performance of her job.

This type of nanny takes pride in raising stoic male babies and sensible female ones. If you intended to feed the baby "on demand" (perhaps to stem relentless crying) and the nanny believes in "a schedule" (feeding every four hours), your offspring will learn the virtue of patience. As a first-time parent, afraid to trust yourself, you'll listen to anyone proclaiming herself a professional in the field. And even if you've had kids before, all of whom were successfully fed on demand, you'll give in. You're savvy enough to understand how inconsequential the timing of a baby bottle is compared to the bigger problems ahead—drugs in the fifth grade and teenage pregnancies. You learn to pick your fights, because you know ultimately the baby will quiet down; the nanny won't.

Having established herself as commander-in-chief of the nursery, the nanny puts out her scent in other parts of the house. "I made the mistake of saying, '*Mi casa, su casa*' to our Guatemalan housekeeper," a mother announced at infant CPR class. "She took me literally. I came home and found our gardener packing up his spades and trowels. Consuela didn't like the way he looked at her. An acre and a half to mow," she said, shaking her head, "and he's on his way back to Kyoto. My husband is fed up. He says with Consuela running things, he feels like a fraud checking Head of Household on our tax return."

With our son's first birthday approaching, my husband and I felt it was time for me to stop nursing and resume working. We started making inquiries about childcare. Friends asked their nannies if they knew anyone looking for work. Although five nations were represented among the neighborhood help, this effort was unproductive. "In all of NATO," said my husband, Martin, laughing, "there's no one to take care of Nicky."

"Scout the parks," we were advised. "If you see a nanny you like, make an offer." I couldn't follow through. Not because of ethics, but because it was winter and the parks were deserted except for a couple of three-card-monte hustlers.

An agency was our final option. The receptionist at International Domestics told us their fee was 75 percent of a month's salary.

"Hers or mine?" Martin joked. Hearing that graduates of nanny schools get upwards of $400 a week, we decided to go for a housekeeper, someone experienced in caring for children who would also do some cleaning. The first to emerge from the back room was Rosario. In her late 50s, she shuffled in slowly, as if her knees were tied together. I ruled her out; Nicky could swallow an entire bottle of Windex before she'd get to him.

"We can only pay $150 a week," I volunteered, hoping Rosario would turn *us* down. "Is that enough for you?"

"*Sí*" Rosario mumbled, studying her lap.

"Talk to *them,*" the receptionist instructed, "in English."

"Jes."

"We're vegetarian"— me, trying another tack. "There's no meat in our house. Do you eat tofu?"

"Sì . . . jes."

While I wouldn't expect a recent arrival from Central or South America to finish the London *Times* crossword puzzle, I wanted someone who could make herself understood to 911 and be able to read instructions on the bottle of Ipecac.

The parade of candidates continued. After we'd met all the possibilities, the receptionist, perhaps perceiving our indecisiveness, offered a suggestion. "If I were you, I'd hire Gloria. She's happily married. With a young baby, you don't want a girl who runs around with a lot of fellows. She'll catch something. Next thing you know, the baby's got it."

If she was trying to scare us into hiring Gloria, it worked. Immediately upon leaving the agency, we picked up a copy of Linda Wolf's *Tell A Maid Child Care, Spanish/English* so I could give instructions like, "*siempre mantenga cerrada la puerta de la piscina*" (always keep the pool gate closed).

We lucked out. Gloria was a good choice for us. The hours she selected approximated those we would have picked ourselves. She's gentle and loving with Nicky. After two years, she's an essential part of our household. Her assertiveness is useful: Gloria's the only one who can persuade Nicky to take a bath, wear shoes, and chew his vitamins. She alone knows where the parts of Mr. Potato Head are buried.

Gloria may not have the panache of a British nanny, and Nicky doesn't sing operettas, but he leaves the twins in the dust when it comes to "*Quando Caliente El Sol.*"

~ *Sybil Adelman*

Nanny Dearest

~Anne Gibbons

I Am the Green Lollipop: Notes on Stepmothering

Lisa and Alex, ages six and three, were standing in a fountain in the middle of the Santa Monica Mall. I insisted they get out. They refused. Again I insisted. Lisa put her arms around her brother and drew him closer to her.

This is what happened the first time I was left alone with my future stepchildren. I insisted they get out of a fountain that did not have water in it. I have given this act of mine considerable thought. At the very least, it indicates a certain amount of panic on my part. A tendency to overreact. Certainly a lack of playfulness. I could have gotten into the fountain with them. I also could have ignored the whole business, waited for their father to return, and let him deal with it or not. But I couldn't wait. I had to seize an opportunity, any opportunity, to assert my authority.

My claim to authority at that time was tenuous—I was not yet their stepmother. I must have wanted to prove just how tenuous it was. Why else would I try to stop two children from doing nothing? Naturally they refused to obey me. But more was at stake here and we all knew it—our futures. Lisa and Alex were seizing an opportunity themselves: They were taking a stand against me, the intruder. It is one of the few moments in their lives when they have been in agreement. And I, in my muddleheaded way, continued to insist, "Get out," when what I really meant was, "Let me in."

~

Lisa wanted a horse desperately. She had been talking about it for weeks and then said she would give up Christmas for three years to get one. Larry said, "Lisa, I don't think you realize, it's very expensive, not just to buy a horse but to keep a horse. It costs several thousand dollars a year."

"My friends will give me the food free," said Lisa.

"Lisa, that's impossible," said Larry, exasperated. "We can't afford a horse."

Lisa stomped up the stairs, then halfway up yelled very sarcastically, "Thanks, Delia."

I would like to point out that I had not said one word.

It doesn't matter. I am the cause of her pain, whatever it may be, perhaps because she blames me for her much greater hurt, that her parents are no longer married. I am not the reason they are divorced, but I am evidence of it, as well as being a hindrance. How can they get back together if I am here? I am also privileged to be the adult that Lisa can most risk being angry with or, put another way, that she can most afford to have angry with her. Life is less secure than it used to be and she isn't taking any chances. So when Lisa feels mistreated, she thinks of me.

The only problem with her point of view from my point of view is this: How can I be her persecutor if I am her victim? For I *am* her victim. My identity as a stepmother is amorphous at best, and if she takes this away from me, what will I have left? Consider:

Larry and his first wife got divorced. Both stayed involved with their children so Lisa has two mothers because she has her regular mother and she has her father. Now that he sees the children alone, Larry is doing a lot of mothering—feeding, soothing, bathing, reading, setting limits (well, sort of—more on this later). Then I arrive and suddenly Lisa has three mothers.

Two were difficult enough. Lisa is in the peculiar position of being overloaded with mothers and deprived of family. And she is possessive and protective of her father, feeling vulnerable to losing him altogether now that the family has fallen apart. And how do I fit in? Who am I, as far as Lisa is concerned? Unwelcome and unnecessary. Unfortunately for her, I am also unstoppable—though that won't keep her from trying.

When I first arrived, I checked out the territory. I wanted to participate. I wanted to be helpful. Well, truthfully, I wanted most to become indispensable. To Larry, not to Lisa, who, at least in the beginning, was simply a means to an end. So what did I seize upon? Cooking and chauffering. (And one other task—criticizing—but we'll get to that later.)

Even if I had known I was cooking my own goose, I would have taken on these jobs; they were the only ones available. The problem that developed was this: When I cooked my own goose, Lisa wouldn't eat it. Because I can cook all I want, but I can't feed. Feeding is what mothers do, and here Lisa drew the line. "I'm not hungry," she said, or something equally upsetting, like, "I just feel like eating yogurt tonight." It was her way of saying, "You can't mother me." So, at least in part, my efforts were thwarted. I was getting little payoff for my hard work. Though I succeeded in becoming indispensable to Larry, I wasn't satisfied. I wanted love. Lisa's love. I wanted this even before I loved Lisa myself, for its symbolic meaning, that I belonged in the family. Oh, what an unreasonable expectation. The self-centeredness of it. Of course, I might have settled for gratitude or respect, but good luck to me.

So the inevitable took place. I began to feel used. The rest of the world may see me as a wicked stepmother, but I see myself as Cinderella in a fairy tale that goes something like this: Once upon a time, there was a handsome prince who fell in love with a beautiful princess (me). He took her away to his castle to live with him and his two children from a previous marriage. Here things quickly went to pot, and the princess became known, at least to herself, as Cinderella. Now she could have given up cooking and driving the coach-and-four, but then she wouldn't have been Cinderella. And what would she be?

A problem, you see, of options.

It happens, however, that there is another role, besides that of victim, that is available to me: the outsider. The problem is, Lisa has a stake in this identity too. She feels driven out by my relationship with her father, while I feel doomed never to be allowed full membership in the club. It occurs to me that one of the unappreciated side effects of all this

uncoupling and recoupling is the endless opportunity it offers all participants to feel sorry for themselves. I was at the door of our house one day having a conversation with my husband's ex-wife. She complained about having to miss *The Jewel in The Crown* on television that night. I said we were going to miss it too. "Oh, but you can tape it," she said. "Why don't you?" I asked, falling into the trap. "I don't have a tape machine," she said mournfully.

This conversation wasn't about a television show. She was actually saying, You have more money than me; life is so much harder for me; I am the victim. Well, let me say this about that: Hands off my role!

~Delia Ephron

How to Talk to Your Stepmother

Your stepmother answers the telephone.
"Hi, is my dad there?"

Your stepmother has just announced that it is time for dinner.
"I'm not hungry."

Your stepmother has just put a bottle of salad dressing on the table.
"This isn't the kind we have at Mom's."

Your stepmother has just put the chicken on the table.
"I don't like chicken in funny sauce."

Your dad, your stepmother, and you are going to the movies. You don't want to see the movie she wants to see.

"My mom says that movie is too violent for me."

Alternatives

1. "My mom says that movie is too scary."
2. "My mom says that movie is too sad."

You want to watch television. Your stepmother says no.

"I'll ask my dad."

You ask your dad if you can watch television. Your stepmother informs him that she already told you you can't.

"I'm not talking to you. I'm talking to my dad!"

Your dad is out in the afternoon and you turn on the television. Your stepmother says to turn it off.

"You're not the boss of me."

You want your stepmother to take you to a movie that she thinks your dad doesn't want you to see.

"Look, you're my stepmother. You're in charge. You don't have to ask him."

Your stepmother picks up you and your friend after the movies.

"Hi, where's dad? Why didn't he come?"

Your dad says you are not allowed to sleep over at your friend's. Absolutely not. It's out of the question. Tomorrow's a school day. Your stepmother says nothing.

"That was your idea, wasn't it?"

~Delia Ephron

Wild Things

THEY'RE FREE RANGE CHILDREN.

~ *Yvette Jean Silver*

Hedge(Hog)ing Our Bets

Your son has fallen in love, my friend calls to report. They have just come from the pet store.

Alden gets on the phone, breathless. "Please, Mom. Please. I saw this pet and I have to have it."

I thought our pet issues were over. I'd heard about the lizards. The hamsters had come and (mercifully) gone. We had succumbed to the cat. The beagle has topped the wish list for months, though temporarily displaced by the pig from Vietnam. Even Alden knew that the pig wouldn't fly.

"It's a hedgehog. It comes from Madagascar."

Half an hour later, Alden is home. A child possessed.

"Mom, it's so cute. I have to have it. Mom, I'll do everything for it. I'll clean its cage. I'll wash it. I'll feed it. I'll do everything for it. It eats cat food."

It *eats* cat food? To the cat, I'm sure, it *is* cat food.

"No, Mom, I asked. The man said it would get along with the cat. He said they wouldn't mess with each other."

No problem. We'll just tell the cat not to mess with it.

Alden, these are wild animals. They belong in the wild.

"They're very friendly. The man said so. He said they only bite if you mess with them."

From his vocabulary it is obvious the helpful gentleman in the pet store is a native of Madagascar and thus an expert in hedgehog behavior.

These animals are not meant to be kept in cages, I tell him. It's not natural: a hog in chips.

"I don't have to keep it in the cage. I figured it out. I can buy a used playpen and it can be in the playpen all day."

When it's not out of the playpen. Or in the cat's stomach.

"And it's very inexpensive to keep, Mom. It only eats cat food. And not that much of it. Just cat food. And worms."

What could be simpler?

How big is it, Alden. (Knowing that asking will be regarded as the first step in a process of capitulation.)

"Not big. Two inches. Or two feet. Or something. Mom, I just have to have it. I'll do everything for it. I'll find out all about it. I'll read everything about it. I'll do *research*."

The kid knows how to push our buttons.

"Mom, did you ever feel that you just had to have something? You just had to or you didn't know what would happen."

Yes, Alden. That's how people feel about their romances.

"But those are just people, Mom. You can always get another one. But I don't think there will be that many hedgehogs after they sell this one. This might be the only one."

How much is it, Alden?

"Well, it's sort of expensive. But Mom, I'll give up my allowance forever. Or at least until next year. I'll make my bed. I'll take a job."

How much, Alden?

"Three hundred dollars."

Three hundred dollars? Don't worry, Alden, I don't think they'll sell it so fast.

"Mom, I've figured it out. I can take money out of the bank for it."

No, Alden, you cannot raid your bank account to buy a hedgehog.

"I'll never ask for anything again."

He promises to give up his allowance. He promises to work for it. He promises to give up all claims to his parents' estates if he can have the hedgehog.

We don't need a hedgehog.

"You never listen to me. You don't care how I feel."

I do. And I do.

"Then please, just think about it."

I'll think about it. (I've thought about it.)

"Mom, I've looked it up. It's not really a hedgehog. It's a kind of hedgehog but it's an insectivore like a hedgehog. It's actually called a tenrac. There are two kinds, the long-tailed kind and this one. Mom, it's so cute. And in winter they hibernate."

They hibernate all winter?

"Yes, Mom. It's hibernating now."

Three hundred dollars for a hibernating animal?

Alden, I just had another thought. How do you know it's alive? Come June, it's time to wake it up, maybe it won't wake up. As a matter of fact, I'd like to get into this deal. Direct line to Madagascar. Hello, I'd like another few dozen of the "hibernating" hedgehogs. Yeah, regular air is fine. The cargo hold will keep the bodies—oh, pardon me, the hedgehogs—cool.

Sunday morning. Long face. Distracted air. Announces he can't even watch the cartoons and has no appetite. Has been raving about the hedgehog almost nonstop for the past thirty-six hours.

"Mom, Dad. I can't get it out of my mind. It's just so cute. And I would do everything for it. I just love it."

Father feigns snoring.

"DA-ad. You're not being nice. You're not listening to me." Tears. Storms out of room.

Alden, don't you see? Your father is just pretending to be a hibernating hedgehog. He's trying to amuse you.

"Can I have it. Please?"

Alden . . .

"Please. Just consider it?"

Alden.

"Please."

Okay, I'm considering it.

"When will you know?"

Bring up old theme: I don't approve of keeping animals in a cage.

"But Mom, look at it this way. It's already in the cage. No one is going to send it back to Madagascar. And we'll be so nice to it."

Oh, Alden.

"Just consider it. Just think about it."

I'm thinking about it.

Monday morning, though I know this is probably one of the dumbest moves I've ever made, right up there with starting those tap dancing lessons, I go to the pet store to see a Madagascar hedgehog. Sure enough: a sign for $299—not $2.99, as would seem reasonable—on the cage. It looks like a miniaturized anteater. It's hibernating but it does seem to be alive. Moves very sleepily. Sort of like Alden and his father in the mornings.

Afternoon. Phone rings at office.

"Mom, you went to see it?" Excitement in the voice.

Who told you?

"Dad did. And I told him that we would give it such a loving home. And he said that these were noble feelings, so we could reopen the issue and talk about it tonight."

I don't want to be home tonight. As a distraction, offer to take child to dumb, violent movie. Hedgehog matter put to rest. Momentarily.

7:30 a.m.

I go to Alden's room to wake him up. For the first time in memory, the bed is made. And made neatly. Alden is feeding the cat, another rare event. He is completely dressed.

8:00 a.m. leave for school.

"I made my bed and got dressed so I could get the hedgehog."

Naturally, this information stuns me. I thought that Alden's behavior was simply the result of a decision he'd made to lead an exemplary life.

"Do I have any after-school plans?"

Not that I know of.

"Then we could go get the hedgehog today."

H Day plus fifty-six hours. Still hedging.

~ *Dale Burg*

Billie's Parents

"You must be Billie's parents. I'd recognize you anywhere!"

~ *Brenda Burbank*

Notes From My Life

Everyone thought I was a midget. I thought I was a kid. I was around six years old and doing a Carmen Miranda act between showings of the movie *King's Row* at a vaudeville theater in New Jersey. My costume was blinding red satin. I wore a turban with different-colored feathers sticking out of it like a dust mop, a brief bralike top over my nonexistent bosom... over my non-existent bosom. . . Why am I saying that twice? That's how it comes out. The skirt was tight over the hips, with a cascade of ruffles to the floor. It had a wide split down the middle which revealed my truly unformed legs.

My father would walk out from the wings to the upright piano at the side of the stage as soon as "The End" flashed on the movie screen. Garish red and blue lights came up and he would start playing your regulation 1940s South American vamp. Then, I sambaed on, all no foot three of me, and sang my tiny heart out. I rolled my r's just like Carmen.

"Ow would you lahk to spend a weekend een 'avana? Ow would you lahk to see the Carrrr-eeeee-beeean shore?" They laughed when I wanted them to. I wasn't a joke. I sang and danced well, my patter was amusing, they got their money's worth if you throw in the movie.

My poor daddy played my musical arrangements very badly. He wasn't much of a pianist, but he made my whole career as Baby Phyllis possible. He invented me, along with hypnotizing cats, hand-painted hats, and a fortune-telling mother, so let's not look a gift daddy in the . . . well . . . at least not too closely . . . yet.

The first time I sang in Atlantic City was 1939. That year my mother was known as Marvelle and was reading palms at the Merry-Go-Round Bar of the Ritz Carlton Hotel. My father was called Dr. S.A. Newman or Gabel the Graphologist, and he was analyzing handwriting at an open stand on the boardwalk. We were just your ordinary all-American family trying to make a buck in the summer before the "Big War."

My father's stand looked like... well, let's see. Do you remember carnival stands where you threw the ball at the stacked wooden milk bottles, or shot the nice little man and his ducks as they went back and forth making the clang-chika-chika-ring sounds? Well, it was like those, but only four or five feet wide and deep enough for one man and possibly his child to stand comfortably. It had a high counter so you could lean on your elbow while you tried to write a brief message and your name unselfconsciously and normally, so my father could analyze it.

When I hung out there, I'd be lifted up onto the counter. I'd sit there for hours watching the people go by on the boardwalk, watching my daddy do his "work" at this funny little spot. It wasn't brilliantly decorated. The facts were painted on the front with some stars scattered among the words. On the expanse of white painted wood behind my father's head there were photographs of him with Jack Dempsey, Gene Tunney, and the Three Stooges.

My father bent over the woman's piece of paper with a magnifying glass and said, "You see the way you don't quite finish the last letter of each word? See, the T and the W? They're incomplete. That shows a problem with seeing things through. You're a dreamer. You start a lot of things and then you lose interest, probably in romance too. I see a somewhat flightly romantic person in your writing."

The stout, graying woman in her sensible cotton print dress, sandals, and stockings looked puzzled. "Gee, I don't think that's so. I've been a nurse for almost twenty years. I've hardly ever missed a day. No... No... I would say I'm the opposite. Yes, exactly the opposite from what you're saying." She was beginning to get upset.

"I don't think you know what you're doing. This is ridiculous. Just give me my dollar back. I never believed in any of this... garbage. I thought, oh well, it's my vacation. I never should have... Just give me my dollar back."

"You don't understand. This shows the real you ... underneath. Your handwriting doesn't lie. We know these things."

"Keep the dollar... Thank you, I've had enough. Why is that child staring at me? She's too young to be hanging around a place like this."

I said, "That's my daddy and he's very good. You should listen to him. He can do anything. He knows everything."

He crumpled up the piece of paper with her "sensible" note and kept it inside his fist as he banged on the counter. He stopped himself, threw the paper down, and said, "Come on, it's going to be slow for a while. I'll buy you a soda." He lifted up part of the counter to get out, then he took me down. He put the pads and pencils in the pocket of his short-sleeved shirt and put up a sign: THE DOCTOR WILL BE BACK IN HALF AN HOUR.

He asked the souvenir man who had the other half of the stand to keep an eye on things. What things? We went down the block off the boardwalk to a "shoppe." He had coffee and a toasted English with lots of butter. I had a chocolate milk shake.

I don't remember how I felt about him then. Was I embarrassed or just sad? Did I feel both superior and threatened? Or did I think he was the greatest daddy in the world? I hope so.

Momma was very attractive that year, her thirty-ninth. Her hair was wavy and dark blond. She was just beginning to be plump. She wore rayon crepe dresses mostly in blue with big shoulder pads and plunging necklines. Her nails and lips were dark bluish red. She always had a charming flirty quality until anyone took her remotely seriously. She had that nonaccent accent and why can't I remember her voice? The thing is she was not a fake, she really wasn't. You'll wind up believing me.

"What do you see in that ball, miss?..." He picks up the triangularly folded shiny card from the center of the table. "Hell, I can't read your name without my glasses."

"Marvelle." My mother laughs a soft musical laugh and looks down into a small crystal ball. "I don't see anything at the moment. You look into it, and really concentrate on what you want me to see."

The man looks slightly uncomfortable, but Marvelle's manner is relaxed and sure. They both look intently into the ball. She closes her eyes for a moment. She opens them and keeps them on the ball.

"Who's... R?... I see an R who's very strong, very important to you. But there's some trouble with R... Yes, I see trouble recently." She looks up at him. "Do you know an R? Do you have an R close to you?"

The man doesn't answer for a few moments. He stares at Marvelle. His face and eyes go from middle-age genial to American tough to little boy, loose and watery.

"An R?... Yes. That's very good. Yes... very good." He's deciding whether to go on with it, whether to reveal himself to this stranger, this fortune-teller. He laughs, but it would not stand up in a court of law.

"What else do you see? Do you see anything else more concrete... about this... R?"

My mother looks at the man. She says gently: "You should say good-bye to her. It's never going to work out. You're never going to give up... everything... everyone else, and R is beginning to make other plans. She is seeing someone else. He's older... Yes... She won't be around. I don't see her around. I see you... Bill...Is that your name, Bill?...I see good things, good health, yes, good things. Listen to me... let her go."

She opens her eyes and puts her hands in her lap. Bill grabs my mother's hands and kisses them. This doesn't embarrass her. Men and women often have to touch her, to thank her, to feel her realness, to hide their amazement, to have an extra few moments to decide what their next move should be. Do they listen to her? Do they believe her? Is it a trick? Was she just lucky this time? Should they tip her? How much? Should they hire her? Who is this woman? Why is she doing this? She's refined. She always tells men, if they ask, that she's married, happily married, and has three gorgeous daughters. Two of them already grown up. Her regulars at night see her husband hanging around a back table at the club. He never takes his eyes off her. His body tenses and he starts walking around if a man sits too long with her. It tenses only slightly less if it's a woman.

"Ray (he called her Ray, or the Yiddish version of Rachel...Rucchhel — guttural)... you should only give them ten minutes... tops. This way they'll come back. Those old bags take advantage of you. They have nothing else to do but hang around."

This is not a first-time exchange. Variations on this theme are recurrent. It always gets to my mother. He has to do it. They play it out.

"Sig, please! Why do you watch me? Why do you time me? I can't stand it. I spend as much time as I have to. I help them. They keep coming back because I help them. They pay me. *They pay me*, Sig!"

Now the nerve has been uncovered and poked at in both of them. Is that the spot where the cancer that killed both of them was nurtured? Is that what it does? Is that how it works? I don't know, but it feels like that to me now.

My father's anger is uncontrollable, my mother can't stop. She's crying.

"A lot of them want to be my friends. They're good to me, Sig. They'd do anything for me. You never understand. You never let anyone be my friend. Not anyone. You're jealous!"

My father is not crying. He is screaming. He has a vein that comes straight down the middle of his thin-skinned forehead. It is enlarged. It looks like a blue thermometer.

"*Jealous! Jealous!* Of a fortune-teller! You sit there pushing your shoulders at them, laughing, flirting with them, trying to make me look like a fool. You think I don't see what you're doing? Always belittling me. Making me feel like nothing. I taught you this. I taught you everything. You should *pay me*! You were an ignorant greenhorn. You . . . you and your snooty selfish family . . . they never liked me. You've held me back. You're always holding me back. I can't trust you. I can't trust anyone!"

"*Sig, please. The baby . . . shah . . . Sig . . . shah . . . please*!"

I cried in my room, in my bed, in the dark every time I heard them. I "vowed" that when I grew up, I would never fight with anyone, especially my husband and children. Well... they are practically the only people I do have knock-down-drag-outs with. So, there's absolutely no lesson to be learned from all this.

—Phyllis Newman

Fire and Bad Clothes

One of my most vivid memories is that when I was a kid our house burned down. "Oh my God, you poor thing!" It always gets quite a reaction. Especially if you say "burned down." It's so dramatic. People even try to trip you up... "*To the ground?*" ...

Let me tell you about my house on fire. I was doing my fifth grade homework and I saw smoke coming out of the closet ... I should have done like the movies and yelled "FIRE!!!" Instead I was *a very cool, laidback, preteen.* "Oh Mom, there's smoke coming out of the closet." With that signature preteen disgust . . . "Just thought you might like to know." My mother raced downstairs. "Oh my God!!!! KIDS! Grab your coats and get your hat ... there's a fire in the basement" ... Sounded like a song cue. My mother always loved musicals.

Now this next moment crystallizes my childhood. We all ran to the closet to get our coats. But being good kids, we all chose our bad coats. Is this a Midwest thing or what? I was always taught, you come home from school and you take off your good clothes and put on your bad clothes. I never understood this philosophy. But I got so used to wearing my bad clothes that my entire childhood was spent in hand-me-downs; and anything nice was reserved for an audience. In fact that's why I became a performer. So I could wear my good clothes.

So that night February 1, 1963, (I have a great memory) *we ran out of our burning house into three foot snowdrifts* with our one possession: our bad coats. My brother even picked a bad hat. We didn't think to wear gloves or scarves. It was our first fire. You make mistakes.

I knocked on Helen Fortney's door: "Hi, Mrs. Fortney. Can we come in your house because our house is on fire." Once again, my attitude was very cool preteen kind of "Sorry for the cheap drama, Helen, but we're in a bind." "Holy Toledo, Earl, did ya hear, did ya hear, did ya hear. The Dillon kids say their house is on fire." Earl Fortney said: "Did you call the

fire department?" Duh. Thanks alot Earl. "Where's your Dad?" Geez, Earl. Where's my Dad? "Hey everybody, drinks on me, Bill Dillon." Where do ya think my Dad is Earl? Thanks alot, thank you for sharing. . .

Then the fire trucks came roaring down my boring dead-end street. I sat in Earl's recliner chair where the footrest shoots out and stared out the huge living room window. It was very exciting. The perfect seat to watch my house burn. It was like watching a Fellini movie. The fire trucks, the flashing lights, my hysterical optimist mother screaming: "This means we'll get all new furniture". *Positive Thinking or Denial Queen . . . You decide . . .*

Then in the middle of the madness, my Dad drives up: three sheets to the wind. "Hey, what-the-hell is going on?" The fireman says to him: "Are you the man of the house?" "Yeah, I'm Bill Dillon!" "Bill Dillon! Hey everybody, it's drinks on me, Bill Dillon."

The next day I went to school and told my fifth-grade teacher Sister Boniface: "Hi, Sister. I'm sorry I'm wearing my bad clothes, but last night my house burned down." She stared at me in pity: "To the ground?!"

Then my classmate, Beanie Gallagher, showed me a newspaper. My house was on the front page! "House on Fire . . . Survivors are Mr. & Mrs. Bill Dillon . . . and their children Kathe, Laurie, Sean & Denny Dillon . . ."

I lit up!!! *My name was in the paper*!! I know it was just a survival mention, but . . . *my name was in the paper*. It looked great. I imagined the letters popping off the page and onto a marquee:

Broadway Tonight: DENNY DILLON—SURVIVOR!!!

~ Denny Dillon

Babes In Toyland

The news that Barbie had been caught shoplifting sent shock waves through the world of little girls.

"Why did she do it?" said one. "Barbie had everything. She had jumpsuits, business suits, and an astronaut uniform with a lavender helmet. She had a Corvette, a beach cottage, and Ken."

Quickly I riffled through the newspaper, where there was a sidebar to the main arrest story by a child psychologist: "Barbie's Booboo—What to Tell Your Children." It said that petty theft often masked deeper problems and was a cry for help.

"It was a cry for help," I said. "A manifestation of some need, perhaps unmet in childhood, for affection and a feeling of belonging."

I thought of Barbie, with her impassive feline face and one-and-a-quarter-inch waist. I wasn't buying it. I explained that it might have been a mistake, that Barbie might have slipped those pantyhose into her Sun-n-Fun tote bag intending to pay for them, and then had just forgotten. It occurred to me that Barbie might have been set up by foreign toy manufacturers who wanted to flood the market with cheap imitations, dolls named Ashley or Melissa with lounge-singer wardrobes and boyfriends named Rick.

Like so many parents, I had learned my lesson from the Pee-wee Herman scandal in 1991. Over the years, the people in children's television have usually fallen into one of three categories: father (Captain Kangaroo, Jim Henson), puppet (Big Bird, Lamb Chop), or animated (Daffy Duck, *et al.*). Despite the suggestion by the Reverend Donald Wildmon some years back that Mighty Mouse appeared to be snorting cocaine in a cartoon, these characters rarely get in trouble with the law.

But Pee-wee Herman was none of these. Suddenly that summer there were stories everywhere telling parents how to explain to children that the weird little guy in a bow tie and lipstick who appeared on Saturday-morning TV with a talking chair and a pet pterodactyl had wound up in the clink, charged with exposing himself in a triple X movie theater.

At seven one morning, looking at the tabloids, I knew that before my first cup of coffee I was going to have to face two small boys and explain the difference between cartoon characters and real life, a difference I was a little fuzzy on myself, having lived through the Reagan years. So I did what anyone would do under the circumstances: I hid the papers.

"If they don't get their questions answered by their parents, where will they?" one child psychologist said to a wire-service reporter.

Simple: They'll get their questions answered on street corners and in the back of the bus to day camp.

After archery, I did explain the difference between characters and the actors who play them, the difference between being arrested and being convicted, the difference between private and public behavior, as well as the rules for keeping your pants on, which I can assure you we've been over a hundred times.

I explained that even grown-ups make mistakes, and that despite published reports, what the actor who played Pee-wee was accused of doing was in no way comparable to mass murder, although in his mug shot he did look like a member of the Manson family. This made it easier for the kids to separate television and reality, although for a long time afterward they kept asking who played Peter Jennings on the evening news.

Pee-wee, of course, was history. This is a very unforgiving country, particularly after you've been famous enough to be made into a doll and sold at Toys 'R' Us.

So when the Barbie story broke big, it occurred to me that I might be witnessing the twilight of a career. I was not sorry. I had never wanted American girls to have a role model whose feet were perpetually frozen in the high-heel position.

Well, as you know, that's not the way it turned out. The next day Barbie's agent started spin control, and before you could say "dream house" there was a Sad-n-Sorry Community Service Barbie, with the navy blue shift and the open letter about how even dolls make mistakes. Little girls read it in the toy aisles and their eyes filled. "It wasn't a cry for help," I said. "It was a public relations stunt." But by that time the little girls I knew had gotten Community Service Barbie from their grandmothers, and they didn't care.

~*Anna Quindlen*

Mom Is Always Right

~*Gail Machlis*

CHAPTER 4

Taxes, Freedom and Gefilte Fish
A Passover Story

Last week, I was startled to realize that Passover and tax time occur around the same time of year. Now, you might not see the incredible coincidence in this. After all, Passover is a celebration of freedom and rebirth, while tax time is a season of frustration, dread, and remorse over shoddy filing habits. And yet, as I began preparing my return, a childhood Passover ritual came to mind and suddenly the relationship between these two sacred events became clear.

It all started with memories of the search for leavened bread or *chametz* (which is pronounced by making a brief gargling sound, then saying "mates." Guess you'll just have to wait for the audio edition). You see, according to tradition, during Passover no foods containing flour are allowed in the home. So what are Jewish families supposed to do with their loaves of rye bread, Entemeyer pastries, and boxes of rigatoni? Well, back in the old country (or so the story goes), the Jews gathered up such food and gave it away. Of course, in 1970s suburban New Jersey where I grew up, this was a little trickier. I can't quite picture my family driving over to the local mall and passing out half full boxes of Ritz crackers and loaves of Wonder Bread. I think my mom ended up stashing much of it in the freezer.

But back to tradition. The night before Passover begins (all Jewish holidays start in the evening—it's a lunar thing) there's a ceremonial search for any last crusts. (It's kind of like an Easter egg hunt, except it will never take place on the White House lawn.) When I was growing up, my dad would hide pieces of a bagel and we kids would hunt them down with a dustpan and broom.

But whether it was my great-great-etc.-grandmother in Russia cleaning between the floorboards (if she had floorboards) or my mother scrubbing with Top Job, the result was the same: Passover cleansing becomes spring cleaning.

So what does this have to do with taxes? you wonder, enthralled though you are with this small piece of Jewish culture. Well, while Jewish families around the globe were searching for bread, I was searching for business receipts. And while most were in my accordion folder, I was fully aware that a slew of errant receipts lay hidden elsewhere, just waiting to be discovered. And discover them I did, neatly folded in my wallet, stuffed in the recesses of my checkbook, serving as bookmarks in unfinished novels. In my search for tax write-offs, I searched through Visa, phone, and insurance bills; duplicate check stubs, lots of drawers (including silverware and sock drawers), not to mention several jammed manila envelopes still lying around from my last move.

Amid this paper hurricane, I felt a sudden desire to recycle the small edifice of newspapers growing under my desk, to arrange and label my computer diskettes, to even, yes, clear out and reorganize my filing cabinet! Momentarily, I considered that this is just an avoidance technique for ignoring my taxes, but then revelation struck! Just as Passover is the impetus for kitchen cleaning, tax time is the stimulus for office rebirth!

The Passover Seder itself is a long, formal, ritual-packed meal containing as many courses as it does prayers. In fact, Seder is Hebrew for "order." So, as I began filling out tax forms, I was again stunned by similarities: the word order kept leaping into my brain.

Consider this. During the Seder, prayers over the wine, the matzo, and the green vegetable must all be said at very specific times. So too is there a specific time for the asking of the four questions, the reciting of the ten plagues, the eating of the gefilte fish. And, it's exactly the same with taxes! I started filling out the popular 1040, but right around line 12 where it asked for Business Income, I had to beat a hasty retreat to Schedule C. This is the place where I put to use those 783 receipts I've located, classified, and totaled. My efforts paid off until about line 13, where I had to fill in my depreciation figures, so I headed over to Form 4562, then back

to 1040 until I got to line 25, which sent me scampering to Schedule SE. The whole thing reminded me of *Had Gadya* a song about a goat that we sing at the end of the Seder: "Then came the fire that burned the stick that beat the dog that bit the cat that ate the goat my father bought for two *zuzim*."

My version? "Then came the Schedule SE that satisfied Line 25 that completed Schedule C that contained line 13 that needed Form 4562 that will bring us back to "doe"! Doe, a deer, a female . . . " Oops. Wrong song.

I could go on drawing comparisons, but it wouldn't be fair. Figuring one's taxes isn't really like wandering in the desert for 40 years; it just seems that way. And various IRS evils (self-employment tax, limits on home/office use) don't really measure up to the magnitude of vermin, locusts, or any of the other ten plagues. (Then again, considering what the military does with our money . . .)

But finally, there comes that moment when the final calculator key is pressed, the final box filled in. Suddenly, the Red Sea parts and a completed tax form emerges! Next Year in Jerusalem! Next year . . . it all goes to an accountant.

~ *Ellen Orleans*

Mommy Dearest

~ *Wendy Wasserstein*

CHAPTER 4

Make Me A Grandmother

All anyone talked about were biological clocks. The whiners on TV's "Thirtysomething" chewed it over like a piece of tough meat every week.

They talked openly of artificial insemination, surrogate mothers, and frozen sperm. (Giving new meaning to designer genes.)

I didn't care about any of this. I wanted to be a grandmother and I was teetering between senility and death. My interest span was becoming limited, patience was in short supply, and I was beginning to forget all the cute games and nursery rhymes. I was out of touch with new toys and TV shows for children. In a few years, I'd throw the baby up into the air and forget to catch him.

All my friends had grandchildren. Me? I was as out-of-sync with my contemporaries as I had been in the '50s when they were dropping babies like lottery balls and I was burning candles to Our Lady of Impossible Conception.

I didn't want to labor it or put pressure on my kids. I just called them every day and left a message on their answering machines, "Why are you punishing your mother?"

It wasn't like I was asking for major sacrifices. All I wanted was for them to get married, live in borderline poverty, drag around for nine months with a little nausea and eight pounds of stomach to stuff under a steering wheel, and surrender two weeks of pay to present me with a small bundle I could play patty-cake with and buy cute presents for when we traveled.

I fancied myself as Auntie Mame. There was so much to teach them about life and *so little time*. I wanted to show my grandson how to bluff his way out of an inside straight. I wanted to take my granddaughter to the mall and dress up like dance hall girls in a saloon and have our pictures taken together in a little booth.

I wanted people to stop me in a supermarket and say, "Your baby is beautiful!" and I would fan myself with a pound of bacon and protest, "Oh puleeese, I'm the grandmother."

I probably wanted revenge.

It is a fact of life that your children never appreciate all you've gone through until they've been quarantined with three kids with measles . . . during Christmas . . . when the washer isn't working . . . and neither is your husband.

They have to experience the exhilaration of kids spitting out their gum in their hands . . . or washing three small faces with one small handkerchief full of spit . . . or having their offspring take their checkbook to school for Show and Tell to have the proper respect for the profession.

Actually, I did lust for the smooth little bodies with breaths that smelled like milk and little heads with the faint aroma of baby powder. I wanted little fingers to grab onto mine like they needed me and little eyes that followed me around the room when I came into it.

I was beyond the point of just talking about it; I was beginning to have dreams of what life would be like with Grandma Bombeck.

The dream always started out the same. My son would kick open the door and drag in a hobby horse (taking a large chunk of wood out of the wall) and yell, "Mom! You home? We'd have called first, but we were running late and couldn't get the real sitter. We knew you wouldn't mind watching Christopher for a night."

"You didn't have to bring the rocking horse, dear," I smiled. "You already left the corral and we eat off the space ship stored in the kitchen."

"He wants the hobby horse, Mom. Reach in my pocket. See that list? He has a small cold. Give him a spoonful of the red stuff three times a day and a little white pill just before he goes to bed. The vaporizer is in the bag and all the doctors' numbers. He *has to take* the pills on a full stomach and he'll spit the syrup in your face, but keep throwing it in until he swallows it."

As he leaves, his brother is coming up the walk with his two children in tow, Velcro Fingers and Terminator II. Within thirty seconds, they have taken the bathroom door off the hinges, clogged up the toilet with a shoe, put meal worm in the refrigerator for their hamster, which is in the middle of the coffee table, crayoned on the fireplace, flooded the patio, and sold me two chances on a pony.

My teenage granddaughter stops by to tell me she wants to move in with us where she'll have more freedom. Besides, my car isn't run often enough and she'll take care of that. It's okay with her mom if it's all right with me. She introduces me to her boyfriend who wears an earring and has a four-letter word on the bumper of his pickup truck.

The baby falls off the hobby horse. Velcro Fingers wants to know if he can keep the wax apple he has already taken a bite out of and Terminator II has drawn a picture of his hand on the wall behind the sofa.

They move on to the piano where they play "Chopsticks" over and over. I threaten to destroy their puppy. The baby wipes its nose on the new slipcovers.

I promise to read them all a story, but they want to sit in the middle of the floor and play poker. They all cheat.

As the teenage grandchild makes a long-distance call that lasts sixty-five minutes before she splits, I try to get up from the floor when one of them comments, "Grandma, you oughta lose those thighs."

I tell everyone it's nap time. They tuck me in and crank up the TV set.

I always awake from these dreams in a cold sweat. What am I thinking! This isn't the way grandparenting is. It's a high-level consultant's job. Grandparents criticize when things aren't being done right, exchange wet bottoms for dry ones and crises for fun times. Grandmothers have three major objectives: keep billfold pictures current, buy whatever their grandchildren are selling, and give kids impractical gifts that parents have forbidden them to have.

The reality is the first child to place a baby in my arms that grabs my finger, stuffs its foot in my mouth, and smiles at me when I say, "This is your grandma"—gets it all.

~ *Erma Bombeck*

Babysitting

~*Cathy Guisewite*

CHAPTER 4

Exit Laughing

A Lighthearted Tale About a Family Plot

My mother calls to tell me she doesn't want the plots. At first I think she's saying *plotz.*

"We live in Florida now," she says. "It doesn't make sense to be buried in Westchester."

The family plot. My grandmother loved it. "The view!" Nana would say, visiting it Sundays. "Have you ever in your life seen such a view?"

"Anyway, I've decided," Mom says. "I'm signing them over to you."

"I have to be buried by myself?"

"There are four plots," she says firmly. "You have two. Your cousin Joan has two."

"*Joanie?* I only see her Thanksgiving!"

We laugh. A week later, the deed to Plot 034, Section 24, comes in the mail.

Down in Florida over Christmas, my mother takes me shopping. She's discovered it's easier to drop bombs in the car when she's looking straight ahead. "You got my letter?" she says, tooling down Palmetto.

"If this is about the plots again, Ma, I don't want the plots. I've decided. I'm getting cremated."

"*What!*"

I remind her of the last time Dad took me to see his father's grave in Brooklyn. Jacob Volk's stone was listing. The plot was overgrown. Swastikas were sprayed all over the place, and every piece of glass that protected the photographs on the headstones was smashed. I remind her how somebody had Granny Ethel exhumed and moved next to Great-

Aunt Ettie, who was buried with two decks of cards so they could play in the afterlife.

"I'm going to be cremated, Ma. No one's going to vandalize my grave."

"Still," she says "the thought of it . . ."

I tell her about my friend Madeline, who keeps her parents in matching urns in the basement. She waves to them every time she does the wash.

My mother cracks up. What I really want to say is: *You can't die until I can't make you smile.*

"I checked out the local crematorium down here," she says a few weeks later. "I asked the fellow if I could see how it's done. He said no one had ever asked him that before. I had to explain I didn't want to actually *watch,* I just wanted to make sure the place was nice. You know me—I like people to be comfortable." We howl.

Saul Bellow calls death "the dark side of the mirror that allows it to reflect life." This is no surprise coming from the man who wrote *Mr. Sammler's Planet.* But that's Saul Bellow, and these are my parents. I've always had my parents. I can't imagine not being able to pick up the phone and talk to them. Should I be trying to? Why is my mother thinking about death so much? Just because she's in her 70s? She just got her master's and has a nice practice, so what's with all this death talk?

I check out the books on my night stand. There's Ellen Currie's *Moses Supposes,* which opens with a story about a man who suspects his father is suicidal. There's the insomniac's companion, the *1989 Guinness Book of World Records,* which lists ten categories under Death. (Tonga has the lowest death rate.) There's *A Doctor's Visit,* by Chekhov, whose death in Badenweiler, Germany, at age 44, is fictionalized in the last book, *Where I'm Calling From,* by Raymond Carver. What's going on? All these books about death? Everything I'm reading now is about death?

I go into the living room and look at the shelf where I keep the books that churn my heart. There's Nathanael West, Dostoyevsky, Virginia

Woolf, William Kennedy, Louise Erdrich, Don DeLillo, Joyce Cary, Toni Morrison, and Bruce Chatwin. So I look at my Paris-in-the-30's shelf, and there's Hemingway, Joyce, Fitzgerald, Jean Rhys, Ford Maddox Ford, and Gertrude Stein. So I look at my Southern shelf, and there's O'Connor, Welty, McCullers, all of Walker Percy and Faulkner. Is it possible that death informs everything? Are we born, as Beckett wrote "astride the grave"? I decide to find one book, any book, that doesn't have to do with death. There are two: *Basic Italian* and *The Films of Mae West.*

Studying the slim, chestnut-haired 20-year-old in the photo Mom has always kept on her dresser, I ask if Dad still looks like that to her.

"He seems just like the day I met him," she says.

Sitting on his patio, overlooking a lake, my father says: "This isn't a bad last view, is it? This isn't a bad way to go."

"Where'ya going?" I say.

Knock wood, ward off the evil eye, I can't picture anything happening to them. They both love their work. They both play killer tennis. They've both had run-ins with scary things, but what does that mean? Most people I know would be dead if it wasn't for modern medicine.

"We're not afraid to die," they've told me. "There comes a time when you're ready. We couldn't have imagined that at your age either."

Sometimes I see myself at my father's funeral. Gripping both sides of the lectern, I pause the way Dad would. I develop eye contact. Then I launch into the one about the man who tells his wife he wants his ashes scattered in Bloomingdale's so he can be sure she'll come visit. The idea that something could happen to them won't seem real until it has to. Why should it? What good does it do to taint the present with the inevitable?

The elevator door slams. I get the mail. There's a letter from the university I went to asking to be remembered in my will. There's a bulletin from the Authors Guild; they'd like something too. There are bills, magazines—and what's this from Florida?

RE: Florida Statute 765.05—Living Wills

I, Audrey Volk, willfully and voluntarily make known my desire that my dying not be artificially prolonged under the circumatances set forth below....

I consider the misspelling. Is this document valid? I'm supposed to let my mother go?

I punch her number. "Ma? I got your present today."

Silence.

"I wanted to get you a Hallmark card. Something appropriate like:

Your living will means lots to me.
A gift that suits me to a T.

Or maybe:

You gave me life!
I help you die!
You're as sweet as
Apple pie!

We laugh. Hurtling toward the apocalypse, we gasp for air. After we hang up, I start flipping through the magazines. Right there, in a column called "What's Hot," is an item about a man in the town my parents moved to. He's bringing mummification back. Prices go from $7,700 for your basic linen wrap to $150,000 for a jeweled sarcophagus. I send it off. Mom will get a kick out of it. I can hear her laughing now. Meanwhile, know anyone interested in prime Westchester real estate, one six-hundredth of an acre, nicely landscaped, riv vu?

~ *Patricia Volk*

Modern Vacation

~*Libby Reid*

CHAPTER 5

The Clock Is Ticking. Can We Tock?

CHAPTER 5

Something's Happening Here

My jeans are shrinking.
The president of the United States is young enough to be my husband.
I need reading glasses.
My thighs are falling.
Trolls are back.

I never expected to live past thirty, and now I've shot past thirty-something right into the great unknown middlesomething.

How can this be happening to me? And, please, I need to know:

Am I Ever Going to Be As Dorky As My Parents Were When They Were Middle-Aged?

No? You really mean it? Thanks. That's the way I feel about you, too. None of us can be that dorky, ever, because we're part of the hippest generation that ever lived. Time is on our side. We were born during an incredible wrinkle in history, when anything was possible, and it still is. Sure, we're getting a little older. But that doesn't mean we've turned into June and Ward Cleaver. We're still cool. We're still the biggest generation of rebels that this world has ever seen.

We invented sex.
We invented drugs.
We invented rock and roll.
The next step for us boomers?

We Will Invent A New Middle Age

Sure, why not? There are 76 million of us, and if we say HELL, NO, WE WON'T GO, we won't. Who says we have to plunge into the midlife doldrums like our folks did? We're much better prepared. We've got stair-climbing machines, Retin-A, and spandex. Most importantly, we've got ATTITUDE. (Sure, our parents and the Generation X people behind us might prefer to call it "denial," but that's just sour grapes.)

So let's begin deconstructing this traditional middle-age myth right now. If you're special, like we are, you never have to be *really* middle-aged, driving big cars and buying the Mrs. a mink and cooking tuna casseroles and actually liking Lawrence Welk and talking about the weather and falling asleep in a Barca-Lounger with your mouth open and wearing ugly eyeglasses on a string around your neck.

Of course, we do drive minivans and buy our beloveds shearling coats and cook pasta and listen to Harry Connick Jr. and occasionally watch the Weather Channel. But hardly any of us fall asleep in front of Letterman since he moved up an hour. And some of us do wear glasses around our necks, but they're designer glasses with neon strings or handwoven attachments made by natives, and part of the money goes to save the rain forest.

So, it's clear: we're different. These years ahead of us are going to be a *truly unique experience,* much cooler than anything our parents ever went through. This is not your father's Oldsmobile. This is a vibrant, fulfilling, hip time of life for us. Call it New Middle Age. Or, if you cringe at the mention of *middle* and *age* together in one sentence, call this time ahead of us the Relaxed-Fit Years. Whatever you dub them, these are the crowning years of our mature young adulthood. The attitude? I'm stuck in the middle with you, and I plan to have a hell of a lot of fun while I'm here.

Checklist: Signs That You Might Be Halfway Up That Stairway to Heaven

- ✔ You've started musing about the shallow value system of people in their twenties.
- ✔ You tune in more often to the local news than to MTV.
- ✔ You wince when the scanner hits a rap station.
- ✔ You find yourself telling your babysitter about your first boyfriend/girlfriend.
- ✔ Many of the doctors in hospitals look like Doogie Howser to you.
- ✔ You suddenly desperately need your first reading glasses, crown, arthroscopic surgery, extramarital affair, Armani suit, elastic waistband, fiber-laden cereal, sports car, baby, inheritance, root canal, dye job, hotel getaway . . .
- ✔ You truly enjoy the Disney Channel specials featuring ancient rock stars of the past who look—"hey!—pretty good."
- ✔ There are house repairs you've been meaning to do for over a decade.
- ✔ You know the difference between Sinead O'Connor and Sandra Day O'Connor.
- ✔ All of the professional athletes you admire are at least ten years younger than you.
- ✔ You no longer care as much if you don't go out on Sunday night.
- ✔ You yearn more wistfully for former repairmen than for certain ex-lovers.
- ✔ You've begun to go toward the *lite*—lite beer, lite rock, lite butter, lite literature . . .
- ✔ You are too old for Doc Martens, but too young for Doc Kevorkian.

~ *Cathy Crimmins*

True Story

This guy calls me up, asks me out on a blind date, then says, "Okay, so how will I know you? What do you look like?"

I said, "I don't know. Uh—I have brown hair. I'm five-four . . ."

He said, "Oh. Five-four. So you should weigh about a hundred-twenty pounds."

I said, "Yeah. I probably should."

True story.

~ Mindy Schneider

Butter

Butter, I remember butter
We were once like lovers
We were quite a team

Sugar, I remember sugar
Not much of a looker
Oh, but what a dream

I remember coffee-flavored Häagen-Dazs
Sweetening my lips
Now it's just a memory
Right here on my hips . . .

Pasta, I remember pasta
Now, I'm not anti-pasta ...
It always did the trick

Chocolate, I remember chocolate
But it became a habit
That was hard to lick

Oh, yes, and I remember Fannie May
But from where I'm standing now ...
Looking at my fanny may
Remind one of a cow

Ohhh, butter, I remember butter
We were once like lovers
We were quite a team
I'll take some butter-smothered pasta please ...
In a vat of ... chocolate ... cheese! ...
Butter.

~ Megon McDonough

Can We Tock?

I'm sick of hearing about my biological clock. I can't pick up a magazine or eavesdrop on a luncheon conversation without detecting its inexorable tick. No one, however, is telling me what I really want to know about this internal, infernal, timekeeper. Does it come with a snooze alarm? What if it turns out to be a biological clock-radio: Is there any chance that my ovaries could suddenly begin blaring out traffic reports or "Born in the USA" while I'm at an important business meeting or arguing with my landlord?

Sure, I understand that basically we're all on Genetic Standard Time: the body's DNA programs precisely how long we remain fertile and indeed, barring accident, sets the hour of our bucket kicking. Science has recently found the masterclock of our daily rhythms, a section of the hypothalamus called the suprachiasmatic nucleus, not much bigger than a pinhead. It seems to govern the hundreds of bodily functions that ebb and flow in a regular pattern throughout the twenty-four-hour cycle of our waking and sleeping. These include body temperature (it peaks at 4 P.M.), levels of various hormones (high tide for testosterone is 9 A.M.), and tolerance of pain (greatest in the afternoon).

But how come we never hear anything about the other interior chronometers that are just a important as the Big Ben of babymaking and the Rolex of rhythms? What about, for example,

The Botanical Clock: Perhaps regulated by the pituitary, the Botanical Clock fixes the precise point in a relationship at which a man stops sending flowers. It is closely related to the **Astrophysical Clock,** which controls the length of time a loving couple will have stars in their eyes.

The Tautological Clock influences redundancy, repetition, and redundancy. It is also responsible for making an otherwise pleasant friend or mate say things like, "Well, listen, you'll either get the job or you won't."

The Ontological Clock: By maintaining a delicate balance of brain chemicals, this clock determines how long you remember the definitions of really rather simple words that won't stick in your head, like *nonplussed* and *ontology* (the one that does *not* recapitulate Phil Donohue; that is onto*geny*. Ontology is, of course, the branch of philosophy dealing with being, something I can tell you with great confidence, having just looked it up for the third time this year.) Nutritional deficiencies can cause some genetically vulnerable individuals to forget the difference between *oligarchy* and *plutocracy*.

Not all body clocks are governed internally. We all own a **Cultural Clock,** which has to do not with how soon we get fidgety at the ballet, but with how our culture views time. Never mind the globally acknowledged oscillations of the atomic clock, the transit of the sun, or even the vaunted suprachiasmatic nucleus: we pick up the tick tocked by our parents and grandparents. Thus, while in remote parts of Brazil it is acceptable to appear at a dinner party several decades late and feign surprise that the host and hostess have passed away, in some Swiss cantons it is considered rude for a guest to enter a room in such a way that his hat arrives before his shoes.

Intimately related to the **Cultural Clock,** is the one that controls differences in the way the sexes perceive time. I call it the **Genderological Clock,** and who are you to stop me?

I must thank the late Lorne Greene for leading me to the discovery of this clock and, ultimately, to the Alpo theory of rapprochement between the sexes. One night I was watching his classic dogfood commercial, idly wondering whether those mutts get their residual checks figured in dog-years or people-years, when all of a sudden I thought, "Hey! I wonder if there are man-years and woman-years!" That could explain a lot. For example: A certain man tells a certain woman he will call "in a couple of days." Two weeks pass. He dials her number—and is shocked by her cold response. She's wrong to think he's been toying with her. He said two days—*and for him, that's all it's been!* Applying a formula very similar to the one Lorne Greene uses to figure out the age of a golden retriever, you can convert man-time into woman-time. (Roughly seven woman-days = one man-day, when you're dealing with relationships. Different formulae apply to work situations and personal growth issues.)

Looking back, I can see unheeded hints of these divergent perceptions of time in my own true life. When I was sixteen, for instance, my boyfriend and I stayed late at a riotous New Year's Eve party in a town about an hour from home. Rather than risk the roads that night, we stayed, quite chastely, with friends. I called my parents to tell them where I was and that I'd be back in the morning.

When we pulled up at 11 A.M. the next day, my father was raking so furiously in one spot that the lawn was bald. "Where the hell have you been?" he barked. "I said I'd be home in the morning," I whimpered. My father's reply, now famous in our family: "Eleven o'clock isn't morning where I come from!" Since I know for a fact that my father comes from Boston, I should have realized right then that man-time and woman-time are out-of-sync.

Maybe it's because so many little boys first learn about time from games like football, in which an announcement that there are ten minutes left in the final quarter means you have the leisure to catch several trout, finally finish *Sister Carrie,* jog a mile, shower, and reestablish yourself on the couch just as the two-minute warning sounds. Whatever the reason, it is a scientific fact that just because a man and a woman share a zip code, that doesn't necessarily mean they live in the same time zone.

~Judith Stone

Egg-Cups

Why do they make bathing suits with those stupid egg-cups on them anyway? Is there a woman on earth they're designed to fit?

I consider myself to be average, okay? Average, average, average. By the time one's age-o-meter has clicked past forty, "average" is considered to be a plus. There are millions of us out there—and whenever we're not juggling careers, chaos, and the challenges of raising teenage children, what are we doing? We are trying to track down a garment manufacturer who sews for the body that is ***@!*?!!average**!!!

What's with the mastiff shoulders, gorilla-length arms, six-inch waists, and skirts designed to gird the loins of an undernourished twelve-year-old boy?!! And . . . what's with the bathing suits?

Summer fashions appear at the exact time we are trying to find clothing for spring. March is when the bathing suits arrive. March is when the average female begins the fruitless foray into the land of Lycra, hoping to find a bathing tog that will (A) cover, (B) flatter, and (C) allow for some participation in water sports.

Hoping for two out of three, we search once more for a suit that's suitable. Hah! This is a project for the Discovery Channel!! Two years ago, I accidentally found a three-out-of three!! Shocked and grateful, I ordered four of them (all the same) so I am set now for multiple seasons to come!! Alas . . . this doesn't mean that I don't still (on a "thin day") try on those high-thigh, egg-cupped disasters with the hope that maybe I can look like the siliconed sylph in the window.

Why do we do it? Every year, we allow our self-esteem to be reduced to the size of bacteria. Every year we struggle in Port-a-John-sized cubicles, trying to get into and out of a garment that's guaranteed to disgust. And, every year we do this (heaven forbid) at the risk of exposure!

It's that old nightmare, isn't it? The average person's worst fear (aside from public speaking) is to be seen naked, or nearly naked, by someone other than one's spouse!

The fear of being seen in one of these egg-cupped creations was the catalyst for this Sunday strip. As a form of therapy, I guess, I had a hapless heroine streak through a shopping mall in "the bathing suit from hell."

After all . . . isn't it nice to see the things we fear most . . . happening to someone else?

~Lynn Johnston

For Better or For Worse
By Lynn Johnston
BATHING SUIT SALE
50% OFF TICKETED PRICE
CAN I SHOW YOU TO THE CHANGING ROOM, MA'AM?
WAIT....
...I HAVE TO PSYCH MYSELF UP FIRST.
I'M GOING TO TRY THIS ON, APRIL... BE A GOOD GIRL AND WAIT FOR MOMMY.
I'LL JUST BE A MINUTE, HONEY. -PLAY WITH YOUR TOYS AND I'LL BE ALL DONE.
TYPICAL...I LOOK GROSS.
WHAT WOULD MAKE ANY SELF-RESPECTING WOMAN WEAR THIS IN PUBLIC ?!!
APRIL?
APRIL?!!
5-2
LYNN

The Swimming Suit

There are moments in every woman's life
When she faces the humiliating fact
That time is no longer on her side,
As she performs the simple, yearly,
Humiliating, death-defying act of ...

Buying a swimming suit.
I can't believe I'm here
Buying a swimming suit.
I do this every year.
Putting myself through
Eight kinds of hell
Searching through spandex
And nylon fortrel for a

Flattering swimming suit ...
Oxymoron ...
A flattering swimming suit.
I feel like a moron.
Take a deep breath ...
A prozac ... a pause ...
And try to remember
The swimming suit laws.

Rule number one ...
No stripes horizontal
Unless you weigh thirty-five pounds.
Rule number two ...

Accentuate the good parts.
Make them look up . . .
Never look down.

Buying a swimming suit.
There are questions when
Buying a swimming suit.
Here's one suggestion.
When thinking of ways
to improve the bra size,
Remember that foam
Is the last thing
That dries.

Rule number three . . .
Keep them distracted
With ruffles and sequins and belts.
Rule number four . . .
Don't squeeze the flab.
If you pull it in here
It comes out somewhere else.

And the lady who helps you is seventy-five
With glasses and rolled-down hose.
She says, "dahling, this one is so good for the thighs."
I look better naked than I do in those.

Still . . . I'm buying a swimming suit.
How I hate this!
I'm buying a swimming suit.
I can't . . . wait!
Here's a nice little speedo.

Maybe I'll take this one after all.
Or maybe . . .
I'll just stay inside . . . till fall!

Could I see something in a wet suit, please?

~*Amanda McBroom*

Dieter's Prayer

Lord, won't you help me?
It's that time of year.
Winter has come and gone.
Springtime is here.
In this season of flesh,
Won't you show that you care?
Lord, won't you heed
This dieter's prayer?

Teach me tonight
To love cottage cheese,
Grapefruit, and celery,
Lord, if you please.
Make me believe
That tofu's a food,
And not something you made up
When you were in a bad mood.

Lord, won't you help me?
Show that you care.
Lord, won't you heed
This dieter's prayer?

Make me believe
That ice cream's just awful.
That the devil is hiding
Inside every waffle.
That mayonnaise is nothing
But a communist plot.
That broccoli is good for you
And chocolate is not.

Keep me away
From the refrigerator door
When life is a trial
And love is a bore.
Save me from nachos,
And tacos, and chips.
For what goes in my mouth
Always lands on my hips.

Oh, pizza, oh pasta,
Oh popcorn, oh pork!
Get thee behind me,
Oh knife and oh, fork.
And chicken fried steak
 from the deepest of south . . .
Oh, lord, if you love me,
Won't you please shut my mouth?

Oh, lord, do you hear me?
Honk if you're there.
Lord, won't you heed . . .
You know my need . . .
Oh, lord, won't you heed
This dieter's prayer?

~*Amanda McBroom*

A Perfect Model Keeps Her Full Mouth Shut

I normally don't buy fashion magazines, pretty much for the same reason I don't subscribe to *Nuclear Fission Monthly.* Unless I'm going to suddenly grow about seven inches and lose about four pounds per inch, or if it's discovered that plutonium can safely rid your shower of nasty soap scum, why should I read these publications?

Last week, however, as I was trying to calculate the unit price of my pork-rind value pack while waiting in the grocery store checkout line, an issue of *Vogue* caught my eye. One of the headlines on the cover read: "Nobody's Perfect: Five Supermodels Face Up To Their Flaws."

Feeling fat, ugly, unintelligent, unsophisticated, inarticulate, short, nearsighted, old, and out of shape (and this is my post-PMS state of mind), I thought this article might lift my spirits. Maybe Christy Turlington, Naomi Campbell, Linda Evangelista, Cindy Crawford, and Nadja Auermann would admit that they, too, are convinced that a hideous, beer-bellied, troll-like creature resides in their bathroom mirror.

Okay. Maybe that's just my own problem. But at least they might own up to a pimple, a split end, or the hint of a wrinkle.

So I read the article. And while I'm still thoroughly disgusted with myself, I've let go of my hope-your-miniskirt-splits hostility toward Christy, Linda, Cindy, and Nadja. These four supermodels had the good sense not only to point out their flaws, but to wisely emphasize that they exercise like maniacs and diet constantly.

Naomi Campbell, on the other hand, apparently has an intense desire to be hated by every woman in America. As the article's author diplomatically points out. "There's virtually nothing about Campbell that she isn't, shall we say, extremely fond of."

That's an understatement. I know it's healthy to have a good self-image, but this woman is head-over-stiletto-heels in L-O-V-E with herself.

For starters, she just *loves* her backside: "My butt is high. I also like the point where my legs meet my butt. In certain pictures you can see it. It's quite defined."

Is anyone thinking about now that Naomi really needs a hobby?

Butt there's more.

"I can wear almost anything, and it can look good. People always say, "We'll give you the worst outfit, Naomi, because we know you can make it look good."

Well, Naomi, that's your take. It's equally possible, though, that while you're strutting down the runway in a gunny sack and combat boots, members of the Paris practical joke society are having a major hoot.

At this point in the interview, I'm guessing the reporter is thinking that four supermodels would have been plenty. But Naomi's on a roll: "I have a little button nose. My lips are quite full, but they're not huge . . . like my shoulders . . . My face is very animated. My smile is very genuine. My waist is 22. My hips are 33 or 34 . . . my body's in proportion."

Okay. If Naomi would have stopped there, I could have cut her some slack. After all, several studies have shown that repeated exposure to flash bulbs, pancake makeup, and push-up bras can result in a condition known as BIMBOS (Boring Inane Mindless Body Obsession Syndrome). In fact, from Milan to Manhattan, BIMBOS benefit concerts are being held in conjunction with the new fall fashion season.

But Naomi crossed the line. Without even a hint of apology, she matter-of-factly noted that she neither exercises nor diets.

It's time someone has a little chat with her.

Maybe she's not aware that if she ever wants to have a woman friend, this is the type of information you take to your grave. Since only .005% of the female population stands over 5 feet 9 inches and weighs under 97 pounds, I think I speak for many women when I request that, in the future, Ms. Campbell, do us a big favor.

Wearing one of your genuine smiles and using your quite full, but not huge, lips . . . lie.

~ Carrie St. Michel

Spiro Agnew and I

Monday. My birthday is coming up and not having had a midlife crises at 40, I'm planning to have one now. I will be *over* 40 now! I can't focus. I have no energy. I think about Spiro Agnew more than other people do. Whatever happened to Spiro Agnew? Has he opened a restaurant, the way retired baseball players do? Spiro Agnew's Ribs. Or a used-car dealership? I can see his face so clearly, his hair combed straight back. It is the face of my youth.

Tuesday. Did you know that an anagram of Spiro Agnew is "Grow a penis?" Did you know the lead singer of the Red Hot Chili Peppers was convicted of sexual battery because he waved his penis at a fan after a concert? I heard this on MTV. I think it would be dangerous to wave it at a fan. I was always told to keep my fingers away from fans. And I always have.

Wednesday. How old was Spiro Agnew when he fell from power? Not much older than I am now. In the 60's, even the old people were young. But now! My birthday is *next week:* I don't have much time to determine exactly what form my midlife crisis will take. This is urgent. I could join a cult. But which one? And it seems a little strenuous for someone my age. Daydreaming about Spiro Agnew—I remember his tie clips best of all—I turn on the TV. "Mystery Science Theater 3000," my favorite. That's it! I could become a "Mystery Science Theater 3000" groupie! Groupies are so youthful. You can do it from home in your spare time. No investment necessary. No special equipment. And I already watch the show twice a day, every weekday. A man and two robots sit in front of a big screen and we watch the backs of their heads as they watch bad movies and make wisecracks. Once, some devils in red leotards were writhing around plotting the demise of Santa Claus and one of the robots said: "Oh! Hell got an N.E.A. grant."

Thursday A.M. Maraschino is an anagram for Harmonicas, Roast Mules become Somersault. Someone told me those, I didn't figure them out myself, I hate anagrams. "Mystery Science Theater 3000" is also on for an hour at 8. What am I doing? Anagrams? Four hours of bad movies a day? I must take up a more constructive hobby, a life-affirming hobby for my midlife crisis. Got a Smith & Hawken catalogue today, as I do every day. I will order English gloves and French watering cans and Japanese pruners. I will make things grow.

Thursday P.M. Yorba Linda, C-Span 2. Richard Nixon is standing in front of the Presidential Library and Birthplace. It's the 25th anniversary of his inauguration. My heart pounds with excitement, rejuvenated by the sound his voice. He poses in front of a fountain with Gerald and Betty Ford. Does former President Ford really count as a vice president? Where is Agnew? Oh, it's all wrong. Nixon doesn't even look like his face masks anymore.

Friday. *US* Magazine says the "deck is stacked against today's younger actors." Sounds promising. Perhaps I can take up acting. Although I'm sure I read somewhere else that actresses over 40 can't get any parts. So back to gardening. I already have several oddly shaped aloe plants the kids brought home from school as cuttings. I never water them. Maybe that simulates the harsh life of the desert. I wonder if Spiro Agnew gardens? If he doesn't already, he should. Gardening is what every celebrity does when he sinks into obscurity. Or do they raise horses? It seems so unfair that Agnew gets so little exposure, and he's not even a younger actor.

Saturday. I don't have to have a midlife crisis after all! I have discovered true immortality. I read in Audubon that ecologists in northern England are planning a "forest of the dead." People will be buried beneath trees to help enrich the soil, instead of wasting all those nutrients in crematories or cemeteries. You can choose your tree and the species of wildflowers you want to have planted above you. Pushing up the daisies, the Indian paint brushes; though blue bells and bunchberries might be more appropriate, more discreet. I've never had much luck with wildflowers, myself. I once bought one of those cans of seeds from the Smith & Hawken catalogue and sprinkled it on my mother's lawn near the septic tank, which had just been dug up, but the seeds washed away with the first rain or were eaten by birds, and she planted grass again instead. I wonder if the gardeners in Echoing Green, as the corpse forest will be called, will order their seeds from Smith & Hawken.

Sunday. A birthday present has arrived! A pot of narcissus from Smith & Hawken, the first of a series of plants to come. Now I don't have to garden at all, just open cardboard boxes once a month. Well, it's 10 A.M. "Mystery Science Theater 3000" is on. But so is "The McLaughlin Report." What will I do? Which will I choose? Life is so full, so ripe with possibility. And I am only in the middle of it! The scent of narcissus drifts through the room. I hate the smell of narcissus. But the name is so historically and psychologically suggestive, so rich with meaning. And they're awfully pretty in the windowsill by the twisted aloes. I am content. I have made up my mind. Someday, as I lie decomposing in Echoing Green, it is this species I will feed. For now, I could just sit here and gaze at narcissus forever.

~ *Cathleen Schine*

Goldilocks

~ *Liebe Lamstein*

What Was I Thinking?

It was a last minute invitation
I did not have a thing to wear
I ran into the store I said I need something black
something formal
other than that . . . I don't care
I made it to the theater as the lights dimmed
the first act was brilliantly fun
but when I caught my reflection during intermission
I thought [pause] . . . what have I done?

CHORUS:
What was I thinking?
what was I, blind?
when I bought this outfit
was I temporarily out of my mind?
What was I thinking?
just look at this dress
I'm taking up drinking
my life is a mess

*My good friend said
I think you're gonna hit it off
I've known him for a long long time
and if I wasn't happily married myself
in a heartbeat I would try to make him mine
so I figure OK I'll take my chances
what harm could it do?
makes you wonder 'bout the motives of your married friends
when something like this happens to you

CHORUS: What was she thinking?
who is this guy?
maybe I'll just choke on this porkchop
and conveniently die
What was she thinking?
quick, sharpen this knife
my endorphins are sinking
I'm taking my life

BRIDGE: Oooh, oooh oooh
Ach! du lieber!
Ooohooohoooh
Ah! Wat da tien na!
Oooh oooh oooh
¡Oh, muy boja!
Oooh oooh oooh
¡Qué lástima, La Vie, au revoir!

(That's an international segment, so people will think this is world music, which I think is going to be the next big thing to sweep the nation and I want to ride that wave right into the beach . . .)

It was late
I had insomnia
that TV stair-stepper started to look good
I thought to myself should I buy it?
I heard Bruce Jenner say
"yes, you should."
And that Snackmaster, that BeDazzler, that Thighmaster and
that Victoria Jackson makeup kit
now I can barely get around my apartment
it's so filled with all this stupid stuff

CHORUS:

What was I thinking?
look at this junk
I can't blame it on drinking
I've never, uh, hardly ever, uh,
right now I'm not drunk
what was I thinking?
when will this end?
what was I thinking?
when will this end
what was I thinking?
this song has no end
what was I thinking?
this song has no end!!!
what was I thinking?
this song has no end . . . etc.

*Alternate second verse:
My hairdresser said it's time for a new 'do
you've had that look for way too long
so he showed me a perm in a magazine
and I thought sure, what could go wrong?
I should have known by the sounds he was making (ho boy)
something was going awry
after two hours I put on my glasses
I could not believe my eyes

CHORUS:

What was he thinking?
I can't believe what I see
I look in the mirror
Art Garfunkel's looking back at me
What was he thinking?

quick, steal me a hat
I should look on the bright side
unlike Art, it will grow back

~ *Christine Lavin*

Juanita Craiga

For Juanita Craiga Weight Loss Centers

(JUANITA is an attractive Mexican woman in her forties with big hair and a slim bod. In fact, she looks a lot like Jenny Craig. She stands in front of a large color portrait of herself. Her manner is intimate, chatty, and incredibly positive.)

JUANITA: *Buenas tardes, chicas—y chicos!—yo soy* Juanita Craiga, and I like to tell you about the Juanita Craiga Weight Loss Centers featurin' the all-new Authentic Mexican Diet Program. But first . . . let me tell you what I first ate when I came to this beautiful country from Mexico, and gained about a hundred pounds. Remember, *m'hijitas*, this is what I ate when I was just Juanita Craiga, fat bored housewife and short-tempered mother, before I became *Juanita Craiga* incredibly skinny Diet Goddess and multimillionaire!

(Rattling it off)

Chicas, I used to get up and have a nice big plate of chilaquiles, with the sausage and the cheese, a big cup of Mexican chocolate, five or six flour tortillas—*(Remembers)* and a pack of Hostess Snowballs. For lunch, I'd go down to

the Taco Bell, put away a couple of chicken enchilada/
chile relleno/tostada *combinaciones*, a side of rice and beans
and guacamole—

(Remembers)

... and a cherry pie for dessert. For a snack—I'd just have a
bag of Doritos and a Coke and a container of Häagen-Dazs
Lite, *chicas*. And for dinner—some tamales, and *ropa vieja*,
or maybe a steak and a nice piece of fried pork with fries and
a salad with ranch dressing, and whatever the kids left
on their plates ...

(Remembers)

and some flan

(Remembers)

and a Sara Lee pound cake.

(Incredulous)

And *chicas*—I was getting *fat!*
So, I went down to this mini-mall in Hollywood, and
I saw this *gringa* Diet Goddess, LA JENNY CRAIG, with
her 7 billion dollar diet kingdom in mini-malls across the
nation, *Chicas* there's even one in Queens—And she gave me
this diet which cost 300 dollars—plus another 5,973 bucks for
the food and positive thinking tapes. Then I starved to death
and became the incredibly skinny and positive *viejita* goddess
you see before you.

In fact, *chicas*, I got so skinny and so positive, I got to thinking
I could be a Diet Goddess too! And, after a whole lot of research,
I came up with a diet that I know works ...'cause it's
the exact same diet I ate in Mexico before I came to this great
country and got fat.

Okay, *chicas*, for breakfast you get ... "*Huevos Mexicanos*!"

(She holds up a giant color photo of one pale sickly-looking fried egg.)

This is the egg from a real Mexican chicken that ain't been shot up with *gringo* hormones. And, on Juanita's Cuisine, you also get . . .

(Holds up a photo of one tortilla)

A tortilla! Mmmmnn. Now, listen *m'hijitas*, 'cause this is *muy importante*. With your breakfast, and every other meal, and in between, you got to drink eight ounces of . . .

(Holds up photo of bottled "JUANITA WATER.")

"Juanita Water." One hundred percent Imported Mexican Tap Water.

(She tales a swig.)

Mmmmnnn. Refreshing. And for you *gringa* dieters, this is gonna help you lose weight *fast*! Okay, *chicas*, how 'bout some lunch? An Authentic Mexican Lunch is . . .

(Holds up tortilla photo #2)

A tortilla! And . . .

(Takes a swig of Juanita Water)

Mmmmn. And, for a snack in the middle of the afternoon?

(Holds up photo of Chiclets)

Chicles! Not *gringo* "chicklets," *chicas*, *chicles*. Just like the skinny kids sell on every street corner in Mexico. You eat like they do—you gonna be skinny too!

Okay. Now comes . . . dinner! Some nice *frijoles* . . .

(Holds up disgusting clump of beans.)

Another tortilla . . .

(Holds up tortilla #3)

And for dessert? A "*Chocho*."

(Holds up picture of Hostess cupcake)

A real Mexican eats one of these every single day—and they never get fat! I don't know why, it's a miracle of the diet so just eat it.

That's it! It's so simple! No variety to worry about, 'cause on the
Authentic Mexican Diet you eat the same thing every single day.
Even pregnant *chicas* and diabetics eat this diet.
And, *chicas*, we ain't gonna ask you to do no aerobics, or nothing.
All you got to do is what we do in Mexico . . . *work*. You get
out in the sun, you do about ten to twelve hours of work . . .
you don't need no Jane Fonda.
Plus, we gonna sell you inspirational tapes just like the
gringo programs. We got tapes you could use while
you're working, with real Mexican "*dichos*"—sayings like . . .

(Thinks)

*"Pobre Mexico, tan lejos de dios, tan cerca de Los
Pinche Estados Unidos."* Which means, "Poor Mexico, so
far from God, so close to the United States."
And . . . speaking of God, *m'hijitas*, Juanita Craiga also
recommends the Catholic Church. You start going to church,
you gonna feel so guilty you won't even *wanna* eat!
Plus they gonna tell you to have lots of kids, and the more mouths
you gotta feed—the less food you got to stuff in yours!
That's it. State-of-the-art tapes combined with authentic
Catholic guilt—plus a diet real Mexicans been eatin' since
the *Conquistadores*. And I'm offerin' it to you this week, and
this week only, for only a hundred and twenty-nine
bucks . . . or two million and ninety-nine pesos.
Come in to one of our conveniently located centers in the
barrio nearest you . . . or call 1-800-JUANITA today!
Get off your *nalgas* and do it!

(Swigs Juanita Water)

Salud!

~ *Lisa Loomer*

One Cranky Customer

~ *Paige Braddock*

Sometimes More Is More

Oh, I appreciate the plain black dress,
The uncluttered room.
The bare wood floor.
The Rothko painting, yes,
But sometimes lately, I'll confess,
It seems to me that less is less
And more is simply more.

Would a palace be a palace if it were small?
Would the Great Wall still be great, or just another wall?
How about the Taj Mahal—would it still impress?
I think not
Sometimes less is less.

Would a quarter pounder be as filling as a half?
Would a little titter be as thrilling as a laugh?
Wouldn't you trade one perfect rose for twenty-four?
I'd say yes.
Sometimes less is less.
Sometimes more is more.

Oh, I adore a simple meal—
Half a sandwich—cafe au lait
But once in a while I might
Have a larger appetite
Then, baby, gimme the grand buffet!

A small Niagara Falls would simply be a drip.
Shrink the great Titanic, you've got one more sinking ship.
A miniature Grand Canyon would be just a crack
Face the facts—
Sometimes more is more—
Sometimes max is max.

And if you want a chic affair
Keep it sweet and simple and mature
But why try to be smart
Cause in matters of the heart
Less—is not—*l'amour*.

Oh, why does Schwartzenegger pump it up before a shot?
Why do we bring the trumpets in when the music's getting hot?
Why would a gal add silicone to what she's got?
What for?

Honey, can't you guess—
Sometimes less is less.
Sometimes more is more.

~*Michele Brourman*

CHAPTER 6

The Coast Is Not Clear

CHAPTER 6

The Coast Is Not Clear

I don't know. I really miss California, but my hair looks better in New York. It's the water. In NYC the water is soft and life is hard; in California it's the other way around. Out West, I'm a woman of simple needs and complex carbohydrates, serene and centered. Back East, I'm caffeinated, careening, and so crazed I worry I'll confuse control-top stuffing with stove-top panty hose and race into a meeting with giblets on my legs.

But I get so much more done in New York; I'm smarter and more interesting. Or am I mistaking histrionics for vitality? Maybe, but better melodrama than mellow.

My brain is a battlefield, Eve West and Eve East fighting for supremacy. In ten years on the right coast after a lifetime on the left, I fear I've become a hybrid, unfit for either. I move too fast for California, but I'm too cheerful for New York. (Although a couple more years here should take care of that.) Californians think I'm rude because I've picked up a New York practice that I call "participatory listening" and they call "interrupting." New Yorkers assume I suffered some sort of early-childhood citrus-induced neural damage that causes me to wait until they're *nearly finished* with a sentence before I respond.

Habits I've formed here get me into trouble there. Roach vigilance, for example, is part of even the toniest New Yorker's life. So finely tuned has my peripheral vision become that I reflexively swat at any small dark object on a countertop. On my last visit to my parents' house in California, I didn't even realize I'd struck without missing a conversational beat until mother asked gently, "Dear, why are you killing that raisin?"

I'm perpetually committing bicoastiality in my heart, measuring my two homes, my two selves, against each other. Though I miss it fiercely, I see now that leaving California's Edenic climate may not have been such a bad thing. Living in an eternal golden present makes folks think they're immune to mutability; decay and death come as shocking affronts, not natural events.

Living through the four seasons forces Easterners to wake up and smell the cosmic coffee. California can be a fool's paradise. But on days when my feet are freezing and sleet is performing unauthorized acupuncture on my face, I sometimes think, "Better a fool's paradise than a fool's hell."

The coasts come out even in the "How-can-you-live-there-aren't-you-afraid-of—Olympics. I worry as much about psychopathic Manson-type killers as I do about psychopathic Son-of-Sam-type killers; I'm about as afraid of earthquakes as I am of muggers. Since I've breezed through a dozen tremors but never been mugged, I tilt toward the devil I know. But my greatest terror is not having an all-night photocopy place within walking distance, so New York may have a slight edge after all.

The West Coast is soothing, but deceptive. The ratio of good men to narcissistic, infantile louses is about the same as in the East—1.5 to 3—but it takes longer to find out who's who. Only in the West have I been wooed with the promise of a romantic Frisbee weekend. Only in the East have I spent a first date at the vet's with a man whose cat was on dialysis. What does this mean? You tell me.

More people live on my block than live in my parents' entire town. In one morning's pass through Grand Central Station, I see more souls, and the bodies encasing them, than my best friend in Oregon sees in a year. I don't think human beings were meant to lay eyes on so many of their species at once. You'd think the sight would be humbling and inspiring, like a night sky full of stars, making you feel small yet part of a grand plan. But gazing daily at a Milky Way of fellow citizens makes me feel like part of a large ant farm.

I've gotten kind of used to it, though. Now, when I'm out West I get lonesome. I just spent a couple of months in San Francisco looking out the window and thinking, "Where is everybody?"

A QUIZ

1. On which coast did I see a sign on a grocery-store bulletin board inviting shoppers to gather and "raise a cone of energy to summon the goddess Astarte"?

2. On which coast did I see a very young Brooks Brother point excitedly at the horizon and cry to his companion, "There! That's the kind of jet I want!"?

ANSWERS

1. right and **2.** left. See? You can't always tell. I've come to understand that the brusqueness of New Yorkers can mask a sweet sort of no-nonsense kindness. I've come to see that California "sharing" often turns out to be about as open as Donald Trump's ledgers. I believe the mix of nice people and human-waste products is equal on each coast.

But I keep having to fight with people who insist geography is destiny. Or density: Westerners think East Coast crowding creates a constant surge of stress hormones that eventually erode the brain's niceness centers, and I can't always offer solid evidence to the contrary. Easterners insist that the West's wide-open spaces are duplicated between the ears of its inhabitants, and that California's official nickname should be the Persistent Vegetative State. New York thinks if you're not there you're nowhere. California thinks it's more highly evolved than thou.

I can come up with ten stories supporting each stereotype—and ten in rebuttal. I'm the Cassandra whose prediction is that soon the only thing the coasts will suffer from is irreconcilable similarities.

New Yorkers mock me because I can't remember what "regular" coffee is. To Westerners I'm a figure of fun because I ask for a bagel with a schmear. "Wouldn't your prefer a smudge?" they chuckle, poking each other knowingly in the tan. West Coast friends can't believe I still live in a form-fitting studio apartment; New York friends can't believe I'm dissatisfied with a rent-controlled anything, however tiny, even in a city where one in ten suicides is attributed to a lack of storage space.

I passionately defend both edges of the country against detractors and curse them both beneath my breath. I love them both. I hate them both. I work better in New York, but I sleep better in California. I say yes better in California, and no better in New York. Where does this leave me? On the continental shelf. In a holding pattern over some existential Omaha. I'll always be a misfit. The coast will never be clear.

Ah, well. Home is where the answering machine is, and that's New York at present. For good or ill, this town's given me something I never had before: attitude. As a Californian, if I felt wronged, I'd think to myself, "They'll be sorry when I'm dead." Now, after a decade as a New Yorker, I think, "They'll be sorry when I kill them."

~Judith Stone

Santa Fe Chic

"I LOVE THE SOUTHWEST, PARTICULARLY HERE IN THE DEN."

~Mary Lawton

CHAPTER 6

Rural Delivery

November 19, 1992
One Week Before Thanksgiving

I'm not entirely optimistic. Bill Clinton says he's a new Democrat, but I liked the old Democrats just fine. Still, the twelve-year reign of the Republicans is over, and, to my mind, that is reason enough to be thankful.

Another reason to be thankful is this day; the sun is shining, the air is crisp. Rudy, Lorraine's child, is spending the weekend with family in Farmville, so Lorraine and I can travel across the border into North Carolina to the Blue Ridge Mountains.

Chase City, where Lorraine lives, is flat. It's tobacco country. Whenever I come to visit her, she promises, "Next time. Next time you come, we'll go to the mountains."

I like mountains. The way some people find the beach to be idyllic, I seek my solace in tall, craggy peaks, in the dip of a valley or a hollow, in the dark pine trees shrouding the landscape. A person can lie low in the mountains, whereas at the beach there's no place to hide. At the beach, you're a sitting duck. New York City, my home, is level ground, but the skyline—building blocks of refuge—is not unlike a mountain range beckoning you to look up.

Lorraine's got a map spread out on her kitchen table. "Here," she points. "This is where we'll go. Pilot's Mountain. Mount Airy."

Although I couldn't have ever been there, Mount Airy has a ring of the familiar, like I know someone from there, which I don't.

"Of course it sounds familiar," Lorraine says. "Mount Airy is Mayberry. From 'The Andy Griffith Show.' Everybody knows Mayberry. It's famous. Like Pamplona."

Mayberry. I'm going to Mayberry. As a child, I had extensive and elaborate daydreams about living in Mayberry, of sitting on my front porch, of knowing everyone in town by name. I'd begged my mother please, please can't we move to Mayberry, but my mother said, "That's television. There's no such place." Evidently, my mother was wrong.

Despite that Mount Airy is only a few hours' drive from Chase City, Lorraine has never been there before either. Except to visit kinfolk, Southerners tend to stay put. They settle into that red soil like it's quicksand. Lorraine has been to the Blue Ridge Mountains only to go to Galax where her father's family is from. So much so does Lorraine stay in one place that, although she lives in a big house, she rarely ventures from the living room. She sits, eats, sleeps, reads, watches television all in one chair in front of a wood-burning stove. "You don't need this big house," I tell her often. "All you really want is a studio apartment."

The funny thing is that when Lorraine lived in New York, she was the most mobile person I knew. In eight years, she lived in six different apartments. Moving as if there were a fire underfoot, she fled from Manhattan to Brooklyn to Queens and back to Manhattan. Lorraine worked as a travel agent only because she got free airfare. She went to the Mid-East, to Europe, to South America the way she now goes to the Red Lion Supermarket and Judy's Beauty Salon. To meet Lorraine in Chase City, you'd never know she'd been practically everywhere, that she'd taken the most circuitous road home.

Mount Airy/Mayberry
An Altered State

It doesn't say Floyd's, but this *is* Floyd's Barber Shop. There's a pole out front and the sign "Two Chairs. No Waiting." Lorraine and I venture inside and, sure enough, there's Floyd. He's older than when I last saw him twenty-five years ago cutting Andy's hair on my black-and-white television. But that's Floyd. I'd know him anywhere.

He leaves his customer with one sideburn longer than the other to chat with Lorraine and me about the weather. Just as he did when I

watched him on TV, Floyd rambles, which gets on my nerves. "We have to be going now," I tell him.

"Well, you all come back tomorrow," Floyd says, "so I can take your picture."

We walk along Main Street, and Lorraine says, "I'm confused. Was that an actor playing Floyd the barber? Or is he a barber they put on TV?"

"I don't know," I say, but I do expect to see Barney and Thelma Lou strolling hand in hand, and Andy and Opie—fishing poles over their shoulders—heading out to the lake. I also think that if I were to telephone my mother right now, Donna Reed would answer, and my father would say to her, "Give my love to Kitten." I'd have a brother named Beaver, and the worst thing that could happen to me is I'd get handcuffed to Lucy.

We don't look when we cross the street—there are no messy accidents in Mayberry—to go to the drugstore where we sit at the luncheonette counter. I assume the ice cream here is homemade, but I ask for scrambled eggs and toast.

Lorraine leans in to tell me that in the South you don't eat breakfast for supper the way you do in New York. However, the woman at the griddle is happy to oblige me, and in that case, Lorraine will have eggs and toast and sausages, as well.

While we wait for our food, the mayor comes in for pie and coffee. Florid-faced and fat, he's stuffed into a lightweight suit. He wears white shoes even though it's well after Labor Day, and he takes the seat next to Otis, the town drunk. Sporting a five-o'clock shadow and wearing last week's clothes, Otis nurses a hangover and grins like a jack-o'-lantern at Lorraine. The mayor eyeballs me.

That mayor is as greasy as the eggs slithering around on my plate. "You see," Lorraine says to me, "the ones with the money always go for you. He's got money, that one. I can tell. And look who goes for me. The good-for-nothing drunk. Isn't that always the way?"

I eat my toast and drink my coffee while Lorraine tries to cozy up to the mayor. "Could you recommend a place for us to stay the night?" Her tone is suggestive.

He directs us to a motel which is on the outskirts of town and where he probably gets a kickback. I know a sleazeball when I see one.

"Yeah," Lorraine says, "but a sleazeball with money."

I shake my head at her, and Lorraine says, "Come on, admit it. Some money would help."

"Help with what?" I ask, but Lorraine can't answer that. "Everything," she says.

The Next Day It Dawns on Me You Can't Live on Television Even If You've Got Cable

Episodes of "The Andy Griffith Show" come flooding back to me—Aunt Bea gets canning jars for her birthday, Otis rides a donkey, Andy captures escaped convicts, Opie shoots a bird—even though I haven't seen the show for years. Lorraine, on the other hand, has cable and sees Mayberry in reruns. For her, it's more immediate and less like a dream.

Snappy Lunch was where Andy and Barney ate nearly every episode. The menu offers bologna sandwiches and hamburgers (breaded or all-meat), but what Snappy Lunch is famous for is their pork sandwich. I don't eat pork, but Lorraine does. The chop is breaded, deep-fried, and smothered in lard-laden onions between two slices of white bread. Lorraine considers this a good meal consisting of the four major food groups.

Lorraine, an otherwise smart woman, is ignorant when it comes to nutrition. Ten years before, despite how she loathed Ronald Reagan—and she did take his triumphs poorly and to heart—she didn't understand the catsup-as-vegetable fuss. "It is tomatoes," Lorraine had said.

I have seen Rudy drink soy sauce from the bottle and eat Reese's Peanut Butter Cups for dinner. Lorraine encouraged her child to eat broccoli only to smite George Bush.

"This is good," Lorraine wipes grease from her lips with a paper napkin. "You sure you won't have one?"

"Positive." I nibble at my grilled cheese sandwich.

Reflecting on her own situation now as a single mother, her ex-husband out of work and drunk and living in some broken-down trailer, Lorraine says, "Andy was a single parent. And look how fine that Opie turned out. Grows up to be a big movie director."

"That's true," I say. "Ron Howard is a son to be proud of."

We keep our promise to return to Floyd's. He takes three pictures of us with his Polaroid camera. One for Lorraine, one for me, and one goes up on the barber shop wall. Then Floyd tells us to wait. "I got gifts for you pretty ladies."

He shuffles to the back of the shop to get each of us a picture postcard of Wally's Service Station where Goober and Gomer worked until Gomer joined the Marines and got a TV show of his own. That was before everyone knew Gomer was gay. A gay Marine wouldn't have gotten his own sitcom.

Floyd also gives us Xerox copies of Francis Bavier's will. She was the one who played Aunt Bea. After being Aunt Bea for so long, she must've gotten confused and moved from Hollywood to Mayberry as if to stay at home.

Back out on the street, it is Lorraine who mentions the fact that all the people in Mayberry are white. "You notice that? I never saw a Southern town that didn't have some black folk. But look around," she says. "What do you see?"

I look up and down Main Street. I see a picture-pretty little town. Quaint, and like a set. No one's living in poverty. No one lives on the street. There's no graffiti on the buildings. There are no serial killers here. No senseless slaughter. The worst thing that could happen in Mayberry is you get handcuffed by mistake to Barney. I see a town where no one is black or Hispanic or Korean or Jewish or Greek. I see a town so isolated that no one even reads a newspaper. There is no president of the United

States—Democratic or Republican—in Mayberry. Here the only elected officials are the mayor and the sheriff who doesn't even carry a gun. This is a town where, if you've got cable, the people come to life for half-hour segments to go fishing, to go courting, to bake a pie. And I know that my mother was right: Mayberry is not a real place. At least not for me.

~*Binnie Kirshenbaum*

Ambitious Trip

~*Cathy Guisewite*

CHAPTER 6

The Montana Nine: A True Story

I don't remember exactly what year it was that this happened, but I do know it was in the wintertime. I had been on the road in the Pacific Northwest—Eugene, Oregon, Corvallis, Portland, Seattle, Vancouver, Spokane, Edmonton—and on this particular day I flew into Winnipeg. I took a taxi to the hotel—I don't remember the hotel's name, but it was small, maybe four stories tall, near the business district. My room was on the fourth floor. It's funny how some details stay with you while others don't.

As I unlocked my door to enter I noticed that directly across the hall from me was a room where it looked like there was a party going on—except it was not your typical "hotel party" type group. It was all women, all older women, in fact, all older women in flowered dresses with whitish-bluish hair. I waved a friendly "hello" and they waved back. I carried my guitar and suitcases into my room and started unpacking, when I heard a light tap on my door.

I opened it to find two of the old ladies standing there, looking a bit on the anxious side. "Excuse me," one of them said, "but we stayed in this room last night and now we can't seem to find our train tickets. Could we look around to see if they are still here?"

"Of course," I said, stepping aside to let them in.

For the next few minutes we all opened and closed every drawer, looked under the bed, on the desk—everywhere—but no tickets. I asked them what time the train was scheduled to leave and they said 10 o'clock. So, since it was around 2:00, I knew they'd find their tickets. I sometimes absentmindedly stick tickets in some pouch or bag while traveling, then spend what seems like hours searching for them, but they always turn up. I asked them where they were traveling to, and I could hear a note of excitement in their voices when they answered.

"We're taking a four-hour train ride north, then we take a plane up close to the Arctic Circle where the sun never rises!" they answered. I asked them if they were scientists and they laughed. "No, we're friends. Every year we pick a destination, then for one week we leave our families behind—husbands, children, grandkids—and the nine of us have an adventure. Last year we went to Phoenix and that was okay, but this year we wanted to try something a little different, and the Arctic Circle seemed like a good idea, so here we are!" I asked them where they were from and she said they all lived in and around Billings, Montana. I wanted to talk some more, but they were worried about finding their train tickets, so they left.

I went back to my unpacking, and with three hours to go before my sound check decided now would be a good time to organize my purse. I have the kind of purse that turns into a black hole during long trips—things get tossed into it in one city, only to disappear, then re-emerge two thousand miles later. So I emptied it out onto the bed and attempted to sort through a wrinkled pile of credit card slips, cash receipts, boarding passes, checks, American cash, Canadian cash, tissues, candy wrappers, phone messages—a boring task that suddenly made me feel very sleepy. I stretched out on the bed next to the contents of my purse and promptly fell asleep.

I awoke at 4:30—and only had a few minutes to get my gear together for the concerts that night. I splashed water on my face, packed a small bag with my performing clothes, guitar strings, batteries, and headed out the door. Right across the hall were all those old ladies, still crowded into that one room, and even though I was running a little late, I was concerned that they might not have found their train tickets. So I went in and asked.

Yes, the tickets had been found, having slipped between suitcases in their room. I looked around and could see how that could happen—all nine of them were crowded into one rather small hotel room, so I suddenly had an idea.

"Look," I said, "I've got two shows tonight—I won't be back until very late." I took my room key out of my pocket and held it out to them. "At least you can spread out a bit. Here, use my room."

They looked a bit doubtful, but one of them quickly grabbed my key. "Thank you," she said, "We will."

I had two performances scheduled that night—one at 7 P.M. and one at 10 P.M. The first concert ended at about 9:15 and immediately afterward I planned to get my Sharpie pen and autograph CDs in the lobby.

I always keep my Sharpie pen in the same section of my purse where I keep my money, so it came as a shock when I reached into that section for the pen and saw that there was no cash in there. I had been on the road for quite a while and remembered having a substantial amount of money. My mind raced for a moment—could I have been robbed while onstage? Then I remembered—I had been cleaning out my purse at the hotel. What did I do with the money? I tried to reconstruct my moves . . . then I realized I had left the contents of my purse on the dresser in my room . . . *and then gave my room key to a bunch of strangers!!!* What was I thinking?

I immediately told the stage manager what I had done, and he offered to drive me over to the hotel between shows. But there wasn't much time, the old women were probably already on their way to the train station, but more than that, in my heart I knew everything would be all right. The stage manager said perhaps I should have the front desk manager be made aware of the situation, but I declined. I had a feeling there was no need to worry.

I performed my second show that night, and got back to the hotel around 1 A.M. I retrieved my room key from the front desk, went to my room, slowly turned the key, and turned on the light. What would I find?

There, on the dresser, neatly folded, were my clothes. Next to that, in short stacks, was my money—separated neatly by denomination and country (U.S., Canadian). Next to that was a pile of receipts, again separated—U.S. and Canadian. Next to that were checks. Next to that was a sheet tallying up the amount of cash, checks, and receipts. (There was over $700 in U.S. money, over $600 in Canadian. Plus some coins.)

Next to all of that was a handwritten note on a small piece of blue-lined notebook paper. In beautiful script it said:

Dear Christine:
(We know your name because it's on your airline ticket.)
Thank you for your kind hospitality. You are a very trusting soul.

Sincerely,
Elsie of The Montana Nine

The Montana Nine, I thought to myself. The name conjures up images of a gang of outlaws, roaming the hills, stirring up trouble. But in reality The Montana Nine is a gang of old ladies, on their yearly adventure, and I had an encounter with them. They folded my clothes, added up my receipts, counted my money, then stole off into the night in pursuit of the Arctic Circle.

Someday, if you're lucky, you, too, might see them. In their flowered dresses, with their blue hair. *The Montana Nine.*

~ *Christine Lavin*

Moving—Hollywood Style

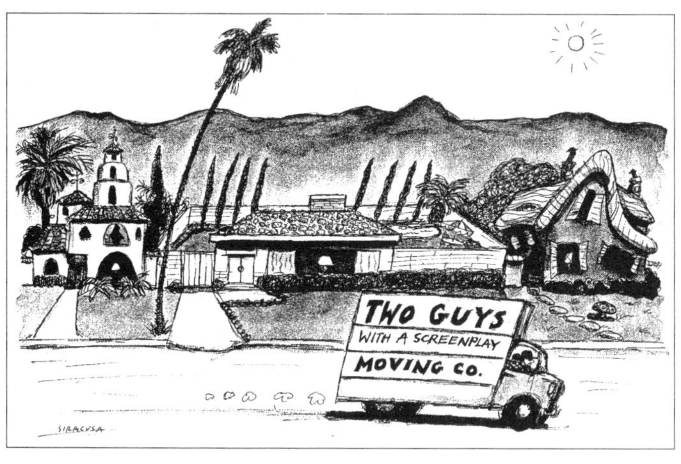

~ *Catherine Siracusa*

CHAPTER 6

Excuse Me For Inviting You To the Plantation

I have a friend, you may know him. He is frequently characterized as being excessively candid. Well, my husband and I were meant to take a trip with him and his wife. They would fly to New Orleans to meet us in my ancestral home, and then we would take a tour of the Louisiana countryside — plantations and Southern gardens and the Gulf Coast. Then my husband found that he had to make a sudden business trip to Paris. He asked me to cancel the trip with our friends and come away to Paris with him.

"You treat me like dirt," I yelled. "You invite me to Paris, you ask me to go first class. How can you treat me this way?"

"Oh, I'm sorry," he said. "Let me apologize for inviting you to Paris. How could I be so cruel?"

But I honestly thought I couldn't let down our friends, who had made all their plans and had unrefundable tickets. So I bravely called our friends and told them, "My husband has been called away on business, but I won't let you down. I know the trip won't be as fun without him but, if you want to go, I'm there and I think it could still be fun."

I went to New Orleans. A few days later, as I prepared to drive my husband to the airport for Paris, my friend, the one who is excessively candid, called me at 8 in the morning. He was supposed to arrive later that afternoon. "I don't think I can be alone with you for six days in antebellum homes," he said. "You talk too much, and I can't drive two women around for six days to antebellum homes and Southern gardens." That was pretty funny. It reminded me of something my hero Walker Percy would have said. It was crusty and Walker Percy, though himself a Southerner, would not have swallowed all that plantation tour stuff, either.

Then my friend told me it would be too claustrophobic because my topics of conversation are so limited because I can only talk about myself. That was pretty funny, too. I don't deny it. But at the time it seemed excessively candid. It was 8 in the morning. I had been up with the baby, who was sick in the night, I was exhausted, I was coming down with a cold, we were coping with some family emergencies, and I had refused to go to Paris for the sake of not letting down my friend. I said, "Fuck you then. Don't come."

I took my husband to the airport for Paris. I came down with a cold. The baby did, too. I tended to other family emergencies. Then my husband returned to New Orleans and took me to the Gulf Coast, anyway, where we had planned all along to spend New Year's. Whenever we go to the Gulf Coast in winter it is freezing and pouring rain. Still the coast road is beautiful, a suave old boulevard along the sea.

We stayed at a bed-and-breakfast in Pass Christian. My friend who is excessively candid had told me how he dreads bed-and-breakfasts — knickknacks, curios, a bathroom across the parlor. He said he would take Motel 6 any time over a bed-and-breakfast. I admit his views are pretty funny. That's why I love him still.

I had actually tried to cancel our reservations, but the bed-and-breakfast proprietor kept calling me, making gentle but firm reminders, insinuations and veiled threats. Southerners are sometimes very firm beneath their gentleness. They are known as iron magnolias. The receptionist at a plantation in St. Francisville said, "You'll still be charged," when I tried to cancel our reservation for three nights. "I can let you talk to Miss Mary," she added doubtfully.

In Southern businesses, the ultimate ruler is always called Miss Mary. She is an iron magnolia. "All right, I'll talk to Miss Mary," I said bravely. "Miss Mary doesn't usually talk until after 5," drawled the girl. "O.K., I'll call after 5," I said meekly.

I spent the next two days fruitlessly trying to get through to Miss Mary. That is part of the drill. You psych yourself up to deal after 5 with an ancient alcoholic matriarch after the cocktail hour, sitting at her desk in the plantation with an old hurricane lamp and a ceiling fan and then you can never get through to her. So, finally, I said to the reception girl in my best Southern tone of incredible gentleness with a tad of a drawl, "I really wasn't able to come due to family emergencies," which was partly true. "And we were so disappointed, but I don't think it's right for me to pay for the whole three nights for both rooms" (the other couple's reservations included). Silence. Whispering drawls. Static electricity. The hum of ceiling fans, the crackle of ice cubes in Miss Mary's drink.

"So how shall we leave it," I persisted. "Shall we say that I'm willing to pay a small portion of it for good faith but I don't think it's fair for me to pay the whole thing?" Silence. The hiss of hurricane lamps. Night sounds from the plantation. The clink of glasses, the whir of the fan. "Or are we going to get into some sort of dispute," I closed with my best Southern manner. "Oh, no," said the girl phlegmatically. Nothing would be more unseemly than a dispute. I await my credit card bill.

The proprietress of the Gulf Coast bed-and-breakfast was a similar type. One night, she called me and said, "Do you want me to rent out the Bluebonnet Room?" Of course, the Bluebonnet Room is exactly the name to make the hearts sink of those who dread bed-and-breakfasts. "Yes, do. I don't think we'll be coming." "But you're not in the Bluebonnet Room. You're in the Rose Room," she said. "Then why are you asking me about the Bluebonnet Room?" I asked innocently. She launched into a lengthy and incomprehensible explanation, which I had to ask her to repeat several times. It had something to do with asbestos and a bathroom on the other side of the parlor. She explained it again and something dawned on me — we would have to go there.

When we got there, it turned out she had gently but firmly misrepresented many things. She said it had a view of the Gulf. It had a view of McDonald's. She said it was a lovely room with all the conveniences. It didn't have a bathroom and you had to go through the parlor to get to one. You also had to share it with the Bluebonnet Room. They were building a bathroom in the Rose Room, but it would be finished next week. Meanwhile, they had just tried to dry the asbestos from the construction work, and maybe we should leave the windows open for a while.

Nevertheless, we celebrated the new year there and drove home in a blinding rain the next day along the suave old coast boulevard. I received several ingratiating messages from my excessively candid friend who is now trying to get back in my good graces. I think I will let him writhe in remorse a bit first. Any iron magnolia would do the same.

~*Nancy Lemann*

Paradise Lost

Stranded on a desert island without her Spellcheck, fiction writer Alicia Root is too inhibited to send off her rescue plea.
machlis

~*Gail Machlis*

CHAPTER 6

Will I Ever See a Picasso Again?

New people are moving to the South in droves—some kicking and screaming because they've been transferred by their companies. Give them a year and they become more Southern than the Southerners. But they sometimes refuse to believe they can even live here when they first find out they have to leave Chicago or Los Angeles or Boston.

They've never been South and they don't know what life is like in "the provinces."

Will they ever eat another decent gourmet meal?

Will they ever see another decent play? Will they ever experience real culture again?

"I moved to Jackson, Mississippi, from Philadelphia," says Jan Carmichael. "The first time some of my relatives were to come down to visit, they were having a fit. They couldn't imagine what we'd have here in Jackson to keep them entertained.

"Well, right off they were charmed by all the hospitality of my new Southern friends. But my cousin Donald still wasn't convinced that he could take this place culturally. He saw an ad for a ballet competition and was very condescending. He thought it might be something like a ballet recital.

"I explained this was the International Ballet Competition. It rotates among only four places in the whole world—Varna, Bulgaria; Helsinki, Finland; Moscow, Russia; and Jackson, Mississippi.

"And if you were attending in Moscow, it wouldn't be as much fun because you wouldn't get to eat catfish and fried dill pickles."

Some people take a little more convincing. Charles Higgins threatened a lawsuit to try to keep from being moved to Dallas from New York when his company decided to transfer him. Much to his horror, it did no good.

"I thought I was going to die from culture shock," he admits. "My friends gave me a good-bye party and wore black armbands. At that point, I would have believed anything. I even considered carrying a Christmas tree on the top of my van when I drove to my new home. Someone told me you couldn't get a decent tree anywhere in Texas."

Was he ever surprised.

"I found trees in every possible texture and color from natural pine to hot-pink sequins," he says. "the green sequined cactus ornaments were a little strange, but I've learned a big lesson. Bloomingdale's doesn't carry everything."

The Texas newcomer also admits he anticipated another big problem with the South. He just didn't believe there could possibly be a decent museum, symphony orchestra or ballet company within miles of a region that practically has made a religion out of something called chicken-fried steak.

"There are fabulous museums in the South." he was told. "You know the King Tut and Catherine the Great exhibits didn't originate in New York or Chicago. They opened in Memphis."

Somehow he just wasn't listening. This was in 1987. Higgins wasn't in Dallas for more than three months when a Russian ballet dancer defected at the transplanted New Yorker's neighborhood Tom Thumb grocery store. Andrei Ustinov of the Moscow Ballet leapt across the expressway, bounded through a parking lot and turned himself in to a Texas beauty who had just gone through the checkout line. They walked to an outside pay phone and called the FBI.

His new Texas friends ruthlessly chided Mr. Higgins about this incident. Talk about cultural deprivation. Not one of these Texans, it seems, could ever remember any *artiste* defecting at Zabar's in New York City.

~*Maryln Schwartz*

Ten Things In Little Rock That You Won't Find in New York City.

1. Ten-cent phone calls.
2. The only diamond mine in the United States just minutes away . . . okay, maybe an hour or so, but who's counting?
3. Sunday brunch at one of the best restaurants in town for under $10.
4. Restaurants where they bring you water with ice without your having to ask.
5. Bars where you won't run into Donald Trump.
6. Cream gravy at the Dairy Queen.
7. Soap containers that read: "Clinton-Gore Cleaning Up America."
8. The Secret Service at the bowling alley.
9. Signs that say "Thank You for Coming."
10. People who mean it.

~*Maryln Schwartz*

GOOD MORNING, FORT WORTH! GLAD TO BE HERE

Hidy, Fort Worth. Think of the fun we're going to have. The statehouse, the courthouse, the White House—mirth, glee, and hilarity to be found in abundance everywhere we look. It requires, of course, a strong stomach to laugh at politics in our time. But the only other options are crying or throwing up, and they're bad for you.

It is not my habit to write columns about writing columns, a subject about which damn few people give a rat's heinie. But since I'm new to y'all and y'all are new readers to me, I thought I'd start by telling you where I come from and a little about how I look at all this—then you can take my diamonds of wisdom with a grain of salt or a pound of salt, depending on your preferences.

I believe politics is the finest form of entertainment in the state of Texas: better than the zoo, better than the circus, rougher than football, and even more aesthetically satisfying than baseball. Becoming a fan of this arcane art form will yield a body endless joy—besides, they make you pay for it whether you pay attention or not.

It's all very well to dismiss the dismal sight of our Legislature in action by saying, "I'm just not interested in politics," but the qualifications of the people who prescribe your eyeglasses, how deep you will be buried, what books your kids read in school, whether your beautician knows how to give a perm, the size of the cells in Stripe City, and a thousand and one other matters that touch your lives daily are decided by the dweebs, dorks, geeks, crooks, and bozos we've put into public office. (You may believe yourself in no peril of ever landing in Stripe City, but should you happen to contravene a law made by the only politicians we've got, this too will become a matter of some moment to you. For example, if you happen to possess six or more phallic sex toys, you are a felon under Texas law. In their boundless wisdom, our Solons decided that five or fewer of the devices make you a mere hobbyist.)

CHAPTER 6

While it is true that I believe all politicians are in a free-fire zone, and further that it is an important American tradition to make fun of people holding high office, I also believe there are heroes in American politics. They're just in damn short supply. I also believe Texas legislators are overworked and underpaid. But that doesn't excuse their performance.

Ronnie Reagan, who was not the brightest porch light on the block, used to go around proclaiming, "Government is not the solution; government is the problem." Me, I think government is a tool, like a hammer. You can use a hammer to build with or you can use a hammer to destroy with. Whether government is good or bad depends on what you use it for and how well you use it. On the whole, it's a poor idea to put people in charge of government who don't believe in using it.

I believe government should be used in order to form a more perfect Union, to establish justice, ensure domestic tranquility, provide for the common defense, promote the general welfare, and secure the blessings of liberty to ourselves and our posterity. God, as the architects say, is in the details.

I believe that all men and women are created equal. That they are endowed by their Creator with certain unalienable rights. That among these are life, liberty, and the pursuit of happiness. I believe that governments are instituted among men and women, deriving their just powers from the consent of the governed, to secure these rights. And that whenever any form of government becomes destructive of these ends, it is the right of the people to alter or abolish it.

I dearly love the state of Texas, but I consider that a harmless perversion on my part, and discuss it only with consenting adults. If Texas were a sane place, it wouldn't be nearly as much fun. Twenty-five years of reporting on Texas and I still can't account for that slightly lunatic quality of exaggeration, of being a little larger than life, in a pie-eyed way, that afflicts the entire state. I just know it's there and I'd be lying if I tried to pretend it isn't.

I am so tickled to have Fort Worth as a home base. I've loved the town for years—it seems to me characteristic of Fort Worth that it still thinks of itself as a town, not a city. Dallas is a city. My great-aunt Eula lives in Fort Worth. Once when I was visiting, I said to Aunt Eula, who's had that same black telephone for at least forty years, "Aunt Eula, have you ever considered getting a new phone? You know they make them now in a lot of different colors and fancy shapes."

Aunt Eula said, "Why would I want a new one? This one is perfectly good." I think "Perfectly Good" should be Fort Worth's municipal motto. Another time, when I was driving for Aunt Eula, she said, "Turn left where the green water tower used to be." I am contemplating writing a guide book to Fort Worth with "Turn Left Where the Green Water Tower Used to Be" as the title, it being the kind of town where everyone knows where the green water tower used to be.

When Jan Morris, the famous British travel writer, wrote a piece on Fort Worth several years back for the *Texas Monthly,* she of course flat fell in love with the place, as all right-thinking people do. For years I've feared that Fort Worth would be "discovered" and become chic and self-conscious. Horrors. I raced over after Morris's gushing article came out to see if any damage had been done. It was the talk of Juanita's, and I joined several prominent citizens, many of whom had been interviewed by Morris, in mid-discussion. They all thought the article was "real fine, real nice."

"So interesting about Jan Morris," I said. "You know she used to be a man." One of the fundamental Fort Worth expressions, benign puzzlement, set on every face. "Yep, she used to be John Morris and she was a don at Oxford and a famous mountain climber, but then she had this sex-change operation and now she's a woman, but she still lives with her ex-wife, 'cause they love each other." Silence ensued. Finally one of them said, "Well, she seems like real nice folks." The others all nodded and said, "Yep, real nice folks."

Fort Worth is a town where people know what's important.

~*Molly Ivins*

CHAPTER 6

Obscenity of The Suburbs

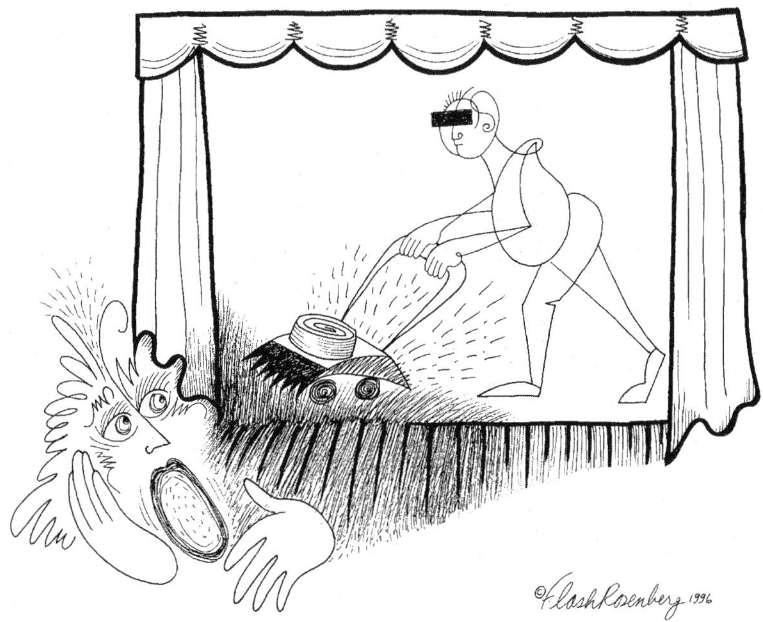

Every day I passed by the Adult Peep Parlor in my neighborhood.
But I never went inside . . . until one night in my dreams.
I couldn't believe it.
It was an immaculate theater. Very proper. Polite. Fat-free popcorn!
Then the lights dimmed . . . *and I was shocked!*
They started showing films of "Daily Life in the Suburbs"
People mowing the lawn . . . Shopping the malls . . . Eating
constantly in front of the TV
To each his own obscenity.

~*Flash Rosenberg*

CHAPTER 7

Are You Having an Interesting Life?

85 Things Every Young Woman Should Know

A Guide To Getting A Grip

10 essential elements for a grown-up home:

- A bed lifted more than six inches off the ground.
- Enough wine glasses.
- Some evidence of personal style.
- A dictionary.
- An answering machine with a no-gimmick, no-music, no-mystery message.
- Enough toilet paper for tonight and tomorrow morning.
- A box of condoms.
- A toolbox.
- A casually displayed photograph of you looking your absolute best.
- A refrigerator whose contents do not require carbon dating.

5 signs it's a good day to go shopping:

- You aren't pre- or currently menstrual.
- You didn't fall in love last night and wake up convinced there's a romantic resort hotel in your near future.
- Debtors Anonymous hasn't advised you to cut up your credit cards.
- You have it on good authority that baby-doll dresses are definitely, finally, *out*.
- Your mom will not be coming along with you after all.

3 good-enough reasons to stay home on a Friday night:

- You're beat.
- You're cranky.
- You're in love.

4 ways to get a strange man to stop staring at you:

- Pick your nose.
- Bellow across the room, "Not getting any at home?"
- Nudge the person next to you and point.
- Remove the can of pepper spray from your purse and read the instructions aloud.

5 items to hide under the sink the first night he stays over:

- Mustache bleach.
- Bag Balm.
- Your retainer.
- Another man's razor.
- Prozac.

7 skills more useful than a Swiss army knife:

- CPR.
- How to knot a man's tie.
- How to measure for window shades.
- The basics of erotic massage.
- How to write a résumé that wildly exaggerates your gifts and achievements but never crosses the line into dishonesty.
- How to gracefully pick up the check.
- How to determine the relevance of the leggy blond he just introduced to you without asking, "Who *is* she?"

4 numbers to know by heart:

- Your target heart rate.
- The percentage of your income that belongs to the IRS.
- The proper tip for the person who cuts your hair.
- Your own personal red zone for credit card debt.

6 reasonable expectations of someone else's wedding:

- Consecutive and sometimes overlapping rushes of happiness and sadness.
- A drunken man who gropes.
- At least one bridesmaid's ugly-dress-rebellion story.
- The opportunity to exercise your acute taste and dazzling judgment as a social critic.
- Poached salmon with that mysterious green sauce.
- A lengthy rendition of "The Wind Beneath My Wings."

1 unreasonable expectation:

- That the man you are destined to marry will appear and ask you to dance.

5 signs you're ready to fall in love again:

- You can't remember what you were wearing the night you broke up.
- "Dr. Quinn, Medicine Woman" just isn't the same anymore.
- You graduated from the Heartbreak Weight Loss Plan.
- You flirted right back.
- You finally found time to get your bikini line waxed.

5 things he thinks you don't know about him:

- Come-from-behind sports movies make him cry.
- Some of the things in the Victoria's Secret catalog scare him.
- He likes to read your *Glamour* when you're not home.
- Half the time when he says "What?" he knows exactly what you just said.
- He sleeps curled up around your pillow when you're out of town.

5 things that aren't worth their consequences:

- Extra mayonnaise.
- Telling off your boss.
- Unprotected sex.
- A deep, dark tan.
- Three-inch heels.

3 things that are:

- A stunningly gorgeous man.
- Coming clean.
- Birthday cake.

4 experiences that will strengthen your character:

- Getting audited.
- Getting fired.
- Waitressing.
- Vacationing with your three best friends.

5 overrated experiences:

- Sex in an airplane bathroom.
- Being the bride.
- Dating a very rich man.
- Shopping in Paris.
- Being the boss.

7 cures for what ails you:

- Two aspirin and as much water as you can drink.
- Black leggings and an oversized sweater.
- "Mary Tyler Moore" reruns.
- Calling home, collect.
- A tape of all the Brad Pitt scenes from *Thelma & Louise.*
- Anything caffeinated.
- A good cry in the ladies' room.

6 delusions to disabuse yourself of:

- "He'll change."
- "Just once can't hurt."
- "Oh, I don't need to have an orgasm every time."
- "Someday my prince will come."
- "Any fool could sell a screenplay."
- "I'll never make it in the real world."

~*Lesley Dormen*

Personal Olympics

~*Jennifer Berman*

Non-Bridaled Passion

SCENE: *The bridal registry of a major department store. In the background we hear Elevator Chimes, Cash Registers, and Soft Muzak.*

ENTER: *A WOMAN in her thirties. She approaches the Bridal Registry Consultant, posted behind the counter.*

WOMAN: Excuse me, are you the registry consultant? Well I'm here to register. For gifts! This is a really big step for me; I'm very excited! I'll bet you hear that a lot, don't you?... When is the happy event? ... Oh, you mean the *wedding* date. There isn't one. I'm not getting married. I'll probably never get married. But I need things, and I think registering is a good way for me to learn to receive... Yes, I know this is the *bridal* registry and that you only register *brides*. Frankly I find that a bit discriminatory. I'm here to register and I really don't want any hassle. No, don't get the manager. I am not trying to cause trouble. *Look,* for months now I've been buying gifts for all of my friends who've been getting married. It's an epidemic. There's been a slew of weddings, not to mention showers, lately, and I've attended all of them, brought gifts to every event. It's not that I begrudge them their happiness—not at all—I'm a very supportive person. It's just that lately I've been feeling that something's a little out of whack, you know, sort of off-balance, and yesterday, while I was attaching tiny silver bells to a spice rack for my friends, Howie and Wendy, this voice inside my head started screaming at me. It said, "Schmuck. Why do you keep buying presents for people who have already found everything they want?" Or words to that effect. I don't remember exactly. I do recall that the voice sounded resentful.

And I had to agree with it. I mean, isn't it enough that they were lucky and found each other? That they fell in love and made a commitment? That they'll be splitting the rent and filing jointly? My God, they've found someone who'll give them a *foot massage* whenever they want! They've already won the sweepstakes, why do they get the door prizes, too? Why do they get to register for things like ... like ... like a cookie jar shaped like a giant eggplant, or a set of "really good knives"? THEY'RE BECOMING A TWO-INCOME FAMILY, FOR CHRISTSAKE, WHY CAN'T THEY BUY THEIR OWN KNIVES???!!! Now, then. I need things. I am not getting married and I need things. I need better towels. Matching luggage. A pasta machine. And sterling silver candlesticks! Since I was five years old, my grandmother promised me hers the day I got married. Well, I didn't get married and last month they went to my cousin Marcy, who did. Why? Why do you only get family heirlooms if you wed? It's no damn fair. Candlesticks! Put me down for *two* pairs! Come on, just do it! You registered Ann and Deena, Lisa, Jane, and Cindy, I *insist* on registering too! ... I *know* I'm single; I confront that fact every day of my life. It's fine! I accept it! But I'm not staying single without the same material goods as my married friends. *My ship is coming in if I have to tow it myself!* ... Do you really want to know when the happy event is? It's a week from Saturday. I'm throwing a shower for myself, officially announcing a life of singlehood. And the beauty of it is, I won't have to return anything if it doesn't work out!

~*Kate Shein*

Decidophobia

I hate to make decisions. I've always hated to make decisions. I used to hyperventilate in our doorway when my mother said "in or out, in or out." And though analysts have tried to pin my decidophobia on two failed marriages and the trauma of having my first sexual experience in an Edsel, I'm pretty sure it all started with crayons.

When I was a kid I liked the box with only seven crayons. There was one brown, one green, one red, and anytime I wanted to color a tree it was a straightforward affair—brown bark, green leaves, red apples, no sweat. Then one afternoon my mother brought home that steroidal box of sixty-four crayons: the CRAYOLA colossus!

For many, this unabridged assortment of colors remains a cornerstone of childhood delight; for me, it reigns in memory as a gift from hell.

Staid colorer of trees that I was (what sunflowers were for Van Gogh, Norwegian pines were for me), I remember innocently opening the flip-up lid to look for my reliable dendrological shades only to find a Pandora's box of verdant choices, a Glocca Morra of green—lime, moss, shamrock, emerald, pea, avocado, olive (there might even have been a *fungus* green); in effect, enough greens to make even St. Patrick queasy and more than enough to set me up for the first of many forays into decision-anxiety.

No matter what shade of green I chose to top off a tree or bush there would inevitably be some friend who'd look at it and say, "Leaves aren't *that* color!" The implication clear as a slap: I had made the wrong choice, a bad decision—I had failed!

If my phobic dislike for decisions wasn't born then, it was certainly borne out when I made the transition from girlhood to womanhood. At that life juncture, I thought the only choice I had to make was between a pad and a tampon, right?

I couldn't have been more wrong if I had boiled sushi.

C H A P T E R 7

Suddenly I was faced with decisions that made Solomon's seem like choosing between vanilla and chocolate. Was it a "light day" or was it a "heavy day?" Did I want a regular or a super? A maxi or a mini? Looking back, though, those were the good old days; the choices escalated with each passing year. Periods were becoming profitable. A multibillion dollar industry was soon thriving between women's legs by leaps and bounds and turning a simple shopping task into a mind-numbing nightmare! Today, I consider PMS a dawdle compared to outfitting myself for the main event.

Aisles in the supermarket literally tower with feminine hygiene products, and every month I find myself more and more in doubt about which is the right one for me! Do I want a slim maxi? A *thin* maxi? An ultra-thin maxi? A super-long, ultra-thin maxi? An extra-absorbent, super-long, ultra-thin maxi with *wings?* Straight, curved, or wraparound? An all-nighter! How about a weekender? I'm ready to just hitch up a mattress once a month and let it go at that! I know all women aren't created equal—but how different can we be?

Not all *that* different. Oh, sure, some of us might love too much or work too much or eat too much, but all of us are pretty much alike when it comes to sex chromosomes and preferring partners who bathe—which is why I think that, for the most part, distaste for decisions is a female thing.

Admittedly, it's an acquired distaste, but it's easy to understand why so many of us acquire it. Men make decisions easily; not correctly, necessarily, but easily. (Hey, it wasn't a woman who came up with "New Coke"!) For instance, a man will buy a dress shirt that is pinned and wrapped—totally sealed in cellophane, with only color, collar, and cuffs showing—and never give a second thought to doing it. For a woman, this is an unthinkable act, tantamount to meeting the ex-husband's new wife without makeup. A woman wouldn't buy herself an expensive blouse without trying it on. At least once! And, even then, chances are she'll still wonder if she's made the right choice when she gets home. Second thoughts are our genetic onus.

Women have to make more decisions in a single day than most men make in a month! Guys can go on date after date without ever having to consider whether they should wear a skirt or slacks, heels or flats, fake it or forget it. And then there are meals. In most instances, a woman has to decide not only what to cook for dinner (including what to serve before and after it) but what to wear for dinner, as well as what to wear *with* whatever it is she's wearing for dinner. This is known as accessory angst and is definitely a distaff difficulty; definitely, because women innately know that choosing the right accessories for an outfit is as important as the outfit itself, although deciding which accessories are "right" can often be more time consuming that choosing an outfit and preparing a meal combined! And dining out is no easier, not for women.

Men make reservations without reservation, at least with other men. ("Hi, Stan. How about Mexican tonight? Casa Rosa, seven o'clock." "Sounds great, Hal. See you at seven.") When a woman is involved it's a different story. And when more than one woman is involved, it's an ordeal in gustatory accommodation that can kill your appetite, like *that!*

Eight words that unfailingly put me in anxiety mode are: "What are you in the mood for tonight?" I have yet to have dinner with a female friend without this query surfacing like the dorsal fin of a Great White, creating an equivalent acceleration in heart rate. My usual response is, "I don't care, anything is okay," which is, of course,(a)untrue, (b) unsafe, and (c) unacceptable as an answer. What follows is a grilling that I wouldn't wish on a war criminal. It goes something like this:

"So, do you want to have Chinese?"

"That's fine," I say. (But is it?)

"Or how about Italian?"

"That's okay, too." (I think.)

"Do you like Mexican?"

"Sure." (I'm not sure at all.)

"Wait, what about sushi?"

"Sushi's good." (Maybe, maybe not.)

"How do you feel about Greek food?"

"Love it," I lie. (Or do I?)

"We haven't had Indian in a long time."

"Then let's." (Then again, let's not and say we did.)

"But you'd probably prefer French, right?"

"Right, French." (At this point, I'd prefer never having agreed to dinner in the first place).

"But it's so rich. What do you say to Spanish?"

"*Sì*," I say, hoping to truncate the volley before arrhythmia kicks in."*Sì*, Spanish!"

And then, just when I think the inquisition is over, I'll hear: "So, do you want to go to that cute little cantina in the village or the place my sister told me about on the West Side? Or there's this new restaurant that the *Times* gave four stars . . . ?"

Generally, I make it a point to steer clear of Chinese restaurants and Greek diners; eateries that offer a choice of more than fifty entrees could seriously compromise my mental health. It's difficult enough for me to make decisions in restaurants, period. I'm always the last at the table to order, and, when I finally do, my sigh of relief is invariably premature. Just when I think that I've aced it, the waiter will ask if I want potato, pasta, or rice? If I say "potato," I'm suddenly on the spot again: "Baked, French fried, home style or *au gratin?*" Then there's the salad dressing gauntlet: "French, Italian, Blue Cheese, Vinaigrette, or House?" I never even look at the wine list; it's enough that I make the choice between red and white without palpitations.

I'm all for options, but when they increase pyramidally on a daily basis, it's scary. I remember when choices at the conclusion of a meal—and standard offering on airlines—were coffee, tea, or milk. Now if you say "coffee," you have to, at the very least, specify regular or decaf. And if you're offered a selection of flavored blends, decidophobia can really start percolating. Where once there was merely the alternative mocha, today there's mocha-vanilla, mocha-almond, mocha-marshmallow, among mucho-mocha others. Say "tea" and you leave yourself open to facing the option of herbal brews, which come in a conundrum of combinations, none of which nature ever intended. Not even milk is just drinker-friendly "moo juice" anymore, not with choices of one percent, two percent, skim, soy, whole, long life, low-fat, no-fat, fat-free, to say nothing of chocolate and cherry-vanilla. All I have to do is look in the dairy case and I find myself craving a beer—a craving, needless to say, that disappears instantly when I reach that aisle!

The more things are supposed to simplify life, the more they complicate it. I remember when there was only one telephone company and I could make a call without thinking twice about whether or not the person I was phoning was in or out of my circle of friends. I've changed phone services more times than Liz Taylor has changed husbands, and, like Liz, I'm still not certain that I've made the right choice.

Packing for a trip, even a longed-for holiday, is a stress test for me. It doesn't matter whether it's three days or three weeks, deciding what—and what not—to take makes me feel as if I'm deciding the fate of a nation (or, at least, a vacation). I run every item through a scenario of permutations. (Hmmm. Evening dress. Okay, we will be whitewater rafting *most* of the time, but if we stop somewhere I *might* need it. I mean, you never know. So, I'd probably better pack a pair of heels, a couple of pairs of pantyhose, earrings, a clutch bag, the beaded sweater, maybe my trench coat in case it rains . . .) And when it comes to first-aid equipment, I'm a traveling triage unit. All I have to do is say to myself, "You never know," and the whole medicine cabinet comes with me. My husband has often questioned the tourniquet, mustard plaster, and emetics—particularly when I'm just going to L.A. on a business trip—but it's less of an emotional strain to schlep them than to decide against them.

Some of my worst moments come at nail salons. The pressure of choosing a single polish from the enormous collocation of colors—in the space of an appointment—is enough to give me the bends (to say nothing of raising the specter of that old CRAYOLA colossus). In fact, it's endurable only because the alternative would be to select one polish for use on a permanent basis, a radical decisive move that I am not yet ready to make.

But I have decided (sort of) that I can keep my decidophobia at bay by cultivating a decidophobia-phobia, a fear-of-the-fear of making decisions, creating confidence by default. This isn't easy, but then neither was learning the lyrics to "In-a'Gadda-da-Vida." Meanwhile, as I wait for the phobia-phobia to kick in, I don't even glance at multiple-choice quizzes in magazines; I avoid Cineplexes: I restrict eye exams to when everything I read looks as if it's printed in Russian; I never ask for the remote control; I shun salad bars; I evade all either-or situations. And, of course, I keep myself as far away as possible from crayons.

~ *Hester Mundis*

Life 102

A book called *Life 101: Everything We Wish We Had Learned About Life in School—but Didn't* made the bestseller lists a while ago. Having read it, I think that much of its appeal was the enticing title, because it seems to me that the authors ignored a lot of the stuff I wish I had learned from *someone*. Thus, my motivation for writing the following tips. These are lessons it has taken me a lifetime to learn.

Being a Woman

Finding "the makeup shade that's just right for your skin tone!" or "the haircut that's perfect for your face shape" or even learning all "ten terrific new ways to tighten your tummy" will still not help you look even a little bit more like the girls in the diet-cola ads. This is because the girls in the diet-cola ads are often *13 years old.* Even they are not going to look like the girls in the diet-cola ads in a couple of months. And so the only way to deal with your female vanity in our society is to remember this important truth: *Mirrors lie. You are much better looking than that in 3-D.*

Men

Men are completely nuts. Women can't understand their behavior because men themselves have no clue as to what they are doing or why. However, there is one incredibly important thing to watch for in the early stages of getting to know a man that will give you all the real information you will need. Men almost always feel compelled to announce their personal deficiencies. The mistake that women make is *we don't believe them.* Learning to listen for a man's usually accurate self-assessment can save a woman a great deal of time and guesswork. If a man tells you that he is a jerk and he doesn't think he is ready to make a real commitment, *believe him.* Spending a couple of months with you is *not* going to be the magical catalyst that will change him. And he almost definitely is *not* going to go into therapy. Men, as a general rule, shy away from therapy because there is no obvious way to keep score. Other danger signals are:

Excessive charm. Men who have a lot of charm have it in place of something real that you are eventually going to want from them and find that they do not have. It is wise to remember that quite a few of our recent mass murderers have been cute guys. Somewhere, some stupid woman probably called up her friend and said, "Ted Bundy hasn't called me in two days. Do you think *I* should call *him?*"

Fast walking. I don't mean fast walking. I mean walking half a block ahead of you, no matter how fast you walk, and never slowing down to accommodate you. An informal poll I have been taking for quite a number of years has convinced me that these fast-walking guys also have terrible tempers and commitment problems. If you don't believe me, ask a friend of yours who is seeing someone with a terrible temper and a history of cheating whether or not her man walks half a block ahead of her and prepare to be amazed.

Dating

Because of what we learned earlier about the essential nature of the universe, it only stands to reason that the more you prepare for a date, the more disappointing the date will turn out to be. In fact, the surest way to make a date cancel or disappear entirely is to go out and buy yourself some sexy, expensive new underwear. And while we're on the topic, it is wise to remember that although many of those underwear get-ups look fetching on the models in the catalog, most of them have the potential to make an otherwise fit and attractive female human suddenly turn into someone who looks like one of the dancing ballerina hippos from *Fantasia.*

One last bit of warning: there is a definite correlation between a man's gift giving and the longevity of the relationship. The more impressive the quantity and quality of gift items early on, the less impressive the chances for the future of the relationship. It's like the guys with the charm. Men who supplement early dating with a lot of swell gifts and prizes are generally distracting you from the stuff they are never going to give you.

Eating

There are four basic food groups: salad, hors d'oeuvres, pasta, and diet drinks. It is appropriate to eat from two of these groups per meal. If you are the sort of person who always thinks she needs to go on a diet, realize this: *everything will always make you fat for the rest of your life.* This is especially true if you live with someone who never gains weight. It is due to a little-known phenomenon called Secondary-Weight Gain, which operates in the same manner as Secondary-Smoke Inhalation. In other words, calories are calories and they have to go somewhere—meaning that *you* will somehow assimilate and convert into fat all the calories that are going unassimilated by perpetually thin people. You get your calories *and* their calories, thus causing you to mysteriously gain weight even when you eat only carrots.

~*Merrill Markoe*

Hair Tomorrow

I've got one hundred and fifty things to do and there just are not enough hours in the day. I've done the "what I really have to do" list, and am on the "what I'm supposed to do but have been putting off" list, so I think I'll go get my hair done.

When the world was made they left out the category of hair stylists, colorists, and cutters. The invisible booth in heaven that creates things had to develop a separate atomic structure for hairdressers. There are, however, a couple of common denominators that run through the genetic makeup of the hair world.

The first is a superior attitude. Everyone who applies for a job in a salon has it. It is astounding to see this in operation because this particular characteristic has no gender, age, race, or nationality. Everyone is welcome to work in the hair field who has a superior attitude. It doesn't matter if you're fat or pale, or have weak ankles, or if your neck is too wide or your upper arms are flabby. Also, it's of no consequence if your own hair is bad: too thin, too curly, too thick, too drab. It doesn't matter a hoot if you have no taste in clothes, if you cannot tell that a protruding stomach looks wrong in tight pants and fat knees look yuck with a short skirt, even if you are wearing only black. As long as you have a superior attitude you qualify.

The second common denominator of hair people is a kind of polished veneer that belies the ability to tell the truth or really communicate about anything. The worst hair people are monsyllabic at best, and the best of them are fiercely verbose on all subjects. Hairdressers know the secrets of the universe and are willing to divulge them to keep you occupied so they can do whatever they want to the top and back of your head.

Last month I called for an appointment only to find my regular hairdresser had gone for the day. I decided to use his assistant since all I required were highlights. When I arrived, the woman at the desk seemed frantic. I walked to the back and ran into my regular guy.

"What are you doing here? I thought you went home for the day."

"I did but they fouled up at the front so I had to come back." He was in a foul mood so I thought maybe serendipity had it up her sleeve and I'd get a great dye job from his assistant instead. But there she was getting a manicure!

"How are you going to do my hair with a new manicure?" I jokingly asked.

"What?"

I repeated my question.

"I'm not doing your hair."

"You aren't?"

"No, I don't think so."

"Well I called for an appointment at four o'clock and they gave me one."

"Oh oh oh no. Let me go check." Sure enough they'd made a mistake and she came hurrying back with lots of apologies.

"That's okay. I'm grateful you'd do it on such short notice. I'm sorry I wrecked your manicure."

"No no no I'd rather have the business." It's a miracle I'd even recognized her because the last time I was there she had black Jean Seberg hair and now today she had Rita Hayworth red, ear-length hair. So I sat in my chair and made small talk. The guy in the next chair had tattooes all over his chest and an "I don't know what I'm doing on this earth but I'll sure as hell fake it" look on his face. He's droning on about how his woman wants to get married.

"You know how it is, she wants a rock."

And then *she* shows up. She's generically dressed in youth fashion with baggy overall shorts and white socks and white Keds. She's radical in her mind. In real life she's just a square, but she has an attitude. They refuse to notice me which is great because I can gape at them all I want. Here they are, feeling cool and being talked to and joked at by the staff and I wonder at the whole scene. The head hairdresser is shaving off practically all the hair of this dark-haired unisex person. I cannot tell if she's a man or a woman because of the severe look on his/her face and the unisex shoes. He/she and the hairdresser seem to have an unspoken agreement that he will do whatever he wants and she'll look tough no matter what. She'd be a perfect candidate for a job here herself but I can tell she thinks she's too good for the place. Oh my God! He's really cut off all her hair and she isn't even flinching! She gets up to leave and comes back with a jean shirt on. I am now clear that she is a she as she casually leaves him a twenty dollar tip.

I never feel thin enough, cool enough, or hip enough when I come here. But it's not just here. It's every hair salon I've ever been to. Why is getting your hair fooled around with such an important thing? The more problems you have with your hair the worse you feel about yourself. If your hair looks great you usually are not extra nervous about living. You probably have organized thoughts. Your moods are not a problem.

I wake up in the morning, look into the mirror and find a unique zebra-style dye job down the middle of my part. I wanted highlights, not stripes. Once again I have been at the mercy of the less evolved.

~Martha Gehman

Trudy the Bag Lady

See, the human mind is kind of like . . .

a piñata. When it breaks open,
there's a lot of surprises inside. Once you get the piñata
perspective, you see that losing your mind
can be a peak experience.

I was not always a bag lady, you know.
I used to be a designer and creative consultant. For big
companies!
Who do you think thought up the color scheme
for Howard Johnson's?
At the time, nobody was using
orange and aqua in the same room together.
With fried clams.

Laugh tracks:
I gave TV sitcoms the idea for canned laughter.
I got the idea, one day I heard voices
and no one was there.

Who do you think had the idea to package panty hose
in a plastic goose egg?

—*Jane Wagner*

Matinee Idol

~*Martha Gradisher*

TV

I'm glad I weren't no pioneer
Ridin' in a wagon 'cross the great frontier
I'm playin' by candlelight
power's out here
And I can't watch TV

I can't do nothin', nothin' at all
Everything come
from a switch on the wall
Drive me nuts when it won't behave
No popcorn from the microwave

Oh, Yeah yeah, yeah
sky's real nice
moon's real big
stars real bright
cable calls and it don't seem right
That I can't watch TV

And it breaks my heart all I'm missin'
Bowling shows, old guys fishin'
How the dogs on the track did
Near death stuff re-enacted
Where to call to talk to strangers
Interviews with hockey players
How to lose a pound a minute
Make big bucks be rollin' in it

Shopping clubs, gladiators,
Cher's make-up, roller skaters
Rhinestone studs in your new shirt
Bald guy stuff, psychic network
Don't you feel bad for me
That I can't watch TV.

~ *Cheryl Wheeler*

Why I Hate Spring And Everything Else

The nearest I have come to spring cleaning is to scroll through some of my more bizarrely titled computer files to find out what they contain. A file called "Possible" turned out to be a list of men whom my friend Sarah and I would consider marrying. Included were Italo Calvino (there was an asterisk by his name for some reason, maybe because he is dead), Toshiro Mifune (I don't even know who he is anymore, but a note next to his name says, "sexy"), Mark Strand (there is an exclamation point after his name), and any king, except Charles if he becomes king, but not Don King.

Another file, called "2," was a letter I had written to the telephone company complaining that when I pressed the 2 button on my telephone the number 4 was activated even though, despite what an A.T.&T. representative had argued on the phone that day, my instrument was not faulty.

The file called "Tramp" comprised notes for a magazine piece I planned to write about a man named Da-vid (pronounced Dah-veed; he told me he chose the name because several years ago he discovered that he "resonated to it"). Da-vid was running for president of the United States and promised to work toward putting a trampoline in every home. I had gone to a political-religious rally where he showed a twenty-minute video that he had worked on for fourteen years. The video consisted solely of water images—waves, droplets, rivers, etc.—and Da-vid believed that if it were shown widely, perhaps as a CNN special, it would transform the world. Da-vid also wanted to convert Alcatraz into a global peace center. I cannot remember why I never wrote the piece.

There was also a file, "$2000," which listed items I though my friend Peter could buy with the money he had been awarded in a legal settlement: 1,650 Big Macs, 2 all-expense-paid ski trips to Aspen, 2,100 bottles of nail polish remover, 1,900 yards of dental floss, 20,000 large eggs or 10,000 small, 1,000 pints of Häagen-Dazs, 1,500 minutes of therapy, 1,500 packages of Oreo cookies, one-eighth of a Honda Accord, 40 haircuts with blow-dry, 1 Flying Dutchman sailboat, 1,400 cappuccinos, 10 years of cable, or 3 days of illegal parking on 57th Street.

. . . Those were not even the files I deleted.

Spring is the season of romance, and last spring, my friend Jon received a phone call from someone he did not know who asked him if he wanted to meet for drinks. "Who are you?" Jon asked.

"We met in the park last week," the caller said.

Jon couldn't remember meeting anyone in the park. "How did you get my number?" he asked.

"It was in your wallet." The caller said. Jon had been mugged in the park the week before.

This Spring—in fact, a recent Wednesday—I was walking down my street in broad daylight. Whenever the term "broad daylight" is used, a crime cannot be far behind. Halfway between Madison and Fifth avenues, a young man approached me and muttered something—I thought he asked which way Lexington Avenue was, so I told him. Apparently he was disappointed with where the street turned out to be, because he pulled out a knife and walked toward me, holding it outward. I hate to brag, but I screamed so loud that many people came to their windows. But there the Kitty Genovese parallel ends, for the young man panicked and ran toward Fifth.

I ran in the opposite direction and then into the street, where I jumped into a car that was driving slowly by. If my life were a Dutch thriller, the driver of the car would have taken me to bleak hinterlands and buried me alive. But instead, the two men in the car—business types from New Jersey—just looked peeved. For the sake of the story, though, I wished they'd asked me which way Lexington Avenue was.

If April is the cruelest month, then nothing is more cruel than a surprise party in April. Surprise parties are organized for people who, it is suspected, wouldn't otherwise attend a party in their honor, or would insist on a different guest list than the host had in mind. I have to confess that on April 1, I co-hosted such a party. I must also confess that it occurred to me more than once as I invited guests to the party that I was somehow being tricked into throwing a surprise party for myself. Suspicious as I was of this possibility, I would have been truly surprised.

I do not just hate surprise attacks and surprise parties (the same thing, in a way); I hate just about any type of surprise, and furthermore I hate people who like surprises. I am always a little irritated, for instance, when pregnant women and their husbands explain that they have chosen not to know the sex of their baby because they feel such knowledge would ruin the surprise. I like to imagine what would happen if these people accidentally discovered the sex of the baby before its birth. "Don't bother showing us the baby," they would say as the doctor tried to hand over the newborn. "We already know it's a girl. What's the point of looking?"

On the 86th Street crosstown bus, I heard what sounded like a frantic cat. Looking around for an unhappy animal pent up in a box, I saw a burly man with a flannel shirt. I'd say he was in his 50s. He sat alone,

looking out the window, and every once in a while, he meowed discreetly. The different cat sounds he made seemed to express a wide range of cat emotions, but they all seemed authentic. Sometimes, he would look around after meowing, as if he, like the other passengers, wondered where the noise was coming from. In my computer, filed under "?'s, I made a note to ask a doctor if Tourette's syndrome can take the form of feline outbursts.

The other morning, there was a note under my door from a neighbor I have never met. He had heard me screaming the other day and had rushed to his terrace, where he saw what he described as "the latter part of the event." He was worried that I might be upset. I am much too insensitive to be upset by something like that. But I have to admit, I was warmly surprised by his concern. Of course some people believe that I overreacted to the man with the knife—my friend Jon says that he was probably just selling cutlery, or about to peel an apple. By the way, a security guard and a couple of onlookers chased the man for a block or two, before he managed to escape into traffic. Maybe he finally made it to Lexington Avenue.

Recently, I saw the movie *Philadelphia.* Sitting behind me were two old women. During the opening montage, one asked, "What city do you think this is?"

"It must be Seattle," the other said. "I think that's where the movie takes place."

~ *Patricia Marx*

Pizza Man

"INSTEAD OF HUNTING TONIGHT, HOW ABOUT ORDERING A PIZZA AND EATING THE DELIVERY MAN WHEN HE COMES?"

~*Theresa McCracken*

Mood Swings

Mom thinks mood swings come from too much caffeine, but I am pretty sure mine come from life.

The man on TV said that humankind is over 3 point 7 million years old. When I think of all I have gone through in my short life, frankly, I do not know how humankind has stood it—just think, all those billions and billions of mood swings.

~*Jane Wagner*

CHAPTER 7

The Story of Z

I've figured out the dirty little secret of women's fantasy lives. And it's got nothing to do with thumbing through *Herotica* or fondling Brad Pitt's backside or soaking in a penthouse Jacuzzi with Richard Gere. Sleep has become the sex of the 90s. Sleep is replacing sex as that obscure object of desire that inhabits our daydreams—if we still have time for daydreams. When I indulge in an out-of-body experience during a particularly dull meeting, my richest, deepest, most rewarding fantasies aren't erotic. They're about checking out for hours and hours of glorious uninterrupted sack time. I'm not mentally undressing my dishy seatmate on the commuter train; I'm wondering whether he'd take offense if I catnap on his shoulder until we get to Hartsdale. My idea of a phone sex line is 1-800-M-A-T-T-R-E-S.

Arlie Hochschild interviewed dozens of working mothers for her book *The Second Shift: Working Parents and the Revolution at Home.* Time and again, they talked about sleep the way starving people talk about food. But this problem is not reserved to working mothers. Far from it. I read a column a few months back about the chronic sleep deficit that's sweeping the country. Something like 80 percent of Americans are seriously sleep-deprived. (Or maybe it was that 80 percent have lower back pain, or 80 percent think Heather Locklear needs to touch up those roots. I nodded off somewhere in there.) Experts estimate that chronic sleeplessness costs the nation as much as $70 billion annually in lost productivity, accidents, and medical bills. There was some maxim that if you fall asleep within five minutes of lights out, you can count yourself among the seriously sleep-deficient. (Wait, there are people who can stay awake for five minutes?)

I don't need Faith Popcorn or Gallup for confirmation. I know a trend when I'm living it. My friends and colleagues concur. Sarah says she would rather lay her head on a pillow than anywhere else. Maria says none of her friends want to fool around on the weekend; they just want to recover from the week (oh God, not another recovery movement). Barb claims that no one she knows is having sex—unless they're on some procreational full-court press to get those babies in before the buzzer sounds.

In fact, the only person to whom I expounded my sleep-as-sex theory who just didn't get it was a single, unencumbered, 20-something guy I work with. As I rambled on during one of my brief moments of clarity (the decaffeinated life is definitely not worth living), he rolled his eyes and said, "Sounds like all you need is a good nap." Which sounded suspiciously like a guy saying that all I needed was a good roll in the hay. Which proves my point exactly.

Obviously, for working parents, small children are the big problem. I guess I should have had an inkling of the trouble ahead when I read a *Parents* magazine survey a few months after our first child was born. In response to the question, "How do you feel about sex after the baby?" one new mom answered, "Fine, just don't wake me."

I just edited this wonderful new book by a physician whose sex therapy clinic has successfully treated thousands of couples. The doctor confirms that fatigue is a big problem in people's sex lives. But when I pressed her for some solutions, I couldn't help but feel a tad disappointed. She explained that we go through these R.E.M. cycles several times a night, one every ninety minutes or so, at which time we become aroused—only we're not aware of it because we're out like a light. She recommends you set your alarm to go off ninety minutes after you fall asleep. The idea is, when you wake up you'll be in one of your R.E.M. cycles, so you'll be in the mood. Yeah, you'll get me up after those precious ninety minutes when you pry my cold, dead fingers from around the pillow.

The women's magazines are certainly no help. *Cosmo* has yet to publish articles for the Exhausted Generation. How about "Douse His Candle: 15 Ways to Rev Up Your Z's" or "I Was the Office Narcomaniac"?

And how long before the Surgeon General realizes that sleep is the ultimate safe sex?

I do see hope on the horizon. Two months ago my husband and I took our first real vacation—three days and two nights—away from our two small children. On our last pre-child vacation, we embarked on an exotic trip abroad with complicated transportation nexuses and an intricate itinerary. This time around, we didn't even bother picking a destination. Our only goal was so modest it was almost pathetic: to go to sleep at night and wake up whenever we happened to wake up—not when a tiny voice shouted "Uppies! Uppies!" in one of our ears.

The first morning we made it to 7:13. The second morning we lasted until almost 8:00. And I was a new woman. For the first time in memory, whenever I closed my eyes, they didn't pine to stay closed. I felt energized, alive . . . sexy! We were, in all modesty, animals. Two days after we returned, however, the inevitable exhaustion crept back in. We're looking forward to re-creating that connubial bliss soon—perhaps when the kids are in their surly, narcotized teenage years. In the meantime, my husband and I comfort ourselves that this too shall pass; we know that one day our lust for sleep will recede and truly smutty thoughts will regain their rightful pride of place in our fantasy lives.

Who knows? Perhaps that day will come sooner than you think, darling. There I'll be, draped in that low-cut black nightgown you bought me on our honeymoon in Florence, my hair back-lit by flickering candles, my limbs still moist from a fragrant tub, awaiting the caress of the massage oil that warms at your touch.

But for now, wake me and you're a dead man.

~Elizabeth Rapoport

Daylight Savings

"I HATE CHANGING TO DAY LIGHT SAVINGS TIME."

~ *Theresa McCracken*

Sleep

You rock the baby, you feed the cat,
You walk the dog, babe, you're good at that
It may be reckless, it may be a sin,
But screw the alarm, I'm going to sleep in

CHORUS: Sleep, sleep, sleep is my good friend
Late in the morning or at the day's end
Pull down the shade, and turn out the light
The only date I have is with the sandman tonight

Don't talk to me about how you need
Only two hours and you're on your feet
Saying where's the fiesta, well you can find me
At the siesta catching some Z's

BRIDGE: Gonna bed down, drop off, got sand in my eyes,
Slumber, repose, get some shut eye,
Get forty winks, nap, hit the land of nod,
Catnap, knock off, go saw some logs

Give me eight hours, give me some REMs
Dreams like diamonds, ten carat gems,
Give me some respite, leave me alone:
It's a nice party, but I'm going home

~ *Debi Smith*

Over My Dead Wet Body

This reporter never thought she would refer to herself as "this reporter." But this reporter has noticed that others writing columns go by that name. And peer pressure is the operative force on this reporter.

This reporter is upstairs in the house she lives in, quiet as a mouse, waiting for the two men who have offices downstairs to go home for the day. These two men are very nice, but still, this reporter feels like Anne Frank waiting for the Nazis to leave. (Except, unlike Anne Frank, this reporter only wants to check the mail.)

This reporter has come to realize how tedious the "this reporter" gimmick can be.

My house is actually a large brownstone in New York City, and I occupy a floor. It is such a nice arrangement that I am convinced I must have been good in a previous life.

As I wait for the men downstairs to leave, I indulge in one of my favorite activities: browsing through annual reports from King's College, Cambridge, where I went to graduate school. The reports contain lengthy obituaries of college members who died that year. The obituaries are usually quirky and catty, even by the petty standards of the English. To illustrate the point, a few excerpts:

"He was very tall (hence the stooping head), dark, with pronounced features, vaguely dinosaurian."

"Already . . . markedly fat, he showed an abundance of the geniality associated with fatness."

"A few of [the songs that he wrote] were quite good, although the fact was obscured by his singing."

"Though he could be tiresome he could also be very amusing . . ."

" . . . [He] was born on 19 May, 1931, and educated at Berkhamsted school where he was remembered for jumping through a window in a blue smock as St. Joan."

"Both his parents were doctors and Eric read Natural Science and medicine, perhaps more to act out parental assumptions than to fulfill a natural inclination . . . Failed examinations came to his rescue and he left King's without a degree, but with friendships, some of them lifelong, originating in the Boat Club and other social activities."

" . . . He also had another pursuit and that was the search for companionship which his nature seemed to deny him. He was a member of at least three London clubs but their secretaries found him generally unclubbable. When he persuaded a guest to accompany him, he would expect undivided attention which he often secured by telling, at length, his latest ghost story. He would be furious if the company became general. Afterwards the cost would be scrupulously divided; or, if the meeting had been in a restaurant, he would consider that he had paid his share by making the arrangements and confirming them, sometimes more than once, in writing."

"He was also much teased over his apparent reluctance to relate to women."

"He had become devoted to the College and its sometimes seemed that his membership of it had freed him from a longstanding feeling of insecurity, grounded perhaps in his Jewish origins and early difficulty in education and in choosing a career."

Rereading these obituaries put me in mind of my one brush with death, which took place five floors below, when, one day, years before the two men worked downstairs, I stepped into the elevator and heard water dripping down below. Actually, it sounded more like the Hoover Dam breaking than water dripping. And so (like an idiot), I pressed the button to the basement, expecting to investigate.

When the elevator reached the basement, however, it did not stop. It descended about six inches farther before coming to an abrupt halt. There was a loud humming sound. As filthy water infused with cigarette butts and cockroaches rushed into the elevator, I tried without success to open the elevator or make it move.

Luckily, there was a phone in the elevator. I called the police and talked to someone whose interest in my plight dropped markedly once she learned there was no assailant with me in the elevator. She promised to send someone over, anyway.

By the time I had hung up with the police, the water had leveled off to the top of my thighs. Vanity set in. Or was it cheapness? I thought: "I can't believe I wore my new Fiorentina shoes!" (which, for once, I hadn't even gotten on sale). Ironically, the last time I had worn the shoes it was drizzling and I had taken a taxi in order to keep them pristine.

I called a friend who had keys to my house. He came over immediately, and informed me that the elevator ceiling was probably detachable. I maneuvered myself to the top of the elevator, as much to get out of the bilge water as to assess the damage to my shoes. I flipped off the ceiling board and shimmied up the greasy wires, praying that the elevator would not remember that I had, only minutes before, frantically pushed every button. Electrocution was a concern, but at least I would become dry. I reached the first floor. The door was locked. (I had not yet seen *Die Hard*, so I did not know that there is a lever that unlocks the door.)

I settled back into the muck. Eventually, the police showed up. My friend pointed them in the direction of the basement. After pulling on the door for a few minutes, one of the police yelled to me, "The door's stuck!" The other added, "And the elevator won't move!"

They called the emergency squad. While we waited, I listened to the police chat gaily with my friend. I felt left out and, frankly, resentful. The mood, I thought, should have been more funereal. I decided to make some phone calls. No one was home, though, so I ended up leaving about a

dozen messages on machines, all variations of "Guess where I am?" My friend told me later that the police, who did not realize there was a phone in the elevator, heard me babbling and thought I had lost my mind. Finally, the emergency squad arrived. With little ado, the door was opened.

The next day, a plumber drained six feet of water from the elevator shaft. The elevator has never been fixed. The melodramatic hand prints left when I clawed my way to the top of the elevator are still vivid. The flood, by the way, seems to have been the result of a water main break caused by Con Edison, which must have a training site on the street outside my house, given how much time they spend digging holes out there.

"You were lucky the elevator stopped where it did." The plumber told me. I'll say. The King's College Annual Report might have read:

"Suffering from delusions of grandeur, she sometimes called herself 'this alumna,' and lived far beyond her means in a large house. In fact, she was probably the poorest person in New York to have a room exclusively for her shoes. She led us to believe she was on her way up, but a police report revealed that she died on her way down."

~ *Patricia Marx*

Mixed Meditation

~Heather McAdams

Who's Calling?

It's six in the evening and I'm thinking to myself:
"Should I take spaghetti or some beans down from the shelf?
Time to cook some dinner, kick back, watch TV—
But what is this I hear—who could be calling me?"

Now, my married name's "Jaworek", which I know's hard to
pronounce—
And I don't mind announcers stumbling on it, when announced—
But when I pick up the telephone and hear someone say, "Ms. Jork?"
There's no doubt in my mind on the other end's a dork

CHORUS: "May I sell you something?
Siding? Windows? Doors?
How 'bout beachfront property at
'Washaway Shores?'"

I say, "So you're going to try and sell something to me?"
He says with pride and confidence— "Absolutely!"
While I'm listening, a little song is running through my mind:
There must be fifty ways to leave this phone salesman behind

Give the phone to your two year old who's learning how to talk
Set it by the parrot who is practicing his squawk
Tell him you're in labor, would he please call 911;
And when you hear a pregnant pause, then you know you've won

Tell him the house is burning and the fire truck's on the way,
Set the phone down on the counter and then just walk away

Tell him you are in your car and a thief is breaking in,
Put the phone up to the car alarm and let the fun begin

Tell him you've been at the dentist for a major overhaul,
(slurred speech) And you are really sorry but you just can't take his call
Pass the phone to your teenage brother who's refining his techniques
Of playing "Feelings" on his armpits and slapping on his cheeks

BRIDGE: Let your kid practice blowing his whistle,
"In the phone, son, have a ball"
Let your dog obey the command, "speak, speak"
and take over the call

When he's finished with his spiel, say, *"Je ne parle pas Anglais"*
Or "My sumo-wrestler husband's in the biz, and you're just in his way"
Or tell him you're so glad he called, you were just going to call him
You're running a deal on cemetery plots . . . would he like to get in?

~ *Debi Smith*

Phone Conversations

I want to talk about the telephone, its use and misuse. People who allow small children to answer the phone should get *the chair.*

It's a real thrill to be late for an airplane and call a business associate from a pay phone where every few minutes you have to deposit another coin to keep the thing going and you have Susie on the line saying, "Hi . . ."

"Put your daddy on the phone, dear."

"Dada gumba lot ak founa."

CHAPTER 7

"What's your name, honey?"

"My nima fa rou al unna las an to."

By the time Daddy gets on the phone I've popped a vein in my head, had three strokes, and blown a fuse.

Another heinous phone crime is the know-it-all who calls your number and says, "Is this Heidi?" I say, "Who's calling, please?"

He says: "Is this Ingrid?"

"No. Who's calling?"

"Is this Phyllis?"

"You called me. You invaded my privacy and you refuse to identify yourself. Why should you know who I am if you won't tell me who you are?"

"Who is this?"

This is when I hang up. To hell with them!

Proper phone etiquette when you are the caller is: "Jane Snoghook calling Jasper Pippingoose." This simple salutation comprising all the facts saves eighteen unnecessary sentences and prevents high blood pressure.

Another egregious error callees make is not to have pad and pencil *by the phone.*

I once called a friend whose maid, who barely spoke English, said, "Wait till I find a pencil." I waited. I was calling long-distance.

She came back and said, "Now I've got to find some paper."

She was gone from the phone so long I felt she must have gone to the store for the paper.

While I waited I wondered if she expected to memorize all messages that came in while her employer was out, including lots of complicated numbers and addresses.

I wish people who hire help who are going to answer the phone would take into consideration that most people calling speak only English in this country.

One day I called and said, "Phyllis Diller calling Joe Dunlap" and got *"Yo solamente trabajo aquí viernes y yo no se quien vive aquí."*

On another occasion I called my friend Bob Hope and got a crisp, breathy 調加上晚上 問：這兩 [illegible]

It is rude to call someone and start out "Is this Joe?" It's none of your business who has answered until you have identified yourself.

Then there's your drunk friend who calls at 3:00 A.M., the night before you're arising at 5:00 to catch a plane to London. He loves you more at 3:00 A.M. than he has ever loved you before and he tells you and tells you and tells you.

"I was just sittin' here thinkin' 'bout you and I thought I ought to call ya and tell ya how much I love you. You know, I really love you. I have always loved you and I will always love you. You know that, don't you? You and I have somethin' wunderful. It's because I love you and I keep thinkin' 'bout how I love you . . ."

Then we deal with the long-winded airhead who suffers from an advanced case of telephonitis. You are busy but he has nothing to do. He is going to go on and on ad infinitum.

I have a little electric push bell by my phone, and after a decent two minutes of senseless prattle I ring it and say, "Excuse me while I get the other line." Then I come back and say, "I have a call from Japan that I have to take. I'll call you back." Then I *leave* for Japan.

Another way to handle the long-winded caller is to have magazines and books by the telephone. One time during a call from my dear friend Helen Hopkins, I finished *Gone with the Wind.*

~ *Phyllis Diller*

Fashion Forecast

ASK MADAME LAZONGA

AND THE CUTEST PAIR OF WRIST-LENGTH GREEN SUEDE...

In old movies, women are always buying silly hats. Today it's shoes. I have 25 pairs of shoes, and yesterday I bought a pair of platform clogs that I can't even walk in! Where do we go from here?
— Teetering

DEAR TEETERING,
RELAX! WOMEN'S SILLY STYLE ZONE HAS MOVED FROM TOP TO TOE AND WILL SOON MOVE AGAIN. PEERING INTO THE CRYSTAL, I SEE THAT THE NEXT OBSESSION WILL BE...

...GLOVES!

...SO I FAXED HIM 3 COPIES...

SALE

LOOK! A SALE AT YE CHIC WRIST!

OMIGOD! LOOK AT THOSE DARLING LACE MITTS!

AND THOSE ELBOW LENGTH GLOVES WITH SEQUINS! TO DIE FOR!

IT'S EMBARRASING! I'M AN EDUCATED, SUCCESSFUL WOMAN...

...BUT I'M ADDICTED TO GLOVES!

THEY DO PROTECT YOUR HANDS...

...WHEN YOU'RE PUNCHING THROUGH THE GLASS CEILING!

© Trina Robbins 93

~ *Trina Robbins*

Just Say "PURL"

Every so often, I get what my mother calls "a bug up my ass" about something. Take what happened when I learned how to knit last fall. It started innocently enough. I was restless. I was frustrated. I wasn't having sex, and I had to do something with my hands (even masturbation gets old after a while). I figured I needed a hobby, so I enrolled in one of those Learning Annex classes where you learn everything you'll ever need to know in four sessions for about forty dollars. Sounds harmless enough, right? Absolutely *wrong.*

The first class was relatively uneventful. We chose our yarn, we got our needles, we made cute little swatches. Then, in the second class, our instructor Brenda—a woman so calm she makes Buddha look like a jumpy neurotic—handed out the pattern for our first project, a sleeveless sweater top. I cast on my ninety stitches in a desultory fashion and started to knit. Suddenly, I realized this thing was growing. I swear I'd never seen anything like it in my life. I was gone. I was possessed. Working, dating, breathing, eating—nothing, repeat, *nothing,* was as important as creating another teal-blue inch of sweater.

Knitting also turned out to be the perfect hobby for a compulsive shopper like me. There are so many wonderful little doodads you need: row counters, stitch holders, cable needles, swatch gauges, and on and on. Ecstatically, I swooped into yarn stores and bought everything I could lay my hands on. Store owners broke out party horns when they saw me coming.

My mother was the first to notice the telltale signs. The poor woman already suffers from latent hysteria because I'm thirty-something and there's not a potential husband in sight. When she called on Saturday night and found me home happily knitting away, she really began to panic. "You're, um . . . you're not giving up your social life to knit, are you?" she'd

ask, desperately trying to sound casual. "Of course not, Mother," I'd lie, guiltily remembering the party at Tavern on the Green I'd skipped because I wanted to finish my armholes. But mothers know everything, and when mine started referring to me as "my daughter, the knitting spinster," I recklessly decided to show her that I had my habit under control. So I went out on a date.

Mike was a perfectly nice guy. A stockbroker with a co-op, he might even be called a catch. We went to a movie, where I busied myself trying to figure out the cable patterns on the sweaters of fellow audience members. At dinner after the movie, Mike told me what he was up to, and I pretended to listen. "Uh-huh," I nodded, wondering how many extra stitches I'd have to cast on to make a double moss Aran panel in a medium-weight cotton.

"So what's going on in your life," he asked, finally snapping me out of my reverie. "Oh," I said, trying to clear my brain. "Well . . . I've been asked to write a book, and I have two plays being published, and I just interviewed Shirley MacLaine, Geraldine Ferraro, and Ivana Trump all on the same day, but the *big* news is I've learned how to knit. Let me tell you about it . . ."

Several hours later, as a bleary-eyed Mike knocked back another scotch, I wound up my saga. Sadly, he didn't know a doctor who could cure me of my wool allergy, thus enabling me to knit in something besides cotton (no self-respecting knitter *ever* uses acrylic), so I didn't see much point in continuing the relationship. Oddly enough, Mike seemed to feel the same way. When I called him the next day to get his feedback on a men's sweater pattern, he muttered something about having to wash his hair and hung up so quickly my telephone rang back.

Things rapidly went downhill from there. On New Year's Eve, I was dying to stay home and start a new sweater, but my roommate talked me into going out. I knit on the subway as I traveled from one party to another. Stumped by a rib stitch pattern I was working on, I cornered revelers at each affair, sticking my swatch under their noses and demanding their opinions. I perfunctorily joined the New Year countdown, then beat a faster retreat than Cinderella when she fled from the ball. Home at long last, I breathed a sigh of relief and ushered in the New Year with four inches of ribbing.

I was fast reaching the point where a month at the Betty Ford Clinic weaning myself from my knitting needles seemed a real possibility. Then I tried on my sweater. Unfortunately, it turned out that I'd accidentally cast on eighty stitches instead of ninety, and the top fit like a slightly loose tourniquet. Staring at myself in the mirror glumly, I began mentally adding the costs involved in achieving this fashion disaster. There was the price of the course, the forty dollars I'd spent on yarn, the umpteen dollars I'd spent on various knitting accessories. Winding up my calculations, I realized that it had cost me about $150 to make a sweater I wouldn't have paid twenty bucks for in a store.

That cold blast of reality quickly helped break my knitting addiction. But have I given up the habit? Hardly. I just bought some great red yarn and a huge kit of needles. At the end of the day, my roommate usually finds me sitting in the old rocker, shawl over my shoulders, granny glasses atop my nose, knitting and purling to my heart's content. I've spent hours in therapy warding off the fear that I would eventually turn into my mother. Whoever thought that I'd actually turn into my *grandmother?!*

~ Ellen Byron

Remote Control

I've got a *Remote* for my TV
so I can see *Remote* broadcasts of *Remote* news.
I order catalog items from *Remote* places with my *Remote* phone.
Why I've even got a boyfriend with *Remote* emotions.
I feel like such a modern woman.
I'm not in control . . . I'm in *Remote* control.

~ *Flash Rosenberg*

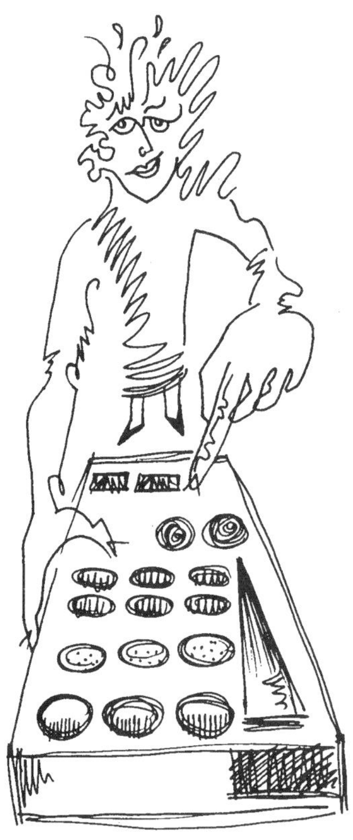

Ambition, And Other Terrible Secrets

I remember the instant that I learned to read.

My family was in the military; we'd been stationed in Barcelona for two years. I'd been attending a Spanish preschool, a sort of paradise where we sang songs and acted out Snow White and the Seven Dwarfs, and I was Snow White.

Then abruptly I was in a different school, a British school, south of Barcelona. My brother and I were brought here for ten days so we would speak English again. Our family was to be transferred back to the States, to a small military base on the Florida Panhandle, where I was to begin first grade.

In the British school, we sat in desks, the kind that lift up. We passed around a *Dick and Jane* reader, each child taking a turn reading aloud the same page, as the book went around the room. I was the youngest in the class, but the British teacher seemed to assume that I knew how to read, and I wanted to accommodate her. When I was handed the book, I fastened my eyes on the page, and repeated from memory what had been read aloud by the girl before me. Then I handed the book on.

This was my huge, mortifying secret—I loved books, but I did not know how to read. Now I was living this lie. At recess, I would squat inside a little clump of bushes, so that no one would talk to me, because I was a liar, a non-reader.

I asked my mother to teach me to read. She was overwhelmed with packing; "They're supposed to do that at school." So every day I went to school, and every day the book came around, and when it did, I fastened my eyes on the page, and repeated what had been said by the girl before me.

If I had committed a crime, I could not have lived in greater fear of discovery. I developed hives.

CHAPTER 7

I had been in the school for eight days when the teacher called me to her desk. My terror was complete. In her hand was the *Dick and Jane* reader. She opened it randomly to a page, and pointed. "Read this."

I stared at the indecipherable page, sick with desperation and guilt. And something happened. A light broke over my forehead, like a wave washing over my head, and a feeling of great warmth and light descended from the very crown of my skull, inside my head, and spread down through my shoulders, to my fingertips.

I was illuminated. As I stared at the first line on the page, I recognized the words as if I had written them myself. I read aloud, "See Spot run. Run Spot run." I turned the page, and read on. I read the entire book aloud to my teacher. Something had happened! A revelation, it was a gift!

If I had received a vision of heaven, I would not have been more ecstatic.

I came home, and said to my distracted mother, "I can read." I seized an American cereal box, and read the thing aloud to her. I was swelled with the joy and power of knowing how. I attempted any word. I was fearless. "I want a book," I said.

This week, a poet, Thomas Lux, was honored with the Kingsley Tufts Poetry Award at the Claremont Graduate School. The award carries with it a monetary prize of $50,000—which gives us a clue as to why poetry ended up in the news.

The *L.A. Times* describes the poet's romantically obscure upbringing: growing up on a small dairy farm in western Massachusetts, his father the town's milkman, his mother answering the phone at Sears, Roebuck, all his other relatives working at a "grim, decaying factory," the article says.

And then this telling sentence: "A bookish boy, Thomas Lux found his way to words at the town library. The Russian novelists, Dostoevsky in particular, unleashed in him joys he could barely fathom."

This is my guess: If we could poll every writer writing today, an enormous percentage of them would say, "It all began for me at the public library . . . "In fact, I don't know where else it *could* begin.

Panama City Beach is in the Florida Panhandle, on the Gulf Coast, tucked right up under Georgia and Alabama. Panama City had a public library, but little Panama City Beach did not. P.C. Beach was a long, skinny, thirty-mile sand spit—more or less connected to the world by a bridge on either end.

And what we had was the bookmobile. The woman who drove the bookmobile— "my bookmobile," as I called it—had a Dickensian name, Miss Lumpkin. She wore a gray crewcut. My military father, who prided himself on his ability to detect homosexuals, referred to her as a "thwarted woman."

I was eight years old, and I knew what Miss Lumpkin was—she was a godsend.

Once a week, Miss Lumpkin drove up in front of the Snake-a-torium next door to our house—this was a dinky little reptile zoo that was open only during the summer. They had a little parking area in front, paved with crushed oyster shells. Miss Lumpkin parked the bookmobile right there on the side of Highway 98, where I was already waiting, with last week's towering stack of books piled up in my arms.

And she had something for me. Every week, Miss Lumpkin had something that she had found especially for me.

In retrospect, I see what a challenge it must have been for her to stock her bookmobile with something new, something that would always take me further as a reader. And I was amazed that she knew just what to bring me—some weeks she brought five, six, ten chapter books, each one more resonant than the last.

"How did you like *that* book?" Miss Lumpkin would ask the next week, and then we would talk books. "It began slow but I liked the middle part a lot—'though I didn't really believe it when that lady let Anne stay at Green Gables . . ."

I knew all the authors' names, I read the cover flaps as hungrily as I read the novels—I wanted the *details* of the authors' lives. They all seemed to live in Connecticut. *Conn-ect-i-cut.* By God, I would go to Conn-ect-i-cut someday.

Miss Lumpkin made me feel extraordinary: in her eyes, I was the sort of child who was worthy of being brought books, books especially chosen for me. I wasn't invisible. Magically enough, I was known to Miss Lumpkin. I had revealed myself to her by what I wanted to read. She was a diviner of souls.

Miss Lumpkin made me real, by asking me the most important question a child can ever hear: "What do you think?"

All my childhood I had an extended fantasy of becoming a writer *and* a librarian, at the same time . . . Driving a bookmobile around as I typed away . . . The freedom of that image carried me a long way, let me tell you.

Later, when I bought a car with my first earnings as a screenwriter, I had a profoundly wonderful dream. I was in my new car, driving on an open highway. It was night, and the car was all around me like a dark, safe place. And instead of a steering wheel, my IBM Selectric II was set into the dashboard, and I steered my course by writing.

From a speech delivered at "The Library Breakfast," during National Library Week.

~Robin Swicord

Oh, Darling!

I remember when I first heard the word "lesbos." It was in the fourth grade. Our two most popular girls, Andrea and Barbara, were taking turns sitting on each other and laughing under the upper-field staircase at lunch. Me and my friend Gloria Iguchi leaned our heads under and said,

"What are you guys doing?" They said, "We're lesbos." After that, me and Gloria said we were also lesbos, and by third recess, it had spread to all the girls. Any girl who couldn't find someone to be lesbos with was out. It was the new main thing of my whole class.

When our teacher found out, I remember how she sent all the boys to Mr. Leclair's room and then pulled down the shades. I thought she was going to show us a filmstrip, but instead Mrs. Hallagan, the school nurse, came in. She told us she had a serious subject to talk about. Then she asked if we understood the word we were using. "Who can tell me what it means?" No one raised their hand. She told us that lesbian was not a joke. "Lesbian is when a girl wants to marry another girl." I remember thinking, what's so big about that? Every girl I knew wanted to marry her best friend. Then she told us it was a hateful idea to God. "God can forgive you for using a word when you don't know what it means, but after that, girls," she said, "He just forgets about you." I remember how some of the girls started crying and how our teacher thanked her, then told us to put our heads down and think about Mrs. Hallagan's message.

It wasn't until the sixth grade that I found out why a lesbo is perverted. It's the girl-opposite of a boy queer.

I was remembering this story because of Vicky Talluso, my best friend who can't sleep over anymore, ever since my mom opened the door to my room and caught Vicky showing me the special way Hector Hernandez does his arms when he slow dances, how he holds one of your hands behind your back and breathes air on your ear in a romantic Mexican way. The song "Oh, Darling" came on the radio and Vicky put her arms around me, showing me the way Hector tries to feel your boobs by holding you tighter and tighter and she was going "Oh, my darling *señorita*" in my ear just as a joke and then I hear the doorknob turn and my mom yells my name the way someone yells when you're about to get hit by a car. "What?" I say. "Come downstairs," she tells me.

In the kitchen my mom whisper-shouts at me to tell her what in the hell was going on up there. "Can you give me one good reason for you and

that Talluso dancing like that?" There was no way I could tell her about the Hector Hernandez Mexican boob feel.

"Mom."

"Don't mom me. It's not right, things could happen."

"Like what?"

"Things."

"Mom," I say, but she tells me to get upstairs and tell Vicky it's time to go home.

"Great," Vicky says. "Now your mom thinks we're lesbos."

"That's not what she thinks," I say. "She has a migraine." It's not that I want to stick up for my mother, I just don't want to get known as someone whose mom thinks her friends are lesbians.

"Oh, sure," Vicky says. "Oh, come off it."

When I walk Vicky to the door, my mom and her say goodbye so normally that for a second I thought I had imagined the whole thing.

After the door shuts, my mother says for me to sit down on the couch. I watched her smoking with her arms crossed and deciding that I was too old to have friends stay overnight anymore. I didn't say anything because a lot of times with my mom, it's just a case of her being in a mood. If you fight with her about it, it only helps the new rule to stick in her mind.

That night I had a dream where I was with Hector Hernandez and he asked me if I wanted to see his coffeepot and his hair kept getting longer and he was wearing a nightgown and then he turned into Jesus. He was kissing me and feeling my boobs and I was getting so excited but I was trying not to because I knew it was wrong to get excited by Jesus. He kept pressing down on me until I noticed he had giant boobs and smelled like Luv's Fresh Lemon Scent and then I looked and his face was suddenly Vicky.

I opened my eyes and freaked out. I wondered which was I going to hell for most, Jesus or Vicky Talluso?

I also had to wonder, was I secretly a lesbian? Dreams don't come by themselves. Anyone who has taken Health knows they are psychological.

The next day at school I kept noticing my eyes going out of control and landing on girls' boobs. When I was changing in gym, Vicky and this other girl Joan were right by me and I was so scared about my eyes that I couldn't even look at them. "You're such a snob today," Vicky said. Then she says, "Can you get this for me?" and what it was, was her earring wouldn't go through.

"Let Joan do it," I say.

"Thanks a lot," Vicky says. "I don't get you today. Are you mad at me about that thing with your mom?"

Joan says, "What thing with your mom?" and I feel my face get hot.

"Okay, okay. Here. I'll do it," I say. "Give it." She hands me the earring.

"She's the only one who can do this ear," Vicky says, and when I lean over I can smell her Luv's Fresh Lemon Scent.

"Hey! OUCH! What are you trying to do, kill me?"

~Lynda Barry

Chain Letters

A chain letter came in the mail the other day. I have never been able to make myself respond to one of these. Nothing in my experience so far has given me any reason to believe that if I agree to send a dollar bill to a stranger and then send a really annoying letter to ten of my "friends" (obviously either really close, incredibly understanding friends, or friends whose opinion of me doesn't concern me a whit), then ten thousand other strangers will each send *me* a dollar bill in the mail. By next week. Right.

Well, suppose it worked? I guess I'd go check my P.O. Box and get one of those little yellow cards telling me I have something that won't fit in the box. Telling me that I have in fact more mail today than I would normally receive in over five years. According to my calculations, this stack of mail would be about 25 feet tall. (I guess the postal workers would just put it in five, 5-foot-tall stacks.) Does a letter weigh half an ounce? If it does, then how am I going to get my 312.5 lbs. of mail out of there? Even if I carry 20 lbs. a trip, I'll still have to make sixteen trips out to the car. Think how ridiculous I'll feel by say even the fifth trip back to the window, grinning at the postal worker, telling him it's some sort of survey I sent out, (since as far as I know chain letters are illegal). How will these ten thousand letters fit in my car? Maybe I'll get a ticket for driving with a totally obstructed view. Then when I do get home (after another sixteen trips from the car to the house), I can open all ten thousand envelopes. I think that will take about 14 hours, allowing 5 seconds per envelope. Guess I'll want to get an early start that day. Of course I'll want to count the money and it would take almost 2 hours to count ten thousand bills. The bank teller will be able to do it faster, I'd probably only be at the window an hour and a half. During the 16 hours I'm sitting on the floor opening envelopes and counting money, I hope no one stops by.

~ Cheryl Wheeler

Edith Ann

my life, so far

Dear Edith

I know you're no expert, but do you know why your mind wanders?

Love,
Puzzled

Dear Puzzled:

The mind gets tired of having to come up with thoughts all the time and so it wanders off to get peace of mind. So it can have a 5-minute coffee break and come back fresh and alert ready to take more of all that stuff your brain drums up.

Edith Ann

I thought this answer was a good one, but there is a lot on this topic I don't get. How can your mind just wander off on its own—with no warning, no "excuse me please, do you mind if I wander?" Does your mind have its own mind? Does your mind make plans to go away from the constant stress of having to wait around till you make up your mind about something?

What's it thinking about when you're not thinking about anything? When you draw a blank and can't remember something, is it your mind's fault? And when you suddenly can recall something you'd forgotten, what's going on inside your brain?

Is forgetting something a relief to the mind? Is it like your memory is taking a vacation or something?

Am I using my brain or is my brain using me?

Where does a new thought come from?

When you want to forget something that happened why can't you just forget it? What is it that won't let you forget?

Your mind will help you make up a lie—then turns right around and makes you feel guilty that you lied.

When you tell yourself, "it's all in your mind," you're telling it all to your mind.

Who else is even listening when we talk to ourselves? We don't have to talk out loud. Does that mean the brain has its own ears?

When you have a closed mind, is it your mind doing the opening and closing or is it the total you?

Why does your brain help you figure out certain things—but on other things may just add to the confusion?

When I say, "What am I thinking?" what do I mean by that and why should I even have to ask these questions about my own mind?

When I understand something, did I just use my brain to help me understand this something or is my brain just making me think I understand?

Why is it so often I don't know what I'm going to think of next? Why don't I know? If our hearts behaved this way, we'd all be dead as doornails.

~*Jane Wagner*

Six Pretty Good Things to Do with the 90 Percent of Your Brain That You Don't Use

or Que Cerebrum, Cerebrum

Since science and watching reruns of "Gidget" show us that we're only using 10 percent—imagine that!—of our brains, here are some useful and entertaining ways to get mileage out of that lazybone of yours. Pick one, or combine them as your enthusiasm dictates:

1. Time Share. Let other people into the back of your head. After all, a little company isn't a bad thing and neighborliness is almost next to godliness. And if you time share now, you have a built-in retirement plan for when you decide to leave that part of the brain that you're in. When you advertise your time share, just remember the realtor's rule of thumb here: LOCATION-LOCATION-LOCATION. Your functional brain is awfully nice to be next to. You enjoy tennis, water sports, and are a fabulous Scrabble player. If that doesn't do it, promise Sony walkmans just for visiting.

2. Add Post-It Notes. Face it, that adhesive on those post-it notes is going to be in our atmosphere forever. So instead of trying to recycle, use that empty 90 percent of brain up there to attach little bits of information to the big stuff you have going on in the other 10 percent. For example, your functional brain knows, "I have to take the dog out for a walk at 9:15 tomorrow morning."

You then add to that:

- 9:15 is when that cute guy next door comes out for his morning paper
- doesn't he work?
- call Gloria who lives in 2F and see if she knows what he does for a living
- and be sure to pick up a half liter of soda while you're out because you want to be prepared in case he gets your bill again for the ungainly sum you promised to PBS during "The Three Tenors, Live at Disney World" and he brings it over in the afternoon.

3. Decorate. Any good interior designer will tell you this can make even an uninhabitable place livable. Of course, these are people who would sell couches to Tarzan if they had half the chance. But if chintz seems too patently busy, think space . . . think open . . . think

CHRISTO!

The empty 90 percent of your brain is THE PERFECT project for you and Christo. Not gauze . . . he's already done umbrellas . . . Why, he could Venetian blind the hell out of your head; and how symbolic, and so perfect for summer! Just imagine, a state-of-the-art "*son et lumiere*" (sound

and light) show every evening. We hear strains of "Evita" as lights play off strategically placed blinds opening and closing, like so many petals of a flower, like so many borders in the Ukraine, like so many doors on refrigerators everywhere. Art is truly universal, and it's being created in your very own brain, not to mention the great kickbacks you'll get from selling souvenirs. And getting decorated is like buying a new outfit—it puts you in a new frame of mind which is, after all, what we're going for here.

4. Install Astro Turf. The Olympics are never that far away, and why shouldn't 90 percent of your brain be the host? The biggest problem is housing facilities but, hey, you're providing the rest of it, so visiting countries can find their own lousy place to stay. Just remember to keep the opening ceremonies as simple and plebian as possible—say a few tarantellas from Aunt Ethel's Tap and Dance School, maybe even throw in some baton twirling in squirrel outfits—and the Olympics should go on without a hitch. And just think, you'll have front row seats!

5. Order Out. Have a phone installed in that cavernous brainspace and hook it up to your central nervous system. *Voila!* The minute you're hungry, you've already speed-dialed an appropriate restaurant with delivery service. If you're really ready to take the plunge, you can have their itemized entrées also programmed so there's no more hemming and hawing over what to get or dealing with itinerant order takers who never really seem to know whether garlic macaroni and cheese is on the menu as an entrée or a side dish. WHO CARES? Your order is quickly taken over the fax machine, with no one to fax but fax itself.

6. Rewrite Your Favorite Books, Movies, and TV Shows. This time give yourself the starring role. You can also create fashion houses, governments, even famous family histories with you in them. It's *Mutiny on the Bounty* starring who? Why, YOU! . . . It's none other than Guess Who as Tina Turner, but it's only Tina-in-the-Good-Years (you know, post-Ike). Okay, or you could be a Kennedy in Tina Turner's body. . .whatever strikes your fancy. Be publicized . . . anglicized . . . immortalized . . . Go on and alter your Ego. Mix and match. After all, you have plenty of space to get it right in your very own "Playhouse 90 Percent."

~Laura Kuritzky Pedegana

The Urban Naturalist

~Roz Chast

CHAPTER 7

In the "Family" Way

Once upon a time, when a woman declared her homosexuality, she could be assured of at least one thing: escaping society's (and her parents') expectation of children. Not anymore. During a visit home a few years ago, my father stunned me by following up his obligatory question, "Think you'll move back to New Jersey?" with a new one: "Are you and Lori considering children?"

His inquiry left me speechless, while at the same time informing me that lesbianism was no excuse for not adding to the pool of grandchildren.

Of course, dykes and their kids aren't really news: there have always been lesbians who have children within heterosexual relationships. After coming out, these women simply raised their children on their own or with a lesbian partner.

And, way back when (before AIDS and trendy lesbian parenting), if a dyke wanted a baby, she merely went to a bar, selected a man with pleasing physical attributes and a reasonable I.Q., engaged in a 3-minute heterosexual act, and—hopefully—found herself pregnant the following month. As detached and clinical as this image might be, it *was* an efficient conception method. The hardest part was dealing with the lesbians who considered motherhood a "manipulative patriarchal construct."

Alas, things are not so simple anymore. Now, there are so many choices! We have doctors providing in-office inseminations with medical-student frozen sperm. Then there are elaborate and complicated sperm banks, where one chooses a donor based not only on physical appearance, musical ability. and favorite hobbies, but also on his answers to required essays such as "Why I Am Donating My Sperm" and "Message to My Future Child."

If all this seems too futuristic, you can bypass the anonymous donor approach and go with someone you know. You can select a donor based on whether he will be a supportive co-parent, won't sue for custody rights, or stay out of your life—depending on your personal preference.

There is also the semi-anonymous donor, in which case you find a trusted friend to run interference. Only this person knows both the donor's and the mother's identity. Additionally, there is the double security method: one middle-person knows only who donated the sperm, and a second middle-person knows only who received it. I'm sure there's a purpose to this kind of arrangement, but I've yet to figure out what it is.

My favorite arrangement is when a brother of the partner not carrying the baby donates the sperm. The neat part here is that one partner becomes the mother and the other becomes the aunt, giving her a legal relationship to the child. Also, both women's parents become grandparents, which can be helpful or problematic depending on their opinion of lesbian motherhood.

Now, you may be wondering why I'm writing about babies. Am I pregnant? No. Is Lori pregnant? No. Are we working on it? No. Am I considering it? Only in the most abstract, eight-years-from-now, if-I-have-a-steady-income-and-stable-emotional-state-kind of way.

Babies? Heck, I still haven't managed to get in touch with my lover's inner child, much less any flesh and blood versions we might create. Right now, feline children are the only babies for which I'm willing to take responsibility.

Still, I like human kids. Just last spring, I signed on for a 3-hour child patrol shift—that is, I told my friend Annie I'd watch her daughter while she went to an appointment.

At the time, Stella was nearly two and immensely fascinated with every aspect of the world. Normally, I would have been content to examine pencils, rubber bands, and shoelaces right along with her; that day, however, I was in "accomplish mode."

Feeling restless, I proposed a stroll to the grocery store, a mere five blocks away. Stella agreed. I asked her if she wanted to ride in the stroller. No, she wanted to walk. So off we went. A half block from the house, I realized I hadn't counted on something: toddlers walk very slowly. Unlike walking an overeager dog, I was not dragged ahead, but instead had to take a step, wait, take a step, wait some more. It wasn't so much that Stella had shorter legs than I; it was simply that just as every pencil, rubber band, and shoelace had been marvelous and mysterious, so now was every stick, pebble, and blade of grass. After two interminable blocks, I had a brainstorm: I decided to carry Stella on my shoulders.

I soon realized there was something else I hadn't counted on: since I'd seen her last, Stella had gotten bigger. And heavier. Nonetheless, through an alternating pattern of carrying and toddling, we eventually reached our destination.

The walk home was even slower, since I couldn't carry both the groceries and Stella, who paused to examine cracks in the sidewalk, large rocks, and a variety of bugs.

Fortunately, Annie met us half way, and with a mother's muscles, hoisted Stella up for the remainder of the walk. As we journeyed on home, she asked, "Why didn't you take the stroller?"

"Stella said she didn't need it," I replied.

Annie laughed. "The point of a stroller is not that Stella needs it. It's that you need it. Unless, of course, you want every walk to proceed at ten inches per hour."

Clearly, I have a lot to learn about being a mother. Guess I'll go practice on the cat.

~ Ellen Orleans

Meet Your Family

I was spending a miserable Thanksgiving in Penn Station.
Trains weren't departing but people kept arriving until the place
was packed with squalling kids and weary parents . . .
and me, strangely envious:
Where's MY husband? Where're MY kids? How does that happen?
And then I discovered the secret:
Will Doris Johnson please come and meet her husband and children
at the Information Booth?
Aah Haa! So I waited there all day listening for:
Will Flash Rosenberg please come and meet her husband and children
at the Information Booth?
So I could rush over and introduce myself.
I always knew I had a family here somewhere.
We just haven't been paged to meet yet.

~ Flash Rosenberg

Caroline's Cremation

It's *Caroline's Cremation*
And we hope to see you there
We're on five nights a week
Plus Sunday matinee—with prayer
It's Off-Off Broadway's newest
Biggest latest hottest show
Come help send up dear Caroline
As she'd have liked to go

It's *Caroline's Cremation*
A bonanza family treat
John Simon gave it three thumbs up,
One finger, and both feet
So come on down and mourn with us
And please do not be late
You know how crazy Caroline gets
When people make her wait

Shake hands with her ex-lover
And his madly jealous wife
And Caroline's dear spouse
To whom she would have owed her life
If when he'd seen her face turn green
He hadn't lost his head
And fled the scene while she lay
Limp and twitching on the bed

Meet kindly Doctor Harris
Whose certificate of death
Was signed before dear Caroline
Had drawn her final breath
And Oscar the mortician
Who with admirable haste
Made all the preparations
In impeccable good taste

You'll hug all nine of Caroline's
Distraughtly weeping heirs
Who held the dear departed's life
More dear to them than theirs:
They'll *prove* they never planned
To push her wheelchair down the stairs

At last—the act climaxes
As the coffin disappears
And Caroline goes up in smoke
With all of us in tears . . .
Now intermission opens with
A long and moving sermon
And solos by the pastor's wife—
Who looks like Ethel Merman

While waiting to reclaim
The former contents of the casket
We're served a catered wake
With home-baked chicken-in-the-basket
Then we pick the dear departed up
At window number four
And as the house lights dim again
We're headed toward the shore

The second act moves quickly
As the mourners gather round
And scatter dear old Caroline
Across Long Island Sound
We hate to say good-bye
But time, alas, is kind of tight:
We must break in a fresh new corpse
From Equity
By eight o'clock
Tomorrow night . . .

. . . For *Caroline's Cremation*
And we hope to see you there
We're on five nights a week
Plus Sunday matinee—with prayer
It's Off-Off Broadway's newest
Biggest latest hottest show
Come help send up dear Caroline
As she'd have liked to go

~*June Siegel*

Scam

> My ex-husband left this morning for Bermuda to play in a tennis tournament, leaving me his dog, who is too big for my house; our kids; and instructions on how to get into his house through a second-story window in case of an emergency.

Here's a sure-fire money maker: a story in less than fifty words. Typed onto index cards, stories like that could hang from the rear-view mirror in a car for something to think about during traffic jams. Or against the Lavoris at the dentist's office to work from during drillings. Or on the bathroom mirror for flossing time.

Well, look: from this one you know a lot about her. You know she's divorced and has kids. If you're paying attention, you know she shares custody because otherwise he wouldn't have left the kids with her, he would have just left.

You know her ex is rich. Relatively. I mean you don't exactly know that some weeks she doesn't have enough money to do the laundry, but you know she has a small house, and he's got a big one plus airplane tickets, and you could surmise that he survived the divorce nicely. You could assume he's got old money, since Bermuda's a place for preppies. And you'd be right.

You know he's an athlete. I mean he's old enough to have kids and he's still gallivanting off to play tennis. From the bit about the second-story window you could assume that she's an athlete, too. Or that he's too much of a schmuck to have made a second key.

If you're still at it, you could wonder whether she always falls for preppies. Whether she's remarried or has a lover. You could wonder about the kids—sex, age, smarts. Are they preppies? Not without constant clean laundry.

But you know that she's a respectable person, because he doesn't expect her to steal stuff from his house or read his diary or anything.

Actually, he's an idiot. Because that's exactly what I'm going to do. There's probably some great material for my index cards up there.

~ *Taffy Field*

Dishwater Rhyme

~ *Sherrie Shepherd*

Three Dreams: South Bronx

1. Three bridges: Whitestone, Triborough, Throgs Neck line up across the Harlem River. I cross one (I don't remember which) into the Bronx and walk up and down Westchester Avenue looking for a dry cleaner. I have one blouse with mud, or blood, some stain. Nightfall, iron gates roar down store windows, streets empty, corners fill up. I find a dry cleaner, but it's really a methadone clinic . . . .They say they do dry cleaning though, so I say okay.

2. School dreams: I beg the principal for my old job back. I was wrong to walk out on 120 students in a district with the lowest reading scores in New York. He says, "I knew you couldn't take the ghetto heat." I protest, "No, it's only I fell in love, went South, and I've never been responsible to begin with." I wait in the lounge with Kathy Kimtis and the 6th grade reading teacher who'd been chasing me since September, calling me Lola, Lola Montez, adventuress and seducer of kings. As if Lola would set foot in the South Bronx. "Lola, Lola, are you back forever?" "Oh no, only until June—correcting my mistake." My classes back: Tariq, Barkim, Evelyn Perez, all the familiar faces, but I don't teach them. I don't talk. I sit on the window ledge staring at vacant lots sprouting rusted mattress springs, refrigerator parts, treadless tires, and the gutted hulls of Art Deco buildings. I won't last two days. I can't teach reading. I can't teach anything.

3. The three bridge dream again: This time I'm on the Bronx side trying to get back to Queens except they've raised the toll. All I have is a two dollar bridge token, but the toll is two hundred. Under the glow of topaz and emerald lights, I wail, "How will I get out of the South Bronx?" The toll clerk says, "Yo, baby, tha's your problem."

~ *Susan Montez*

Unsolved Mysteries

~*Heather McAdams*

Looking Back and Commenting on Stuff

I hung out with a pretty depressed crowd in high school. On Friday nights we'd pile into a car and go joyless riding. I was suicidal at the time, but I didn't believe in violence and was a bit of a health nut. One night I decided to end it all by drinking gallons and gallons of Sleepytime Tea. The doctors said I lived only because it hadn't steeped enough. To this day I have bladder trouble.

My high school days have been on my mind lately because I recently received a letter from my old guidance counselor. That dedicated woman tracked me down after all these years because she discovered that a mistake had been made with my aptitude test results, and it turns out I wasn't gifted after all. In fact, my potential is much, much lower than originally assessed, and she wanted to let me know. I'm still not sure how I feel about this—I've spent years in therapy thinking I'm an underachiever—and now it turns out I'm an overachiever. My analyst pointed out that I was now free to address other issues. So I signed up for a class on self-love through the Learning Annex. It was called "How to Win Your Own Heart." And I did everything they said. I bought myself flowers. And candy. *Lots* of candy. I took long walks in the park. I held hands. After awhile, though, I sensed that it wasn't going anywhere, that there was no real commitment on my part, so I broke it off. I didn't have the guts to do it face to face, though—I called and left a message on my answering machine. I said, "Look, it's nothing personal, I just don't have room for you in my life right now . . . Okay, the *truth* is I was only in it for the sex—*which,* by the way, was *terrific!*" I was hoping I could still be friends, but at this point I'm too angry. I feel used.

Despite everything you may have heard, not all of us have a "child within." I, for instance, have a convicted felon within. I want him out. He won't leave. I've taken steps to have him evicted. He's formed a tenant's association. They're taking me to court. If I lose, I can't go co-op.

I've got this book on obsessive behavior! Couldn't put it down! It said, if you want to avoid obsessive thought patterns, place a rubber band around your wrist. Whenever you catch yourself obsessing, snap the band. It will hurt, and eventually those obsessive thoughts will cease. So I did it. For a while. I did it until my wrists became bloody and desensitized, at which point I decided that it would be wiser to go back to inflicting emotional pain on myself. So I started dating. I had just seen *Beauty and the Beast* for the seventh time, and felt myself strongly attracted to the Beast. I vowed to pay closer attention to cloven-hoofed animals in the future—just the wealthy, literate ones, of course, who lived in castles and dressed well. Certain that there was a Beast out there just for me ("a lid for every pot," as the saying goes), I answered some personal ads. I tried to curb my tendency to project too much onto the other person but I had so much hope that I just couldn't. At last, though, sitting across the table from me one evening was a guy who also projected! He assumed, based on my demeanor, that I had a tragic past, and he was intrigued. Looking deeply into my eyes he said, "Ah, mysterious, sorrowful Kate. Talk to me. Tell me about the great love of your life. The one who kicked your heart out and left you crushed, broken, without a shred of dignity." And I looked right back at him, faith shining in my eyes, and said, "I'm hoping it's you!."

~ Kate Shein

Contributors

SYBIL ADELMAN (185) is an established television writer, recipient of the Writers Guild of America Award, and was nominated for an Emmy for *Lily* (a Lily Tomlin special). A resident of New York City, she collaborates with her husband, Martin Sage.

LYNDA BARRY (332) is an author, playwright, illustrator, and cartoonist. Her play, *The Good Times are Killing Me*, has been performed in New York and throughout the United States. She lives in Evanston, Illinois.

JENNIFER BERMAN'S (75, 167, 288) self-syndicated cartoon "Berman," can be seen in *The Chicago Reader, The Detroit News*, and several other choice publications around the country. She is the owner of Humerus Cartoons, a postcard company which features her work. Jennifer Berman has written three books, *Why Dogs Are Better Than Men, Adult Children of Normal Parents*, and *Why Dogs Are Better Than Republicans*. She lives in Chicago with three dogs and a cat.

JENNY BICKS (50) has written on staff for numerous network sitcoms. She has also written for Comedy Central, MTV, and The American Comedy Network. In her free time she writes jokes for President Clinton. A native New Yorker, Bicks now lives in Los Angeles.

MARY KAY BLAKELY (45) is a contributing editor for both *MS.* magazine and *The Los Angeles Times Sunday Magazine*. Her essays on social and political issues have appeared in *The New York Times, The Washington Post, Vogue, Life, Mother Jones, Mirabella*, and other national publications. She is the author of *Wake Me When It's Over* and *American Mom — Motherhood, Politics, and Humble Pie*. Her latest book is *Red, White, and Oh So Blue, Memoir of a Political Depression*. A native of Chicago, Blakely now lives in Manhattan and teaches at The New School for Social Research.

ERMA BOMBECK (216), born, raised and educated in Dayton, Ohio, became the author of more than a dozen books, her columns syndicated in over 700 newspapers. She began her writing career as a "copy girl" for the *Dayton Journal Herald*, where she found her career niche. She raised three children, and until her recent death, she and her husband lived in Arizona. Her best-selling books include, *The Grass is Always Greener Over the Septic Tank, I Want To Go Home, I Want To Grow Hair, I Want To Go To Boise,* and her last book, *All I Know About Animal Behavior I Learned in Loehmann's Dressing Room*.

PAIGE BRADDOCK (94, 253) is a graduate of the University of Tennessee with a degree in Fine Arts. After working at the *Chicago Tribune* as a staff artist, she moved to Atlanta where she is Graphics Editor for the *Atlanta Journal-Constitution*. She is a full member of the National Cartoonist Society and creator of the cartoon series "See Jane."

BARBARA BRANDON (64), a New York native, is the country's only nationally-syndicated black female cartoonist. Her "Where I'm Coming From" strip, originally published in the lifestyle pages of the *Detroit Free Press* is now carried by Universal Press Syndicate. An alumna of Syracuse University's College of Visual and Performing Arts, Brandon lives in Brooklyn, New York.

MICHELE BROURMAN (168, 253), winner of the 1994 Johnny Mercer Songwriter Award, is one of the featured songwriters on Nostalgia Television's two-hour special *A Tribute to Johnny Mercer*, filmed at Washington D.C.'s Smithsonian Institute. Her songs have been recorded by Margaret Whiting, Olivia Newton-John, Michael Feinstein, Cleo Laine, Amanda McBroom, Thelma Houston, and Billy Stritch. Brourman has composed music for television, as well as the original Broadway production of Stud Terkel's *Working*. Currently completing a new musical, *Josie & the Women of Tombstone*, Brourman is married to television producer Steve Silas. They have two sons, Noah and Luke.

BULBUL'S (27) cartoons appear in labor, feminist, senior, environmental, and alternative publications. Her work has also appeared in many books. Bulbul is her pen name, which in Middle Eastern poetry is a bird of protest. She lives and works in Mountain View, California.

BRENDA BURBANK (201) has, since 1970, sold thousands of cartoons to a variety of publications, including *The National Enquirer*, *The Wall Street Journal*, and *Medical Economics*. She lives on five acres near Alvin, Texas, with her husband Bob, three horses, three loud geese, and an amazing number of barn cats.

DALE BURG (197) most recently co-authored *The Complete Home Reference Book* (Crown, 1994) and *How To Mom* (Dell, 1995) and long-running columns in *Woman's Day*, *Family Circle*, and *Star*. She has contributed to many other publications, including *New Woman*, *Harper's Bazaar*, and *The Ladies Home Journal*. At press time she was still refusing to adopt a ferret.

ELLEN BYRON'S (325) plays have been produced at prominent New York City and regional theaters such as the WPA, Ensemble Studio Theatre, and Actors Theatre of Louisville. Her one-act *Graceland* is included in the *Best Short Plays of 1985* collection. Other published plays include *Asleep on the Wind, Election Year* and *So When You Get Married*. She has also written over 100 articles for magazines including *Redbook, Glamour*, and *Los Angeles Magazine*. As a performer, Byron helped found Freestyle Repertory Theatre, an improvisation company based in Manhattan. A native New Yorker, she currently lives in Los Angeles, where she is a supervising producer for the hit television series *Wings*.

MARTHA CAMPBELL (60) is a syndicated cartoonist. A graduate of Washington University School of Fine Arts, she has written and designed for Hallmark cards and illustrated 19 books. During her 27 years as a freelance artist, Campbell has had more than 15,000 cartoons published. She lives in Harrison, Arkansas.

ROZ CHAST (9, 341), syndicated cartoonist, has been a regular contributor to *The New Yorker* since 1978, and has published collections of her work, including *Proof of Life on Earth*, and illustrated *Now Everybody Really Hates Me*. She lives in Connecticut with her husband and two children, and is currently working on a collection of cartoons about families.

CINDY CHUPACK (151) is a television comedy writer whose credits include *Coach, Empty Nest*, and several other shows that went off the air because only her parents were watching. She also writes humorous essays for *Glamour* magazine's "Sexual Ethics" column. Originally from Tulsa, Oklahoma, Chupack lives in Los Angeles, California.

CATHY CRIMMINS (226), writer and stand-up comic, is the author of *Y.A.P.: The Young Aspiring Professional's Fast Track Handbook, The Secret World of Men, When My Parents Were My Age, They Were Old*, and co-author of *Newt Gingrich's Bedtime Stories for Orphans, Primary Whites* and *The Private Diary of Scarlett O'Hara*. She lives in Philadelphia, Pennsylvania.

CATHY N. DAVIDSON (27, 32) is the author or editor of over one dozen books, including *The Book of Love: Writers and their Love Letters* (Plume, 1996) and, with Linda Wagner-Martin, *The Oxford Companion to Women's Writing in the United States* (1995). She teaches American Literature at Duke University in Durham, North Carolina.

RUBY DEE (164), actress, calls herself a "word worker." Dee was awarded an Emmy for her role in *Decoration Day* and has appeared in numerous film, TV, and stage productions including *Do The Right Thing, Jungle Fever, Just Cause, A Raisin in the Sun*, and *The Stand*. The author of two children's books, *Two Ways to Count to Ten* and *Tower to Heaven*, she has also published a collection of poems and stories called *My One Good Nerve*. Born in Cleveland, Ohio, Dee has been a New Yorker all her life. She lives in

Westchester, New York, with actor husband Ossie Davis, and is the mother of three, and grandmother of seven.

PHYLLIS DILLER (321) is one of America's leading comics. She lives in Los Angeles, California.

DENNY DILLON (207), actress, comedienne, and writer, won a CableAce Award for "best actress in a comedy series" for HBO's *Dream On*. She was nominated for a Tony Award for Broadway's *My One & Only*. Denny writes and performs a one-woman comedy act, *Bi-Coastal Babe*, in New York City where she resides.

LIZA DONNELLY (149) has been contributing cartoons to *The New Yorker* magazine since 1979. Her work has been in numerous collections, and she is the editor of *Mothers and Daughters*, a book of cartoons. She lives in Rhinebeck, New York, with her husband and two daughters.

LESLEY DORMEN (284) writes regularly for *Mirabella*, *Glamour*, and *Redbook* magazines. She is the co-author of *The Secret Life of Girls* and *The Grownup Girl's Guide to Boys*. Dormen lives in New York City.

LINDA EISENBERG (54) is an illustrator who lives in New York City. She also teaches art in elementary school.

JAN ELIOT (25, 80, 154, 160), syndicated cartoonist, has been published in several humor collections, including *Women's Glibber*, *Mothers!*, and *Men Are From Detroit, Women Are From Paris*. Her comic strip, "Stone Soup," is distributed by Universal Press Syndicate. Eliot lives in Eugene, Oregon with her husband Ted. Her daughters, Johanna and Jennifer, now 22 and 26, have been the inspirations for much of her humor.

DELIA EPHRON (191, 194) is an author and screenwriter. Her most recent novel, just published last summer, is *Hanging Up*. She has written many other books for adults and children. Two of these, *How to Eat Like a Child* and *Teenage Romance*, were best sellers. She is the co-screenwriter (with Nora Ephron) of *This Is My Life* and *Mixed Nuts*, for which she also served as Executive Producer. She was the associate producer of *Sleepless in Seattle*. She began her writing career as a journalist for *New York* magazine. Her work has also been published in *The New York Times Magazine*, *The New York Times Book Review*, *Esquire*, *Vogue* and other publications. She lives in Los Angeles and New York.

TAFFY FIELD (349) is a regular commentator on Monitoradio, the broadcast edition of the *Christian Science Monitor*, and for Maine Public Radio. *Short Skirts*, a collection of her fiction, was published in 1989, and her work has also been included in two previous anthologies of women's humor, *Women's Glib* and *Women's Glibber*. She lives in mid-coast Maine.

SALLY FINGERETT (109) is a singer/songwriter and a member of "The Four Bitchin' Babes" performance group. She has made three solo recordings for Amerisound in Columbus, Ohio, where she lives with her husband and daughter. Why Columbus? There's always a parking space and never a line at the movies!!

MARTHA GEHMAN (299) is the daughter of actress Estelle Parsons and writer Richard Gehman. She is both an actress and a writer. She performs her own theater pieces around the country, and is currently at work on a book of short stories.

ANNE GIBBONS (4, 104, 190) is a self-syndicated cartoonist. She lives in New York City.

MARTHA GRADISHER (32, 303), syndicated cartoonist, has an endless list of accomplishments but keeps forgetting where she put it. In her twentieth year of waiting to be discovered overnight, she has amused herself by collecting minor awards for her hideously underappreciated cartoons. Gradisher takes pride in the fact that she has never resorted to using the word "tampon" for a cheap laugh. Her work has appeared in *Ms., Glamour, Business Week, PC Magazine*, and publications of ABC News, NBC Radio Entertainment and Chembank. She lives in South Nyack, New York, with her husband, two boys, a puppy, and a garage full of sporting equipment.

CATHY GUISEWITE (48, 86, 219, 267), creator of the comic strip "Cathy" TM, was born in Dayton, Ohio. A former advertising copywriter, she began her career in comics by doodling her daily life traumas in letters to her mother. Since then, "Cathy" TM has grown to become syndicated in 1300 newspapers worldwide, with an audience of over 70 million readers. Currently living in Los Angeles, California, with her four year old daughter, Guisewite has become a celebrity in her own right, having appeared on numerous talk shows. In 1992, she became the second winner, since 1946, of the National Cartoonist Society's Reuben Award.

CAROL HALL (81, 97) wrote both music and lyrics to *The Best Little Whorehouse in Texas*, and was a contributor to *A...My Name is Still Alice, Sesame Street*, and the landmark children's special, *Free to Be You and Me*. Her songs have been performed by Barbra Streisand, Michael Feinstein, Barbara Cook, Frederika von Stade, and Big Bird, among others.

MARIETTE HARTLEY (10), an Emmy Award-winning actress, enjoys a celebrated career in television, film and theater. Recent television credits include *Caroline in the City*, and her series, *Wild About Animals*. Recent theater credits include *Sylvia*, *42nd Street* and *The Sisters Rosensweig*. Her autobiography, *Breaking the Silence* is among her career highlights.

KATHERINE HEWETT (143), who was born in Royal Oak, Michigan, is a comedy writer for theater and television and is currently a member of the Dramatist Guild and Sisters-in-Crime. She lives in New York City.

GEORGIA BOGARDUS HOLOF (2) is a songwriter who has contributed to *A...My Name is Alice*, *A...My Name is Still Alice*, and *Skirting the Issues*. She is the lyricist for Ray Bradbury's musical version of *Fahrenheit 451* and lyricist/bookwriter for *Internal Combustion*. Her current work, *Taking Care of Mrs. Carroll*, based on a novel by Paul Monette, is being produced in Chicago. Married, she lives in New York City and is the mother of Seattle comedienne Amy Alpine.

PERRY HOWZE (104) is a screenwriter and cartoonist living in Los Angeles. She is the creator of the comic strip heroine, VERBENA, may she rest in peace. Her film credits include, *Maid To Order*, *Mystic Pizza*, and *Chances Are*, all of which she wrote with her sister, Randy.

MOLLY IVINS (279) is a columnist for the *Fort Worth Star-Telegram*, where she writes about Texas politics and other bizarre happenings. Originally from Houston, she began her career at the Complaint Department of the *Houston Chronicle* and rapidly worked her way up to the position of Sewer Editor, where she wrote a number of gripping articles about street closings. Her career as a reporter and columnist has taken her on many travels, but she returns each time to Texas, to write for the *Texas Observer*, *The Dallas Times Herald*, and now for the *Fort Worth Star-Telegram*. Ivins' weekly columns are syndicated in almost 200 newspapers. Her freelance work has appeared in *GQ*, *Esquire*, *Atlantic*, *The Nation*, *Harper's*, *TV Guide*, and many other publications. She has received a number of journalism awards and was a finalist for the Pulitzer Prize three times. Ivins is the author of *Molly Ivins Can't Say That, Can She?*, and *Nothin' But Good Times Ahead*, collections of essays on politics and journalism.

LYNN JOHNSTON (233, 235), award-winning cartoonist and creator of the syndicated comic "For Better or For Worse," was born in Ontario, Canada, where she continues to reside with her husband and children. According to Johnston, the source of much of the humor of her famous comic strip is "life." There have been 18 collections to date of "For Better or For Worse" including *Remembering Farley* and *Love Just Screws Everything Up*. "For Better or For Worse" currently appears in over 1700 publications worldwide and is printed in eight languages.

NURIT KARLIN (163) is a cartoonist and illustrator whose work is frequently seen in *The New York Times*, *The Washington Post*, *The Wall Street Journal*, and a variety of magazines. She is also the author and illustrator of several children's books. Karlin lives in New York City.

MARTA KAUFFMAN (5) is one of the authors of *A...My Name is Alice* and is the creator of the television comedy *Friends*. She lives in Los Angeles, California.

MARGO KAUFMAN (134, 146) is the author of *1-800-Am I Nuts?* a collection of humorous essays about life's little annoyances, published by Random House, and *This Damn House!*, an amusing look at remodeling, published by Villard. Her work has appeared in publications including *The New York Times*, *The Los Angeles Times*, *Good Housekeeping*, and *Redbook*, and she is the Hollywood correspondent for *Pug Talk Magazine*. She can be heard weekly on the Ken and Barkley Company, KABC Talkradio, where she is their official "Gripe Lady." She lives in Venice, California.

BINNIE KIRSHENBAUM (262) is the author of two collections of stories, *Married Life and Other True Adventures* and *History on a Personal Note*, and two novels, *A Disturbance in One Place* and *On Mermaid Avenue*. She is a Barnes & Noble "Discover" author and was chosen by *Granta* magazine as one of the 50 best young American authors. Kirshenbaum, who lives in New York City, is also a recipient of a Critics' Choice Award from the *San Francisco Review of Books*.

LAURA KURITZKY PEDEGANA (338), a freelance writer, is an alumna of the Warner Bros. TV Comedy Writers' Workshop, and has been involved in television development and production for ten years. She resides in Woodland Hills, California, with her husband and screenwriting partner, and their two children.

ANNE LAMOTT (176), who has been the book review columnist for *Mademoiselle* and a restaurant critic for *California* magazine, is the author of *Operating Instructions*, *Hard Laughter*, *Rosie*, *Joe Jones*, and *All New People*. She lives in San Rafael, California.

LIEBE LAMSTEIN (100, 245) is a cartoonist whose work has appeared in *The National Enquirer*, *Good Housekeeping*, *Cosmopolitan*, and *Reader's Digest*, among other publications. Her cartoons were included in Avis Lang Rosenberg's international exhibition, *Pork Roast*, and are presently distributed through Jerry Robinson's Cartoonists and Writers Syndicate. Liebe lives in Brooklyn, New York.

CHRISTINE LAVIN (246, 268) is a songwriter, recording artist, founding member of "The Four Bitchin' Babes" performance group, and contributor to *The Performing Songwriter* magazine. She has recorded eight albums of original material, and her concert schedule has taken her all over the United States, Canada, Australia, and Germany. She is currently working on her ninth album. Lavin lives in New York City.

KATHLEEN ROCKWELL LAWRENCE (20) is the author of two novels, *Maud Gone* and *The Last Room in Manhattan*. Her essays have been published in many magazines and are collected in her book *The Boys I Didn't Kiss*. She lives in New York City.

MARY LAWTON'S (15, 175, 261) cartoons appear in a wide variety of publications, including *Utne Reader*, *Ms.*, *The San Francisco Chronicle*, *Hippocrates*, *The Funny Times*, and *Comic Relief*. Her work has also appeared in several collections including *Getting in Touch With Your Inner Bitch*, *The Best Contemporary Women's Humor*, *Men Are From Detroit, Women Are From Paris*, and *Pandemonium, or Life With Kids*. Her cartoons have been on exhibition in Boston, Berkeley, and at the Cartoon Art Museum in San Francisco. A native New Yorker, Lawton now lives in Houston, Texas.

NANCY LEMANN (272) is from New Orleans, Louisiana. The author of several books, among them *Lives of the Saints*, *The Ritz of the Bayou*, and *Sportsman's Paradise*, she has also written for *Esquire*, *The New Republic*, *Paris Review*, *New York Observer*, and others. Her latest novel is to be published in 1997.

LUISA LESCHIN (161) is an actress/writer/mom. Her television series credits include seven seasons on the Emmy Award-winning PBS series *Square One TV*, *Beverley Hills 90210*, *ER*, and more. She is a founding member of the comedy group "Latins Anonymous," with whom she has toured extensively, both nationally and abroad. Leschin is currently working for Disney Studios under a television writing fellowship.

LISSA LEVIN (64) has been a writer and producer of television for sixteen years. Her credits include *WKRP in Cincinnati*, *Cheers*, *Family Ties*, *Thunder Alley*, Showtime's *Brothers* (which garnered her a CableAce Award nomination), Fox's *Women in Prison*, *Married People*, and *Live Shot*. Her first musical, *Twist of Fate*, is currently running at the Tiffany Theatre in Los Angeles. She lives in Encino, California, with her husband, television writer/producer Dan Gunzelman, and is the mother of two wonderful children.

LISA LOOMER'S (68, 249) plays, including *The Waiting Room*, *Accelerando*, *Birds*, *Bocon*, *Chain of Life*, and *Looking for Angels* have been seen at such theaters as Mark Taper Forum, Arena Stage, The Kennedy Center, The Public Theater, Trinity Rep, and South Coast Rep. Loomer, who is also a screenwriter, is one of the authors of *A ...My Name is Still Alice*. She lives in Los Angeles, California.

GAIL MACHLIS (143, 211, 275) is a syndicated cartoonist whose daily cartoon, "Quality Time," is distributed by Chronicle Features Syndicate. A collection of cartoons, *Quality Time and other Quandaries*, was published by Chronicle Books. Her work has also appeared in *Ms.*, *Cosmopolitan*, *New Woman*, *Glamour*, and many of the *Women's Glib* anthologies. She lives in Berkeley, California.

MERRILL MARKOE (15, 296), former head writer for the *David Letterman Show* is the author of *How to Be Hap-Hap-Happy Like Me* and *What the Dogs Have Taught Me*. She is the creator of Stupid Dog Tricks.

JANE READ MARTIN (111) began her career at *Saturday Night Live* and was Woody Allen's assistant on nine films and Associate Producer of his film *Alice*. In addition to "Rosebud," which was selected for the 1992 Edinburgh Film Festival, she has written two children's books, *Now Everybody Really Hates Me* and *Now I'll Never Leave the Dinner Table* (both co-authored by Patricia Marx and published by HarperCollins.) Born and raised in Princeton, New Jersey, and a graduate of Denison University, she resides in New York City with her husband, screenwriter/director Douglas McGrath.

PATRICIA MARX (305, 315), the first woman to write for the *Harvard Lampoon*, has since published in *The New Yorker*, *Atlantic*, *The New York Times*, and *Spy*. She was a staff writer for *Saturday Night Live* and has written for many other television programs. She has also written several screenplays and a number of books, including *How to Regain Your Virginity*, and is co-author of *Now Everybody Really Hates Me* and *Now I'll Never Leave the Dinner Table*. She teaches humor at The New School in New York City.

HEATHER McADAMS (319, 352) is a Chicago-based cartoonist, illustrator, and filmmaker whose work has appeared in *The Chicago Reader*, *The Chicago Tribune*, *The New York Times*, *Nickelodeon*, *Mademoiselle* and *The New York Press*. She is the author of *Cartoon Girl*, published by Longstreet Press. McAdams has made numerous 16mm films (available for rent through Filmmaker Co-op, New York City, and Canyon Cinema, San Francisco.) Currently, she and her husband, Chris Ligon, are doing animation for MTV.

AMANDA McBROOM (236, 238) is an actress/singer/songwriter, and a heck of a nice girl. She is best known as the composer of Bette Midler's Emmy winning hit song, "The Rose." At the moment, she has six albums and an interesting concert career. She lives in Ojai, California, with her absolutely perfect husband, George Ball.

THERESA McCRACKEN (145, 309, 313), a cartoonist who lives in Waldport, Oregon, runs McHumor, a business dedicated to making people laugh. They charge $1,000 per hour, but have never taken more than seconds to produce a cartoon or article.

Her dog, Sweet Pea, is the receptionist; her cat, Kate, is the prufe reeder, and her other fur ball, Nate, snoozes in the in-box.

MEGON McDONOUGH (229) has been a singer/songwriter/performer for 25 years. She has 8 solo recordings, and is included on 5 compilation CDs of contemporary folk music, including her work with "The Four Bitchin' Babes" performance group. A CableAce Award winner for her performance of Thom Bishop's "Wake Up and Dream" on an HBO special, she has recently composed and performed songs for the award winning children's video, *Concert in Angelland.* Currently, Megon is touring with the "Babes," working on a theater piece, and keeping her "comedy chops" up at The Players Workshop of Second City in Chicago. She lives in a suburb of Chicago, Illinois, with her husband Greg and her son Denvir. She has recently released an album of Jazz standards.

TERRY McMILLAN (82) is the author of critically-acclaimed novels, *Mama, Disappearing Acts, Waiting to Exhale,* and *How Stella Got Her Groove Back.* The last two have been *New York Times* bestsellers and *Waiting To Exhale* has been made into a major motion picture. McMillan is also the editor of *Breaking Ice: An Anthology of Contemporary African-American Fiction.* She lives in northern California with her son, Solomon.

SUSAN MONTEZ (350) is the author of *Radio Free Queens* (Braziller), and has another book forthcoming. She is a full-time faculty member at Norwalk Community Technical College, and lives in New York City.

HESTER MUNDIS (291) is a humorist, a four-time Emmy nominee, and the author of twenty-two books, including *101 Ways to Avoid Reincarnation or Getting it Right the First Time.* She is the mother of two only sons and a chimpanzee.

ROBIN BROURMAN MUNSON (168) is a licensed Marriage and Family counselor, but writing has been her lifelong passion. Her songs have been performed by several distinguished artists and showcased on Nostalgia Television's *Live at The Russian Tea Room* series. She lives in Kingston Springs, Tennessee, with her husband, Art Munson.

KATHY NAJIMY (74) is an award-winning actress, writer, producer, and director. She was co-creator and star of *The Kathy and Mo Show,* an off-Broadway show for which she won an Obie as well as an American Comedy Award Nomination. Her two HBO specials based on "The Kathy and Mo Show" garnered a total of four Ace Awards and an American Comedy Award nomination for Kathy. She is most widely known for her work in such films as *Sister Act* (American Comedy Award for Best Supporting

Actress), *The Fisher King*, *Soapdish*, and several others. Television credits include a starring role in TNT's *In Search of Dr. Seuss*, and a three week featured role on *Chicago Hope*. Ms. Najimy is currently developing a series with NBC and working on a book. She is an AIDS and Women's Rights activist, and in her spare time jumps out of airplanes and sings in her garage band, "Hail Mary" and plays with her two dogs, Al Finney and Miles.

PHYLLIS NEWMAN (201) received rave reviews for her starring role in Nicky Silver's *The Food Chain*. She has appeared on Broadway in Neil Simon's *Broadway Bound* (Tony nomination), *Subways Are For Sleeping* (Tony Award), *Bells Are Ringing*, *First Impressions*, *Moonbirds*, *Pleasures and Palaces*, *The Owl and the Pussycat*, *The Apple Tree*, *How Do You Do, I Love You*, *Last of the Red Hot Lovers*, *The Prisoner of Second Avenue*, *On The Town*, *Annie Get Your Gun*, *Straws in the Wind*, *I Married an Angel*, *I'm Getting My Act Together and Taking it on the Road*, and *The Madwoman of Central Park West*, which she co-wrote with Arthur Laurents. Television credits include appearances on *Thirtysomething*, *Murder, She Wrote*, *Follies*, and *Coming of Age*. She is the author of the book *Just in Time: Notes from My Life*.

LYNN NOTTAGE (61) is a playwright from Brookyln, New York. Her plays include *'Po'Knockers*, *Crumbs From the Table of Joy*, *Las Meninas*, and *Poof*. A contributor to *A...My Name is Still Alice*, she is the recipient of Playwriting Fellowships from New Dramatists, the New York Foundation for the Arts, and Manhattan Theatre Club. Nottage is a graduate of Brown University and The Yale School of Drama.

ELLEN ORLEANS (212, 342) is a writer and contributing editor to several magazines. The author of *The Butches of Madison County*, *Who Cares If It's A Choice?*, and *Can't Keep A Straight Face*, her essays have appeared in the *Women's Glib* series, *Funny Times*, and *The Washington Post*, among other publications. She and her lover, Lori, live in Colorado.

JANICE PERRY (26), aka Gal, is both a writer and performer of theatrical, political, comedic monologues about contemporary world citizenship. She has toured Europe and the United States with her one-woman performances since 1982. Perry teaches and lectures on theater arts and political humor. Her short comic videos have aired on public television channels in the U.S., England and Germany. She lives in Ferrisburgh, Vermont.

PAULA POUNDSTONE (54) is a comedian who, when not attending the Oscars® or figuring out how to fix them, lives in Los Angeles with her two foster daughters, six cats, and two rabbits. In addition to a stand-up schedule that takes her across the country non-stop, she writes a regular, politically-skewed humor column for *Mother Jones* magazine.

ANNA QUINDLEN (94, 181, 209) has been called the "laureate of real life" and "the most eloquent voice" of her generation. Her *New York Times* column, "Public and Private," won the Pulitzer Prize in 1992 and was anthologized as *Thinking Out Loud*. Many of her "Life in the Thirties" columns are included in the collection, *Living Out Loud*. Ms. Quindlen's novels, *Object Lessons* and *One True Thing* were both bestsellers. She lives in northern New Jersey.

ELIZABETH RAPOPORT (310) is an executive editor at Times Books/Random House and a contributor to the "Endpaper" column of *The New York Times Magazine*. She naps in Westchester, New York.

LIBBY REID (44, 67, 224), ex-cheese-hostess, radio announcer, and glamorous fashion model, turned cartoonist because she can't stop noticing stuff. After dwelling many years in New York City, she moved to Portland, Oregon, for the slugs and good manners.

JOAN RIVERS (49)—comedienne, author, actress, playwright, screenwriter, film director, nightclub headliner, television talk show host, businesswoman, and mother of Melissa—is one of the hardest working women in the world of entertainment. She is the author of four bestselling books, *Having a Baby Can Be a Scream*, *The Life and Hard Times of Heidi Abromowitz*, *Enter Talking* (a biography), *Still Talking* (it's sequel), and the forthcoming *Bouncing Back/How to Survive Anything . . . and I mean Anything*. In 1990, Ms. Rivers won an Emmy for Outstanding Talk Show Host for the *Joan Rivers Show*, and in 1994 was nominated for both Tony and Drama Desk Awards for her performance as comedian Lenny Bruce's mother in the Broadway production of *Sally Marr And Her Escorts*, which she also helped write. National spokesperson for the Cystic Fibrosis Foundation and a forceful advocate for suicide prevention, Rivers has also been active in the fight against AIDS since 1982. Ms. Rivers lives in New York and Beverly Hills.

KAREN RIZZO (37) is a comedy writer from New York, now living and writing and driving in Los Angeles. She is currently working on a collection of short stories. "Don't I Know You?" is for Bea Rizzo, who had a great loud laugh.

TRINA ROBBINS (324), a syndicated cartoonist, has been drawing comics for almost thirty years, and writing books since 1990. Her latest book is *The Great Superheroines*. She lives in San Francisco with entirely too many cats, and collects shoes (size 6) and vintage clothing (medium).

DIANE RODRIGUEZ (40, 150) is a playwright and actress who lives with her husband on top of the Elysian quake fault in downtown Los Angeles. She believes in living dangerously. She is a member of the artistic staff at the Tony Award-winning theater, the Mark Taper Forum, where she writes, directs, acts, throws parties, and talks loud in the halls.

FLASH ROSENBERG (91, 150, 282, 328, 345) is an observer who writes, performs, cartoons, sews, photographs, and makes films. Readers of the *Philadelphia City Paper* voted her "Local Comedian Most Likely to Make You Laugh Until it Hurts," so she promptly moved to New York. Her cartoons run in the Jewish *Forward*. Co-producer of the series *Between a Laugh and a Hard Place*, she regularly performs in New York's downtown circuit.

CATHLEEN SCHINE (242), grew up in Westport, Connecticut. She attended Sarah Lawrence College, Barnard College, and the University of Chicago. The author of four novels, *Alice in Bed*, *To the Birdhouse*, *Rameau's Niece*, and *The Love Letter*, Schine is a regular contributor to the "Endpaper" column of *The New York Times Magazine*. She has also written for *The New York Times Book Review*, *The New York Review of Books*, and *The New Yorker*. She lives in New York City with her husband, David Denby, and their two sons.

MINDY SCHNEIDER (229) is a comedy writer whose television credits include *Kate & Allie* and the *Tom Arnold Show*. Originally from New Jersey, she now lives in Los Angeles, California. She is still five-feet-four.

MARYLN SCHWARTZ (276, 278), a native of Mobile, Alabama, and award-winning columnist for *The Dallas Morning News*, is a social observer. Whether she's writing about sports, politics, or a royal visit from the Prince of Wales, she goes behind the scenes of the event to tell a story you aren't likely to hear anywhere else. A frequent guest on major TV talk shows, she has also been featured in *People Magazine*, *USA Today*, *Entertainment Weekly*, and *The Ladies' Home Journal*. Her two bestsellers, *A Southern Belle Primer—or Why Princess Margaret Will Never Be a Kappa Kappa Gamma* and *New Times in the Old South—or Why Scarlett's in Therapy and Tara's Going Condo*, have sold more than a half million copies.

KATE SHEIN (289, 352) is an aspiring writer (greatly encouraged by being included in this book!) A contributor to *A...My Name is Still Alice*, she is also an actress and comedienne. Formerly of San Francisco, and recently of New York, she currently resides in Los Angeles, California.

SHERRIE SHEPHERD (136, 139, 350) is a cartoonist who lives in North Little Rock, Arkansas.

JUNE SIEGEL (100, 155, 346) (member BMI, MAC, Dramatists Guild, League of Professional Theatre Women) has contributed lyrics to many Off-Broadway musicals and revues, including *A...My Name is Alice* (I & II), *The Housewives' Cantata*, and *That's Life!*. Her theater piece, *Life Forms*, appeared at The Theatre for the New City; her mini-soap, *Suds and Lovers*, turned up in San Francisco. A published writer, songwriter, and performer, she lives in New Rochelle, New York.

YVETTE JEAN SILVER (20, 156, 196) is a cartoonist and professional caricaturist. She got her training drawing supply and demand curves as an economics major at Tufts University. Since then, she's become known as the Strolling Caricaturist, having drawn more that 12,000 caricatures at special events, using her trademark mobile easel. Yvette was the publisher of Silver Lining Cards, a collection of greeting cards for people over fifty. *Grandparents Run in the Family*, her first humor book, was published by Pinnacle in 1995. She lives in New York City.

CATHERINE SIRACUSA (271) is a writer, cartoonist and illustrator. Her humorous drawings and cartoons have appeared in many books, newspapers and magazines, including *Cosmopolitan* and *The New York Times*. Among her published books are *Beef Stew*, *No Mail for Mitchell*, *The Parrot Problem*, and *Banana Split from Outerspace*. Her twelfth children's book, *The Peanut Butter Gang*, was recently published by Hyperion. She lives and works in New York City with her husband, author-illustrator Sidney Levitt.

DEBI SMITH (314, 320) is a contemporary singer/songwriter/instrumentalist from Falls Church, Virginia. Her appearances include international radio, television, and performances as a soloist with "The Smith Sisters" and the "The Four Bitchin' Babes." She has won a number of record label awards and has recorded on more than a dozen albums, including her recent solo recording, "In My Dreams" (Amerisound).

JANET SMITH (78) is a published songwriter and performer, and presently owns Bella Roma Music, a publishing company in Berkeley, California. She handles her own repertoire, as well as that of several other composers, and transcribes music, occasionally engraving it on computer for publication. She is currently doing research in the area of ancient Sumero/Babylonian lyre notation with Professor Anne Kilmer of U.C. Berkeley.

YEARDLEY SMITH (87), born in Paris, France, and raised in Washington, D.C., has appeared at Arena Stage in D.C., as well as on Broadway in "The Real Thing." She crashed Billy Crystal's birthday party in the film "City Slickers"; was "Louise" on Fox T.V.'s "Herman's Head" for three years; and is best known as the voice of "Lisa Simpson" on *The Simpsons*. She can also be seen in the feature film "Old Friends" this fall with Jack Nicholson and Helen Hunt.

MARCIA STEIL (140) was born in Glenview, Illinois, into a normal, happy family except "we probably laughed more than most families." She later taught high school English at Evanston Township High School and taught middle school history in Los Angeles, where she currently writes and lives with her husband (who still can't find anything in the refrigerator).

GLORIA STEINEM (137) is a writer, editor, and feminist organizer, who co-founded *Ms.* magazine (in 1972), the National Women's Political Caucus (in 1971), and such other expressions of the modern Women's Movement as Voters for Choice and the Ms. Foundation for Women. She has published numerous articles and books, including *Revolution From Within* and *Moving Beyond Words*. She lives in New York City.

CARRIE ST. MICHEL (76, 240), who resides in Southern California's Antelope Valley, writes a syndicated column, "Laugh Lines" for the *Los Angeles Times*. She is also a frequent contributor to national women's magazines, including *Good Housekeeping* and *Family Circle*.

JUDITH STONE (157, 230, 258) was a contributing editor at *Discover, Health,* and *Glamour* magazines before becoming arts and features editor of *Mirabella*. She was formerly articles editor of *McCall's*, and of *Science Digest*. "Light Elements," the humor column she wrote for *Discover*, won a 1989 National Headliner Award. She is the author of *Light Elements: Essays on Science from Gravity to Levity* (Ballantine, 1991) and co-author, with Nicole Gregory, of *Healing Your Inner Dog: A Self-Whelp Book* (Times Books, 1993), a parody of the inner child movement. She also contributed to the collections *The Nature of Nature* (Viking, 1994) and *Mysteries of Life and the Universe: New Essays from America's Finest Science Writers* (Harcourt Brace, 1992). Her work has appeared in *The New York Times Magazine, The Village Voice, Newsday, Elle, Vogue, Self, Ms., American Health,* and other publications. She was a member of the touring company of The Second City, the improvisational theatre troupe.

ROBIN SWICORD (329) wrote the screenplay for two recent films, *Little Women*, starring Wynona Ryder and Susan Sarandon and *The Perez Family*. Last summer's release *Matilda* is the first film on which she collaborated with her husband, screenwriter Nicholas Kazan. *Matilda* is adapted from Roald Dahl's classic children's novel, and stars Danny Devito and Mara Wilson. Swicord and her husband are also adapting Roald Dahl's *BFG* for producer Kathleen Kennedy. She lives in Santa Monica, California.

JUDITH VIORST (92) is a poet, non-fiction writer, novelist, playwright, and lecturer. She is the author of numerous works of both poetry and prose, among them *Necessary Losses, Forever Fifty and Other Negotiations, When Did I Stop Being 20 and Other Injustices,* as well as fourteen children's books. She resides in Washington, D.C., with her husband Milton, who is the author of several critically acclaimed political books. They have three sons, Anthony, Nicholas, and Alexander.

PATRICIA VOLK (220) is the author of the novel *White Light*, and two short story collections, *The Yellow Banana* and *All It Takes*. Her work has been published in *The New York Times Magazine, The New Yorker, New York, 7 Days, The Atlantic, Playboy, GQ, Redbook, Mirabella, Allure, Good Housekeeping, Cosmopolitan*, and *Family Circle*. A New York writer, Volk wrote the Cityscape column for *New York Newsday*. "Exit Laughing" first appeared as a "Hers" column in *The New York Times Magazine.*

JANE WAGNER (172, 302, 309, 336) has received four Emmys, a Writer's Guild Award, and Peabody for her work in television. She is the author of *Edith Ann, My Life, So Far* and the Tony Award-winning *The Search for Intelligent Life in the Universe*. She lives in Los Angeles, California.

WENDY WASSERSTEIN (108, 184, 215) is a contributor to *The New Yorker, New Woman, The New York Times*, and other publications. She is the Pulitzer Prize winning author of *The Heidi Chronicles* and *The Sisters Rosenzweig.*

CHERYL WHEELER (304, 335) is a favorite singer, songwriter, and raconteur in the contemporary folk music scene. During her public appearances, it is often the witty between-song patter and stories about why her songs were written that receive as much attention as the musical works themselves. Nonetheless, she is considered a songwriter's songwriter with many recordings by well regarded commercial recording artists to her credit and a poetic and melodic writing style.

SIGNE WILKENSON (71, 72) is an internationally syndicated cartoonist whose work appears regularly in *USA Today* and the *Philadelphia Inquirer*. Cartoonist for *The Philadelphia Daily News* since 1985, Wilkinson, in 1992, became the only female ever to win the Pulitzer Prize for editorial cartooning. A graduate of Denver University, she studied at the Philadelphia College of Art and the Pennsylvania Academy of Fine Arts. She has served as a museum art director, and written commentary and book reviews. A collection of her work, *Abortion Cartoons on Demand*, was published in 1992. Past president of the Association of American Editorial Cartoonists, she creates special cartoons for *Working Women* and *Organic Gardening*.

MARION WINIK (127) is a regular commentator on National Public Radio's "All Things Considered," and is the author of *Telling*, a collection of essays, as well as *First Comes Love*, a memoir of her marriage and her husband's death from AIDS. An East Coast native, Winik now lives in Austin, Texas, with her two sons.

A Note on the Charities

AMERICAN FOUNDATION FOR

AmFAR

AIDS RESEARCH

The American Foundation for AIDS Research (AmFAR) is the nation's leading nonprofit organization dedicated to the support of AIDS research (both basic-biomedical and clinical research), AIDS prevention, and the advocacy of sound AIDS-related public policy. Since 1985, AmFAR has invested over $83 million in grants to more than 1,700 research teams.

As a major source of objective, up-to-date information on the AIDS epidemic and its impact on society, AmFAR has been instrumental in educating our country and the international community about issues germane to AIDS prevention, treatment, and public policy, with an emphasis on the global nature of the epidemic and the threat it represents to everyone. AmFAR seeks to be a healing force in society; it is concerned about the rights of all people and strives to be a catalyst for an overall attitudinal change toward people who have, are perceived to have, or are threatened by HIV and AIDS.

Early on, AmFAR recognized that the AIDS virus would have a major impact on the health and well-being of women. Recent statistics on women and HIV testify to the special and growing need now for research that targets this group. AmFAR continues to award grants to investigators who are conducting groundbreaking research on ways to protect women, men, and children from the devastation of HIV infection, including the transmission of HIV from mothers to infants.

AmFAR mobilizes the good will, energy, and generosity of caring people everywhere, and it urges the American people and, indeed, people around the world to unite in supporting the research effort that is the only way to prevail over a deadly epidemic.

For more information about AmFAR write to:
AmFAR
733 Third Ave, 12th floor
New York, NY 10017
Or Call: 212-682-7440

Every Home A Safe Home

The National Coalition Against Domestic Violence (NCADV) was organized in 1978 by a group of activists and women's advocates from all parts of the nation. NCADV continues to carry out its role as a grassroots organization which works at the national level to end violence in the lives of women and children. NCADV represents an active, diverse, and powerful network of coalitions, programs and individuals throughout the country and serves as a nationwide communication link and national voice for battered women and their children and the organizations that serve them.

NCADV carries out important work in the areas of information and referral, networking, public education and awareness, advocacy, public policy, conferences and training and offers a full line of products and publications.

NCADV is governed by a working Board of Directors comprised of women from all across the country and representatives of NCADV's Task Forces which represent women of all social, racial, ethnic, religious, and economic groups, ages, and lifestyles in rural and urban communities.

To learn more about domestic violence or NCADV, please write to:

P.O. Box 18749
Denver, Colorado 80218
Or call 303-839-1852

The Susan G. Komen Breast Cancer Foundation was established in 1982 by Nancy Brinker to honor the memory of her sister, Susan Goodman Komen, who died from breast cancer at the age of 36. The Foundation is a national organization with a network of volunteers working through local chapters and Race for the Cure® events nationwide, fighting to eradicate breast cancer as a life threatening disease by advancing research, education, screening, and treatment. The Foundation is the nation's largest private funder of research dedicated solely to breast cancer. In addition to funding research, the National Grant Program funds innovative breast cancer education, screening, and treatment projects for the medically underserved. Hundreds of thousands of men and women receive the life-saving message of early detection through Komen outreach efforts.

For breast health information call the Foundation's toll-free helpline: 1•800 I'M AWARE (1-800-462-9273).